Virginia Real Estate Postlicensing for Salespersons

2nd Edition Update

PERFORMANCE
PROGRAMS
COMPANY

Stephen Mettling
Ryan Mettling
David Cusic

Material in this book is not intended to represent legal advice and should not be so construed. Readers should consult legal counsel for advice regarding points of law.

© 2026 by Performance Programs Company
6810 190th Street East, Bradenton, FL 34211
info@performanceprogramscompany.com
www.performanceprogramscompany.com

ISBN: 978-1955919982

Virginia Real Estate Postlicensing for Salespersons

Table of Contents

Virginia Real Estate Postlicensing for Salespersons

Course Overview

Welcome to our Virginia Real Estate Postlicensing for Salespersons course, a 30-hour review and applied principles course for newly-licensed salespersons beginning their real estate careers in Virginia. Successful completion of this course will satisfy your one-time postlicense requirement as a salesperson actively practicing real estate in Virginia.

ABOUT THE AUTHORS

For nearly fifty years, Stephen Mettling has been actively engaged in real estate education. Beginning with Dearborn in 1972, then called Real Estate Education Company, Mr. Mettling managed the company's textbook division and author acquisitions. Subsequently he built up the company's real estate school division which eventually became the country's largest real estate, insurance and securities school network in the country. In 1978, Mr. Mettling founded Performance Programs Company, a custom training program publishing and development company specializing in commercial, industrial, and corporate real estate. Over time, Performance Programs Company narrowed its focus to real estate textbook and exam prep publishing. Currently the Company's texts and prelicense resources are used in hundreds of schools in over 48 states. As of 2024, Mr. Mettling has authored over 100 textbooks, real estate programs and exam prep manuals.

Ryan Mettling, partner and publisher of Performance Programs, is an accomplished online curriculum designer, author, and course developer. He is responsible for the company's strategic planning, general management, printing and production, e-pub and retail platforms, and multi-channel marketing. Mr. Mettling is a member of the Real Estate Educators Association (REEA), and graduated Valedictorian from the University of Central Florida's College of Business Administration.

David Cusic, Ph.D., has been a training consultant, author, and Performance Programs Company partner for over forty years. As an educator with international real estate training experience, Dr. Cusic has been engaged in vocation-oriented education since 1966. Specializing in real estate training since 1983, he has developed numerous real estate training programs for corporate and institutional clients nationwide. Dr. Cusic is co-author of the Company's flagship title, Principles of Real Estate Practice by Mettling and Cusic, now complemented by over 20 state supplements and 35 exam prep texts.

KEY CONTRIBUTOR

Kseniya Korneva. Kseniya Korneva is a licensed REALTOR® in Tampa, Florida with a passion for writing and editing. She graduated with a Civil Engineering degree from Clemson University and fell in love with real estate shortly after. Coming from a long line of academics, her love for education runs deep. Kseniya was first introduced to the world of publishing after writing her own e-book in 2019 and realized she wanted to dive deeper. In her free time, she loves to write about personal finance and real estate on her blog (www.TheMoneyMinimalists.com).

UNIT 1:

REAL ESTATE LAW AND REGULATIONS

Unit One Learning Objectives: When the student has completed this unit he or she will be able to:

- Characterize the most essential aspects of Virginia real estate licensure, including regulatory entities, types of licenses and what activities require licensure.
- List and summarize the various non-relationship disclosures that licensees and/or sellers must conduct in a timely fashion, including those relating to property condition, the environment, material facts, and homeowners associations.
- Summarize the local Virginia statutes pertaining to real estate.

THE REAL ESTATE BOARD

The Virginia Real Estate Board (REB) is the regulatory board that certifies and licenses individuals wishing to conduct real estate business. The REB has authority to enforce, amend, and promulgate rules and regulations to execute the law.

The REB falls under the direction and supervision of the DPOR. The Director of the DPOR acts as the secretary for the REB, maintains all REB records, collects fees paid to the REB, exercises specific powers as the administrator of the REB, and enforces statutes and regulations as necessary.

Structure and functions

The REB consists of nine members, two of whom are citizen members and seven of whom have held real estate broker or salesperson licenses for 5 consecutive years prior to being appointed to the REB. Members are appointed by the Governor for 4-year staggered terms and may be appointed for a second term. They elect their own chairman from the membership and adopt a seal to authenticate their proceedings.

The REB does not:

- arbitrate disputes between salespersons and brokers
- arbitrate disputes between brokers
- establish commission rates or commission splits
- standardize listing agreements, sales contracts, or other real estate forms except when charged to do so

Powers

The REB's general powers include the following:

- administering and enforcing regulations under Chapter 21 of the Virginia Code
- establishing real estate licensure and renewal requirements
- determining license fees

- adopting regulations for establishing licensure educational requirements and ensuring related courses meet certain standards of quality
- waiving education or experience requirements when the equivalent has already been obtained
- issuing and renewing real estate licenses
- establishing activities unlicensed independent contractors are permitted to perform
- administering the Virginia real estate transaction recovery fund
- enforcing the Virginia Fair Housing law, conducting investigations on complaints, and imposing penalties on violators
- imposing discipline and sanctions for license law violations, i.e., suspending, revoking, or denying renewal of licenses
- investigating allegations of unlicensed individuals performing real estate activities, issuing cease and desist orders, imposing civil penalties, and reporting the individual to the commonwealth attorney for further action
- obtaining and examining a licensee's documents, books, or records related to any real estate transaction

IMPROPER DEALINGS AND PROHIBITED ACTS

The Virginia Administrative Code identifies the following licensee actions as improper dealing:

- offering property for sale or lease without the knowledge and consent of the property owner or the owner's representative
- offering property for sale or lease on terms not authorized by the property owner or the owner's representative
- placing a sign on a property without the property owner or the owner's representative giving consent
- advertising property for sale, rent, or lease without including the name of the real estate firm or sole proprietorship, regardless of the advertising medium
- entering into a brokerage relationship that does not include a termination date or the means to determine a termination date or that does not allow the client to terminate the relationship

DISCIPLINARY PROCEDURES

Complaints

Anyone who has a complaint against a licensee for allegedly violating statutes or regulations may file the complaint with the DPOR. The complaint must be in writing and received by the Department within 3 years of the alleged act. If a licensee materially and willfully misrepresents information legally required to be disclosed to a complainant and such information is material to establishing the alleged violation, the complaint may be filed within 2 years after the discovery of the misrepresentation. The complaint form can be found online on the DPOR's website at https://www.dpor.virginia.gov/Report-Licensee .

The REB can also investigate any licensee on its own motion, even if no complaint has been received.

Complaint processing. The Regulatory Programs and Compliance Section will review the complaint to determine if the alleged violation is within the scope of the REB's authority. The DPOR only processes complaints against individuals and businesses that are subject to the laws and regulations of its regulatory boards, in this case, the REB. If the alleged violation is not within the REB's authority, the complaint will be referred to the appropriate regulatory agency.

The accused licensee is notified as soon as possible so he or she may respond. The principal broker is also notified.

After reviewing the complaint, the Regulatory Programs and Compliance Section may attempt to resolve the matter informally, investigate further, refer the complaint to the Alternative Dispute Resolution (ADR) for further action, or close the file.

Prior to further investigating the complaint, the DPOR may suggest that the ADR mediate the matter. Resolving the matter through ADR avoids months of formal investigation and potential civil litigation. If the complaint cannot be resolved through ADR, it will be referred to the Investigations section for a formal investigation wherein evidence is obtained to determine whether or not a violation occurred.

If the investigation supports a probable violation, the DPOR may offer the licensee the opportunity to enter into a voluntary consent order with the REB. Consent orders negotiate terms that may include monetary penalties, remedial education, or probation. Cases resolved with consent orders are closed without disciplinary action beyond the terms agreed to by the licensee.

Based on the report of findings from the Investigations section and the licensee's refusal of a consent order, the Board may either hold an informal hearing to resolve the matter quickly and bring the licensee into compliance or hold a formal hearing.

A formal hearing is conducted by a hearing officer who is appointed by the Virginia Supreme Court. A formal hearing's proceedings are conducted in accordance with the Administrative Process Act of the Code of Virginia. The subject licensee may be represented by an attorney, and both the licensee and the Board may subpoena witnesses. A finding of guilty can be appealed to a court of competent jurisdiction within 30 days.

If the investigation does not find probable cause that a violation occurred, the case will be closed.

Sanctions

The REB has the power to impose disciplinary actions on a licensee who has been found guilty of violating or cooperating with others in violating any provision of Title 54.1 of the Code of Virginia.

Consequently, if an investigation or hearing finds probable cause that the violation did occur, the REB may require remedial education, impose a fine up to $1,000, suspend or revoke the license, or refuse to renew the license. However, as a regulatory board, the REB cannot require any individual or business to refund money, correct deficiencies, or provide other personal remedies.

Effect of disciplinary action on subordinate licensees. If the complaint and subsequent investigation regarding a violation by a principal broker or sole proprietor results in the revocation, suspension, or denial of renewal of the broker's license, then the licenses of all affiliated licensees must be returned to the REB until another principal broker or sole proprietor requests the licenses to be reissued.

LICENSED ACTIVITIES

Virginia license law mandates that any time a person, firm, partnership, co-partnership, association, or corporation is provided compensation for any of the following activities for another, that person or entity is acting as a real estate broker or salesperson and must be licensed as such.

Specific permitted activities

- buying, selling, exchanging, leasing, renting, or offering to do any of these activities
- showing property or holding open houses
- answering questions for more information on a property to include questions on listings, title, financing, closing, contracts, brokerage agreements, and legal documents
- discussing, explaining, interpreting, or negotiating a contract, listing, lease agreement, or property management agreement with anyone outside the firm
- negotiating or agreeing to any commission, commission split, management fee, or referral fee

Activities not requiring a license

Unlicensed employees and assistants may perform the following activities:

- perform general clerical duties, including answering the phones, responding by electronic media, provide information shown on the listing, schedule appointments
- submit listings and changes to MLS, have keys made for listings, place signs on properties, order repairs as directed by licensee
- prepare promotional materials and advertisements for approval of the licensee and supervising broker
- prepare contract forms for licensee and supervising broker's approval, assemble closing documents, act as a courier service
- obtain required public information from governmental entities
- record and deposit earnest money deposits, security deposits, and advance rents
- follow up on loan commitments after contracts are ratified
- compute commission checks
- monitor license and personnel files
- receive compensation for their work at a predetermined rate not contingent on the occurrence of a real estate transaction
- perform any other activities undertaken in the regular course of business for which a license is not required

REPORTING TO THE BOARD

Salespersons and brokers must keep the Board informed of their current name and home address, just as each broker must keep the Board informed of the current firm and branch office name and addresses. The Board will not accept a post office box address, so a physical address is required. Any change must be reported to the Board in writing within 30 calendar days of the change. Licensees who use a professional name other than a legal name must report the professional name to the Board prior to using it.

When any licensee is discharged or in any way terminates active status with a sole proprietorship or firm, the sole proprietor or principal broker must return that individual's license to the Board within 10 calendar days of the date of termination or status change, indicating the date of termination on the license.

When any principal broker is discharged or in any way terminates active status with a firm, the firm must notify the Board and return the license to the board within 3 business days of termination or status change, indicating the date of termination on the license and sign the license before returning it.

VIRGINIA RESIDENTIAL PROPERTY DISCLOSURE ACT

The Virginia Residential Property Disclosure Act (§ 55.1-700 et seq. of the Code of Virginia) governs the information property owners must disclose to prospective purchasers of residential real property.

Applicability. The Act applies only to residential property with one to four dwelling units being transferred by sale, exchange, installment land sales contract, or lease with option to buy, whether or not a real estate licensee is involved.

Exemptions. The following are exempt from disclosure requirements:

- court-ordered or involuntary transfers
  - administration of an estate
  - pursuant to a writ of execution
  - foreclosure sale or deed in lieu of a foreclosure
  - by a bankruptcy trustee
  - eminent domain
  - an assignment for creditors
  - escheats
  - owner's failure to pay taxes
  - a judgement for specific performance
- voluntary transfers
  - from one or more co-owners to other co-owner(s)
  - divorce or property settlement stipulation
  - to lineal line relatives
  - from government entity or housing authority
  - first sale of property other than foreclosure

Licensee duties. According to the Act, the listing broker for an owner of residential property has a duty to inform the owner of the owner's rights and obligations.

A licensee representing a purchaser of residential property has a duty to inform the purchaser of the purchaser's rights and obligations. If the purchaser is not represented by a licensee, the licensee representing the owner has the duty to inform the purchaser of his or her rights and obligations.

A licensee has no further disclosure duties to the parties to the transaction and is not liable to any party to the transaction for a violation of disclosure requirements or for any failure to disclose information regarding the property.

Contract termination. If required disclosures are not delivered to the purchaser prior to ratification of the purchase contract, the purchaser may terminate the contract prior to or upon the earliest of the following:

- three days after delivery of the disclosure statement in person or by electronic delivery
- five days after the postmark if the disclosure statement is mailed, postage prepaid, and properly addressed to the purchaser
- settlement upon purchase of the property
- the purchaser's occupancy of the property
- the purchaser's written application for a mortgage loan if the application contains a statement that the right of termination ends with the application for the loan
- after receiving the required disclosure statement, the purchaser providing a waiver of the right to terminate that is in writing and separate from the purchase contract. The purchaser must give written termination notice to the owner by hand delivery; postage prepaid U.S. mail with proof of mailing; electronic delivery; or overnight delivery by a commercial service or the U.S. Postal Service

PROPERTY DISCLOSURES

Sellers of residential property are required to provide a Residential Property Disclosure Statement to the buyer to warn buyers of certain matters that may affect the buyer's decision to purchase the property. This is the seller's responsibility, not the licensee's responsibility.

Although the seller is not be required to voluntarily disclose certain issues, he or she must be honest if the buyer asks questions.

The seller cannot be held liable for errors, inaccuracies, or omissions in the disclosure if the seller relied on information from a professional third party.

The Residential Property Disclosure Statement covers disclosure information and can be found at https://www.dpor.virginia.gov/Consumers/Residential_Property_Disclosures .

Forms to be used for required disclosures are also on the REB's website at http://www.dpor.virginia.gov/Consumers/Disclosure_Forms/.

The Disclosure Statement is a "Buyer Beware" notice that the seller makes no representations or warranties as to

- condition of the property
- use of adjacent properties
- historic district ordinances
- resource protection areas (the Chesapeake Bay Preservation Act)
- sex offender registry
- wastewater systems
- special flood areas
- conservation easements and other items.

The statement also includes affirmative written disclosure requirements, which are covered below. The statement must be provided to the buyer before the purchase contract is executed.

While the Residential Property Disclosure Act limits the licensee's disclosure requirements to the rights and obligations of the parties to the transaction, §54.1-2131B mandates that the licensee handling the property sale must disclose any information about the physical condition that materially affects the property or the property's value. However, this requirement is limited to information the licensee knows about the condition of the property.

The licensee may rely on information provided by the seller and has no legal obligation to perform independent research into the property's condition. The licensee cannot be held liable for misrepresentation if the information was provided by a client, public record, or a regulated professional.

The disclosure requirement applies only to the property itself, not to adjacent properties, land use regulations, or roadways near the property.

Given the limitations on disclosure requirements in Virginia and the Buyer Beware warnings, it is the buyer's responsibility to research the property and inspect it for defects.

If a buyer discovers defects in the property that were not disclosed or were misrepresented in the disclosure, the buyer may take legal action within one year of the disclosure delivery date, one year of lease with option occupancy, or one year of settlement if the required disclosure was never delivered.

Aircraft noise/crash

Any seller of residential property that is located in the vicinity of a military air installation must disclose whether the property is located in a noise zone or accident potential zone. Such zones are designated on the official zoning map for the area where the property is located. The disclosure must use a form found on the REB's website. The disclosure must indicate the specific noise or accident potential zone where the property is located.

Septic system

While no Virginia law or regulation requires inspection of septic systems when properties with septic systems are bought or sold, the seller must disclose to the buyer the fact that the property uses a septic system.

If the buyer or seller chooses to have the septic system inspected before execution of the property sale, it should be noted that the state health department has no standard for inspection and does not perform inspections. The seller must also inform the buyer that it is the seller's responsibility to determine the details about the system and its maintenance requirements.

If the property's septic system needs repair or maintenance and the seller has obtained a waiver from the State Board of Health allow the seller to continue using the system while living on the property, the seller must inform the buyer that the waiver will not apply to the buyer. Consequently, the buyer will be required to have the system repaired before it can be used.

Repetitive flood loss

Virginia law now requires sellers to disclose any real knowledge of repeated flood loss risk. This is defined as 2 or more claims made with the National Flood Insurance Program over a 10-year period, going back to 1978. The claims must be greater than $1,000 to require disclosure.

Megan's Law

Megan's Law is a federal law that requires law enforcement authorities to make information about registered sex offenders available to the public.

The General Assembly in Richmond has also passed a Megan's Law statute intended to provide the public with more direct access to information on sex offenders. As part of this public policy initiative, the Virginia Residential Disclosure Act now requires listing agents in Virginia to ensure that property purchasers are provided with either the Virginia Residential Property Disclosure or the Virginia Residential Property Disclaimer form. Both forms inform prospective purchasers about how to obtain information from the Virginia State Police regarding sex offenders in their area.

Stigmatized property

Stigmatized properties are those that have experienced an event or condition that may affect the desirability of the property while having no effect on the property's physical condition. Such events or conditions include murder, suicide, a felony; a reputed haunting, or a communicable disease. Virginia does not require inspection, investigation, verification, or disclosure regarding these types of events. A buyer has no cause of action against the seller or licensee for not disclosing any of these events or conditions. However, if the buyer asks a specific question, the seller must answer truthfully.

Methamphetamine. Sellers who know that methamphetamine has been manufactured on the property and that the property has not been cleaned up in accordance with statutory guidelines must disclose that information to potential buyers. The seller must use an REB form for the written disclosure.

HIV or AIDS. Just as with other events that affect the desirability but not the condition of the property, there is no requirement to disclose that the property is or has been occupied by a resident with HIV or AIDS.

HOA/POA

Homeowners' associations (HOAs) and property owners' associations (POAs) are considered common interest communities which are governed by The Virginia Resale Disclosure Act. The legislation standardizes all resale documents into a consistent certificate form and includes rules and regulations, procedures and mandates, budgets, and other information. The certificate contains all of the benefits and obligations of living in the association.

Sellers within any of these associations must provide this resale certificate to a buyer before the transaction closing. The seller must also disclose in the contract that

- the lot is located within a development that is subject to the Property Owners' Association Act
- the Property Owners' Association Act requires the seller to provide the buyer with an association resale certificate
- the purchaser may cancel the contract within three days after receiving the association resale certificate or being notified that the association resale certificate will not be available
- if the purchaser has received the association resale certificate, the purchaser has a right to request an update of such resale certificate
- the right to receive the association resale certificate and the right to cancel the contract are waived conclusively if not exercised before settlement

The resale certificate may be delivered to the buyer either in hard copy or electronic format, based on the seller's instructions within the written request for resale certificate. It must be delivered within 14 calendar days after a written request has been submitted. If hand- or electronically delivered, the request is deemed received on the date of delivery. If sent by U.S. mail, the request is deemed received 6 days after the postmark date.

The following are exempt from HOA or POA disclosure requirements:

- condominiums, cooperatives, time-shares
- campgrounds
- disposition of a lot by gift
- disposition of a lot pursuant to a court order
- disposition of a lot by foreclosure or deed in lieu of foreclosure
- disposition of a lot by sale at an auction that already includes the resale certificate
- disposition of a lot to a person or entity not acquiring the lot for his or her own residence but who is obligated to comply with the declaration, bylaws, rules and regulations, and architectural guidelines of the association

Other environmental disclosures

Defective drywall. An owner of a residential dwelling unit who has actual knowledge of the existence of defective drywall within the unit must provide a prospective buyer with a written disclosure that the property has defective drywall.

Pending building or zoning violations. A seller of a residential dwelling unit must make written disclosure to any prospective buyer of actual knowledge of any pending

- enforcement actions related to the Uniform Statewide Building Code that affect the safe, decent, sanitary living conditions of the property as notified by the subject locality
- violation of the local zoning ordinance that has not been corrected within the required timeframe

The seller must use the REB disclosure form found on its website.

Lead-based paint. Federal law requires sellers of houses built before 1978 to make a lead-based paint disclosure before accepting an offer to purchase. The licensee must disclose any known information about the presence of lead-based paint in the home and include a "Lead Warning Statement" either as an attachment to the contract or as a statement within the contract. The licensee must also provide the buyer or lessee with a copy of the US EPA *Protect Your Family From Lead in Your Home* booklet.

Chesapeake Bay Preservation Act. The Chesapeake Bay Preservation Act was originally adopted in 1989 and amended in 1991, 2001 and 2012. The concept of the Act is that land can be used and developed to minimize negative impacts on water quality, such as that of the Chesapeake Bay. The Act balances state and local economic interests and water quality improvement and is the only program in Virginia state government that comprehensively addresses the effects of land use planning and development on water quality.

The lands that make up Chesapeake Bay Preservation Areas are those that have the potential to impact water quality most directly. By carefully managing land uses within these areas, local governments help reduce the water quality impacts of nonpoint source pollution and improve the health of the Chesapeake Bay.

Under the Act, each Tidewater locality is required to adopt a program based on the Act. Recognizing local government's responsibility for land use decisions, the Act's regulations are designed to establish a framework for compliance without dictating exactly what local programs must look like.

SERVICEMEMBERS CIVIL RELIEF ACT

The SCRA was created in 2003 to support active military members with issues concerning rental agreements, prepaid rent, security deposits, evictions, mortgage interest rates, mortgage foreclosures, credit card interest rates and more.

VIRGINIA RESIDENTIAL LANDLORD AND TENANT ACT

Purposes

The Virginia Residential Landlord and Tenant Act (VRLTA) applies to most residential properties and rental agreements in the Commonwealth and supersedes local, county, and municipal landlord and tenant ordinances. The Act was enacted and has been amended to protect landlord and tenant rights and obligations under rental agreements.

The Act in its entirety can be found online as a handbook on the Virginia Department of Housing and Community Development's website at https://dhcd.virginia.gov/landlord-tenant-resources. It can also be found within the Code of Virginia in Title 55.1 Chapter 12 (§ 55.1-1200 – 1262).

A summary of tenants' rights and responsibilities under the Act can be found online at

https://www.dhcd.virginia.gov/sites/default/files/Docx/landlord-tenant/final-vrlta-statement-formatted.pdf

Covered properties

The following properties are covered by the Act:

- single-family housing with a rental agreement
- apartments, regardless of the number of units owned
- motels, hotels, manufactured homes, if the tenant lives in the unit for more than 90 days
- public housing and federally subsidized housing, if consistent with federal regulations (HUD)

Obligations

Landlord. In addition to the provisions of the rental agreement, the landlord has the following obligations:

- provide tenant with a written report of damages already existing in the dwelling prior to occupancy or allow tenant to inspect and provide the written report to the landlord, either to be done within 5 days after tenant moves into the unit
- on the first page of the lease agreement, disclose to tenant all additional fees that may be charged in addition to rent
- disclose to tenant any visible signs of mold in the dwelling and allow tenant to terminate the lease if mold exists

- disclose to tenant the name of the dwelling's current owner or of sale of the dwelling and the new owner's name
- disclose to tenant prior to signing the presence of any military air installation adjacent to the premises or allow tenant to terminate the lease within 30 days of occupancy if no disclosure was provided
- disclose to tenant prior to signing the existence of defective drywall in the dwelling or allow tenant to terminate the lease within 60 days of occupancy if no disclosure was provided
- disclose to tenant prior to signing any previous manufacture of methamphetamine on the premises which has not been appropriately cleaned or allow tenant to terminate the lease within 60 days of occupancy if no disclosure was provided
- comply with building and housing health and safety codes and make necessary repairs
- maintain major systems and appliances in good working order
- maintain premises in a clean condition and in a manner to prevent mold growth; remediate any visible mold promptly
- provide receptacles for trash removal
- supply running hot and cold water at all times
- provide to tenant certification that all smoke alarms are in good working order
- provide locks and peepholes for the dwelling

Tenant. In addition to the provisions of the rental agreement, the tenant has the following obligations:

- comply with building and housing health and safety codes
- maintain the dwelling in a clean and safe condition
- maintain the dwelling free of insects and pests and promptly notify the landlord of infestations
- remove all waste from the dwelling in appropriate receptacles
- maintain the dwelling's plumbing fixtures cleanliness
- use and pay for all utilities as included in the rental agreement
- do not damage or allow others to damage any part of the premises
- maintain smoke alarms in accordance with uniform standards
- maintain carbon monoxide alarms in accordance with uniform standards
- maintain the dwelling in such a manner so as to prevent mold and promptly notify landlord of any sign of mold growth
- do not make alterations, such as painting, to the dwelling without the landlord's written approval
- conduct him/herself in a manner so as not to interfere with neighbors' peaceful enjoyment of the premises
- abide by all reasonable rules imposed by the landlord
- be financially responsible for treatment of any infestations caused by the tenant's failure to notify the landlord in a timely manner
- be reasonably responsible to prevent any personal injury or property damage by an animal owned by the tenant or guest

VIRGINIA COMMON INTEREST COMMUNITY ACT

Creation

Establishing documents. Common Interest Communities (CICs) are designed by developers for community living. The developer creates the community through a set of documents that can later be changed by the membership of the community (homeowners).

At some point, the developer relinquishes control of the community, and the community's homeowners' association takes over governing the affairs through an elected board that is authorized to enforce rules and mandate assessments to pay for maintenance and improvements to common areas of the community, such as roads, recreation facilities, pools, etc. Owners have an obligation to pay the assessments for these expenses as well as for insurance and other shared costs.

Public offering statement. When a dwelling in a common interest community is initially being sold, Virginia law (§ 55.1-1976) requires the developer to provide the purchaser a public offering statement with the contract for the sale. The public offering statement (POS) is a document that fully and accurately discloses the characteristics of the subject CIC and the units within the CIC. It must include all unusual and material circumstances or features that affect the community.

Items required in the POS include:

- a general description of the community and amenities
- copies of the declaration and bylaws
- copies of any management contract
- terms of easements and liens
- the purchaser's right to cancel the disposition within given timeframes (typically 3 business days from signing), and so on.

Governance

CIC Board. Common Interest Communities include condominiums, cooperatives, time-shares, and property owners' associations. These communities all fall under the administration of the Common Interest Community Board which regulates CIC managers and some employees of licensed management firms. The board is responsible for licensing association managers, certifying certain employees of the managers, receiving annual reports from the associations, and registering condominiums and time-share projects. The 11 members of the board are appointed by the governor.

CIC manager. The CIC board licenses managers to provide services to a common interest community association and has the authority to discipline licensed managers for violations of associated regulations. Services that managers may offer include but are not limited to collecting and handling monies and assessments, preparing annual budgets, scheduling association meetings, negotiating contracts, enforcing rules, communicating with association members on behalf of the association board, etc.

CIC Ombudsman. In addition to the CIC board, the Office of the CIC Ombudsman offers assistance and information to association members regarding their rights and processes in relation to their associations. The ombudsman may receive complaints, refer possible violations to the CIC board for warranted action, and offer referrals to alternate dispute resolution services. The ombudsman may not offer legal advice or interpret association bylaws or other governing documents.

VIRGINIA PROPERTY OWNER'S ASSOCIATION ACT

Purpose

The Virginia Property Owners Association Act regulates associations that manage real estate developments with certain characteristics such as a declaration and Covenants, Conditions, and Restrictions (CC&Rs). The Act provides guidelines regarding a POA's powers, required disclosures, and remedies available in the event of a dispute between the property owners and the association.

The Act applies to

- all developments subject to a declaration recorded after January 1, 1959
- associations organized or incorporated after that same date
- subdivisions created under the Subdivided Land Sales Act

Rights

Purchaser's right to cancel. The Act allows purchasers to cancel the contract within three days of receiving the resale certificate. The buyer may also cancel within three days of receiving the packet if it was hand delivered or electronically delivered or within six days after the postmark date if the packet was sent by U.S. mail. The buyer may also terminate the contract at any time prior to settlement if the packet has not been made available or delivered to the purchaser. All rights for the buyer to cancel the contract are waived if they are not exercised prior to settlement.

Property owners' rights. Homeowners have the right to access all association books and records, participate in elections for the board of directors, vote on amendments to the declaration, and to attend meetings of the board of directors. Association members in good standing also have the right to serve on the board of directors if elected.

Disclosure Requirements

Seller disclosure. The POA Act requires property owners who are selling their homes to disclose in the purchase contract that the property is located within a development that is subject to the POA Act. Sellers are also required to obtain an association resale certificate from the association and provide that to the buyer.

Association resale certificate. The resale certificate is to contain at least the following:

- the association's name
- statements of association expenditures and amounts of assessments and fees imposed on property owners including those to cover the cost of construction or maintenance of stormwater management facilities, as well as any other entity to whom the owner may owe fees or charges
- the current reserve report or summary showing the status and amount of all reserve accounts and specific projects to which the reserve funds are assigned
- a copy of the association's current budget or summary and financial statement for the last fiscal year
- a statement regarding any pending action or unpaid judgment related to the association
- a statement showing all insurance coverage provided for owners by the association
- restrictions and prohibitions applied to owners regarding property modifications, signs and flag placements, political sign placement, and solar panel placement

- a copy of the current declaration, articles of incorporation, bylaws, rules and regulations, approved board of directors meeting minutes, any notices to the current owner for violations, and any current project approvals issued by secondary mortgage market agencies
- a copy of the CIC's completed form providing the characteristics of CICs that may affect the buyer's decision to purchase
- certification that the annual report has been filed with the CIC Board

VIRGINIA CONDOMINIUM ACT AND REGULATIONS

Covenants, conditions, and restrictions

Condominium bylaws. Covenants, conditions, and restrictions (CC&Rs) are typically created and used by the homeowners' association of common interest communities, including condominiums, to set the use, appearance, maintenance, and management of the property.

CC&Rs are found within the condominium's bylaws, which are to be recorded with the condominium's declaration. Once the bylaws have been filed, they may only be modified through amendments voted on by the association membership (homeowners) and filed as such with the bylaws.

Common restrictions. CC&Rs commonly include restrictions on what homeowners can do on their property or in their unit. For example, CC&Rs may prohibit pet ownership or restrict the size or type of pet. They may regulate what modifications homeowners can make to the exterior of the condominium unit, such as prohibiting satellite dishes or solar panels on the building's roof.

Statutory requirements. While CC&Rs are included within the condominium instruments, some requirements are found in the Virginia Condominium Act. For example, the Act places all powers and responsibility for the maintenance, repair, and replacement of the condominium common elements on the unit owners' association and of the individual unit on the unit owner.

Unit-owner rights

The Virginia Condominium Act includes a statement of rights for unit owners who are in good standing with the owners' association:

- the right of access to all association records
- the right to vote on association matters that require a vote
- the right to be notified of any board meeting, to record the meeting, and to participate in the meeting
- the right to be notified of any board proceeding against the unit owner to enforce rules, to be heard at the proceeding, to be provided due process in the hearing
- the right to serve on the board if duly elected and a member of the association in good standing

The Virginia Condominium Act may be found in its entirety online at https://law.lis.virginia.gov/vacode/title55.1/chapter19/.

VIRGINIA REAL ESTATE COOPERATIVE ACT

Structure

Regulation. A residential cooperative (co-op) is a housing unit that a group of individuals own and control with equal shares, membership, or occupancy rights. The Virginia Real Estate Cooperative Act, administered by the CIC Board, governs residential co-ops.

Ownership. Each member of the co-op is a shareholder in the entire cooperative community. The members do not actually own their units. Instead, they own shares or interests in the co-op. Just as with other common interest communities, co-ops include common elements and limited common elements, a declaration and an association, and an executive board or board of directors to handle the association's business and enforce the by-laws, rules, and regulations.

Legal requirements. Under the Cooperative Act, co-ops have many of the same requirements as other CICs, such as maintaining an annual budget, using self or professional management, maintaining common elements, charging fees and assessments to co-op shareholders to cover association expenses, holding annual meetings, carry property and liability insurance, and establishing shareholder rights and limitations.

Public offering statement

Cooperative declarants must prepare a public offering statement (POS) prior to offering any co-op interest for sale and provide it to a purchaser before conveyance of the co-op interest and no later than the date of the purchase contract.

Contents. The POS must include:

- name and address of the co-op and its declarant
- general description of the co-op and its features
- number of units
- current balance sheet and projected budget
- assessments and fees
- liens, encumbrances and unsatisfied judgments
- available financing
- warranties
- unit restrictions
- insurances
- land use requirements
- material characteristics
- rights of the owners and lessees
- contract cancellation rights and procedures
- time-share information, if applicable

Purchaser's right to cancel. A co-op interest initial purchaser may cancel the purchase contract within 10 days of signing. The purchaser may hand deliver the cancellation notice or mail it to the offeror or the offeror's agent.

There can be no penalty for cancelling, and all monies submitted by the purchaser must be promptly refunded. If the initial purchaser was not provided the POS prior to the interest conveyance, the purchaser is entitled to receive 10 percent of the sales price, 10 percent of the proportionate share of common expense liability, and any applicable damages.

Seller disclosures

Co-op interest holders selling their interests must provide purchasers a copy of the declaration, the bylaws, the rules and regulations, and a certificate containing information and attachments similar to the POS, as specified in § 55.1-2161.

Purchaser's right to cancel. The purchaser may cancel the contract prior to receiving the certificate, within 5 days after receiving the contract, or prior to interest conveyance, whichever happens first.

VIRGINIA RESALE DISCLOSURE ACT

The Virginia Resale Disclosure Act took all provisions for resale certificates and disclosure packets from the Virginia Condominium Act, the Property Owners' Association Act, and the Virginia Real Estate Cooperative Act and created a single act with all resale provisions. All sellers in common interest communities must now use a standardized form called a resale certificate which can be accessed here:

https://www.dpor.virginia.gov/sites/default/files/boards/CIC/A492-05RESALE.pdf

Buyers and sellers in CICs may negotiate a recission period that consists of any number of days. During this period, buyers may cancel the contract without penalty. If no number is named by the parties, the default window is 3 days from the ratification date.

Buyers may cancel the contract any time before settlement if the resale certificate is undelivered or unavailable. If the resale certificate is delivered but incomplete, buyers may request and update. However, an incomplete resale certificate is still considered delivered. If a seller provides an incomplete resale certificate, a buyer's only remedy is to cancel the contract.

VIRGINIA TIME SHARE ACT

Essential provisions

Regulation. As with other common interest communities, the law governing time-shares in Virginia is administered by the CIC Board. The Virginia Time-Share Act mandates the requirements for creating and selling time-shares.

Instrument. To create a time-share program for a time-share project, the developer must prepare a time-share instrument and record it in the clerk's office in the locality of the time-share. Required contents of the instrument include, but are not limited to:

- evidence of an association created in accordance with the Virginia Nonstock Corporation Act (§ 13.1-801)
- the time-share name and locality
- identification of the project as either a time-share estate or time-share use
- common expenses
- restrictions on use
- description of the time-share real estate
- any developer rights. (See § 55.1-2208 & 2209 for the complete list)

Public Offering Statement. The required time-share POS is similar to that for other CICs, and the developer must file it with the CIC Board. The developer must deliver a copy to a prospective buyer before execution of a purchase contract. It must contain information similar to that contained in statements for other CICs. The POS must fully and accurately disclose the material characteristics of the time-share program and the offered time-share and let each prospective buyer know about all material circumstances that affect the program.

Right to rescind initial purchase contract. On the initial purchase of a time-share, the POS and the purchase contract must both include a statement providing the purchaser with a non-waivable right to cancel the contract and have any deposits refunded.

The cancellation must be exercised before midnight of the seventh calendar day after contract execution. There is no penalty for cancelling within this timeframe. Deposits must be refunded within 45 days after the cancellation notice is received.

Conversion. Existing tenants of a property to be converted to a time-share must receive 90 days' notice of the conversion intent and another 60 days in which to purchase their unit. If the tenant is on a month-to-month lease, the developer must provide a 120-day notice to vacate the unit.

Resale. A time-share owner intending to sell his or her time-share must provide the purchaser a certificate of resale from the developer or association prior to the settlement of the purchase contract.

The certificate must include a copy of the time-share instrument, bylaws, rules and regulations, current annual financial report, liability assessments, and any liens or pending actions against the developer, managing entity, or association.

Right to rescind resale purchase contract. A purchaser may cancel the contract any time before receiving the resale certificate or within 5 days of receiving the certificate or after the time-share transfer, whichever occurs first.

A buyer seeking to rescind a purchase contract on the basis of inaccuracy or misrepresentation in the certificate or other document has two years from the date of the purchase contract to take action.

Deposits. All deposits received for a time-share purchase must be held in an escrow account until appropriate disbursement at the end of the cancellation period, until the buyer defaults on the purchase, or until they are refunded to the buyer.

VIRGINIA UNDERGROUND UTILITY DAMAGE PREVENTION ACT

Purpose

The Underground Utility Damage Prevention Act serves to protect the underground storage and conveyance of water, sewage, telecommunications, electric energy, cable television, oil, petroleum products, gas, or other substances.

The regulated means of storage and conveyance include but are not limited to pipes, sewers, combination storm/sanitary sewer systems, conduits, cables, valves, lines, wires, manholes, attachments, and those portions of poles below ground.

VIRGINIA HOMESTEAD

State and federal homestead laws are intended to protect people against loss of their primary residence in the event of a drastic change in economic conditions. These laws allow homeowners to declare a portion of their real estate as a homestead and thereby to shield some or all of the equity in the home against creditors and bankruptcy actions. Single family homes, condominiums, mobile homes, and manufactured homes used as the owner's primary residence may qualify.

Exemptions

Virginia requires residents seeking homestead exemptions to use the state homestead exemption laws. These laws allow homestead exemptions to be declared as follows.

- single residents-- $5,000, plus $500 for each dependent
- married couples filing together and residents 65 and older-- $10,000
- surviving spouse of deceased homeowner   -- $20,000
- minor children of deceased homeowner with no surviving spouse -- $20,000
- veterans disabled by 40 percent or more -- $10,000

Virginia passed an additional $25,000 exemption applied only to real or personal (mobile home) property used as a principal residence and mandated that exemption amounts are to be adjusted triennially based on the U.S. average consumer price index.

VIRGINIA JOINT TENANCY

Right of survivorship

In a joint tenancy, two or more persons collectively own a property as though they were a single person. The tenancy may or may not include the right of survivorship, under which a deceased tenant's share is divided equally among the surviving tenants.

In Virginia, joint tenancy is automatically established without survivorship unless the term "with survivorship" is included during the titling, registering, or endorsing of the property. Virginia law (§ 55.1-134) abolished automatic survivorship and mandated that a deceased joint tenant's share descends to the tenant's heirs, passes by devise (will), or goes to the tenant's personal representative as though the tenant had been a tenant in common.

A deceased tenant's share may be divided among the surviving tenants only if the property is being transferred to the other tenants by an instrument that indicates the share is to be divided among the others and not passed on to heirs.

When ownership is set up as a joint tenancy with survivorship, a deceased owner's share can be passed on to other owners without going through the probate process necessary with a will. Married couples in Virginia often set up their property ownership as a joint tenancy for this very reason.

The four unities

Virginia, like other states, requires the four unities (time, title, interest, and possession) to create a joint tenancy, with the unity of interest meaning that all parties receive equal undivided interests. However, Virginia in addition requires that all tenants hold the same tenancy. Thus, if one tenant is a tenant for life, all tenants must be tenants for life.

VIRGINIA REAL PROPERTY TAXATION

Property taxes are assessed and collected mainly to fund a local government's operations and services to its residents. Article X of the Constitution of Virginia covers taxation and finance in Virginia, mandating that all property (see exemptions below) is to be taxed. According to Section 1 of the Article,

"All taxes shall be levied and collected under general laws and shall be uniform upon the same class of subjects within the territorial limits of the authority levying the tax, except that the General Assembly may provide for differences in the rate of taxation to be imposed upon real estate by a city or town…"

Taxation process

Local governments or taxing districts establish an annual budget including expected expenses for the year. Any expected income from sources other than taxes is subtracted from the total budgetary amount needed for the expenses. The remaining funds needed are collected from property taxes.

Each local government uses its own method of assessing and collecting property tax. Consequently, while assessments are made at the property's fair market value, there is no one tax rate that applies across the board to all Virginia properties. The average rate varies from 0.74% to 0.80%.

In Virginia, local property assessors determine the fair market value of properties on a scheduled basis, with state law mandating reassessment every two years for cities and every four years for counties. Cities with fewer than 30,000 people and counties with fewer than 50,000 may vote to reassess at longer intervals up to every six years. Tax rates are then calculated based on each $100 of the property's assessed value.

Virginia law prohibits a tax district's total taxes from increasing by more than 1% due to a reassessment, but the law does not limit the increase on individual properties. Homeowners who disagree with the value assessment may contact the local assessment board or file an official appeal with the Board of Equalization and Assessment Review.

Property tax payments

Annual property taxes can be paid in two installment payments. The due dates of those installments vary by county. For example, for Fairfax County, the installments are due on July 28 and December 5. However, Arlington's due dates are June 15 and October 5. If payments are late, counties impose a late payment penalty and potentially other fees such as collection and interest fees.

Tax liens

An unpaid property tax assessment becomes a lien against the property. The lien is recorded in the clerk or treasurer's office and not released until the delinquent taxes are paid. Tax liens are prioritized over all other liens except liens for court costs. If a property is sold with a tax lien still in effect, the delinquent tax payment will be taken from the proceeds of the sale.

Tax sale and redemption

If a property's assessed value is $100,000 or less and its taxes are delinquent on December 31 following one year after the due date or there is a lien on the property, the property may be sold by public auction to pay the taxes. A 30-day notice of impending action must be sent to the property's owner. The owner may redeem the property by paying all delinquent taxes and associated fees and penalties within 36 months of the request for redemption.

Other property taxes

Special assessment taxes are collected to fund a specific improvement for a specific area or neighborhood and so are levied only on properties within the specific area. For example, if a street is being widened in a particular area or neighborhood, only those homeowners in that area or neighborhood will be charged the special assessment tax as they will be the ones who will benefit from that improvement. Notice of the planned improvement must be sent to the impacted homeowners who may then protest both the improvement and the assessment.

Exemptions

A property is exempt from taxation if it is

- owned directly or indirectly by the Commonwealth
- owned and exclusively occupied or used by churches or religious bodies for worship or ministers' residence
- a burying ground or cemetery not operated for profit
- owned by a public library or school and used for literary, scientific, or educational purposes and not operated for profit
- intangible personal property
- used for religious, charitable, patriotic, historical, benevolent, cultural, or public park and playground purposes
- land subject to a perpetual easement permitting inundation by water
- individually or jointly owned and occupied by any veteran and spouse when the veteran has a 100 percent service-related, permanent, and total disability
- owned and occupied by the surviving spouse of a veteran who was eligible for the above exemption as long as the spouse does not remarry
- owned and occupied by the surviving spouse of a U.S. armed forces member who was killed in action as long as the spouse does not remarry
- manufactured homes but not the land they sit on

Properties owned by those 65 and older or by those permanently and totally disabled may be exempt or assessed at a lower rate.

Exemptions for private property, but not public property, are determined on the basis of the property's use.

Taxpayer Bill of Rights

Virginia law includes a Taxpayer Bill of Rights to safeguard the rights, privacy, dignity and property of taxpayers during tax assessment, collection, and enforcement processes. The statute includes the rights to:

- courteous and accurate responses to questions
- assistance when requested
- representation by counsel
- notification of impending collection actions
- confidentiality of information.

The entire Bill of Rights is included in § 58.1-1845 of the Code of Virginia and can also be found in .pdf format on the Department of Taxation's website at https://www.tax.virginia.gov/sites/default/files/inline-files/virginia-taxpayer-bill-of-rights.pdf.

TRANSACTION TAXES

In addition to imposing taxes on real property, taxing agencies in Virginia impose deed transfer taxes, recordation taxes, and other fees when a property is sold by deed. Some of these taxes and fees are levied by the state and others by the county or municipality where the property is located.

Transfer taxes

A transfer tax is an excise tax on a transaction in which the property's title is transferred from the seller to the buyer. The tax is payable before the transferred deed can be recorded in the new owner's name.

In Virginia, the buyer typically pays the state and county deed transfer taxes. The state transfer tax is $0.25 for every $100 of the sale price or fraction thereof. The county or city transfer tax is usually one third (1/3) of the state tax.

Another Virginia transfer tax, known as the **grantor tax**, is paid by the seller. The grantor tax is $1 for every $1,000 of the sale price, or 0.1%. For example, a property sold for $500,000 would involve a grantor tax of $500. In some areas in Northern Virginia, an additional $0.15 is charged per $100 of the sale price, or 0.15%.

Recordation taxes

When the deed is submitted for recording, the buyer pays two deed recordation taxes, one to the state and the other to the county or city. The state recordation tax is $0.25 for every $100 or fraction of the consideration of the deed or the actual value of the property, whichever is greater. The county or city recordation tax is usually one third (1/3) of the state tax.

The state may also impose a recordation tax on a deed of trust or mortgage. The rate for either is $0.25 for every $100 or fraction thereof of the mortgage loan, bonds, or other secured obligations and is paid by the buyer/borrower.

Special fees

There may be a **regional transportation improvement fee** that is paid by the seller at a rate of $0.10 for each $100 after May 1, 2021. **Regional congestion relief** fees imposed in planning districts established by statute are paid by the seller at a rate of $0.10 for each $100.

VIRGINIA HOUSING AUTHORITY

Virginia Housing, formerly known as the Virginia Housing Development Authority, was created by the General Assembly in 1972 to help the state's residents obtain affordable, quality housing. The organization is self-supporting and does not receive funding from taxes. Instead, its funds come from capital markets.

Virginia Housing works with local governments, community service organizations, lenders, real estate professionals, developers, and others to provide housing services to those in need. These services include mortgages for first-time buyers, financing for apartment communities and neighborhood revitalization efforts, free homebuyer classes, assistance for the elderly and disabled in making their homes more accommodating for them, down payment and closing cost assistance, as well as housing counseling. They also provide grants for rental housing modifications for the disabled, Granting Freedom funds to help disabled veterans modify their homes for better accessibility, and voucher programs to help low-income families and those who may be homeless.

Virginia Housing Trust Fund

This Fund was created by the Housing Partnership Network in 2001 to help meet the need for early-stage financing for affordable housing development. The Fund's purpose is to provide affordable homeownership and rental opportunities for low- and moderate-income Virginians. The Fund provides loans and grants to finance the development or rehabilitation of single family, multi-family, congregate, and single room occupancy housing.

Approximately $18 million was allocated to the Fund for 2018-2020, with at least 80 percent to be used for short, medium, and long-term loans to reduce the cost of homeownership and rental housing. Up to 20 percent of the Fund may be used to reduce homelessness.

Members of the Network include regional developers, lenders, and community builders who work together in the belief that stable, affordable homes provide positive benefits to people and their communities.

ADVERSE POSSESSION

Adverse possession allows a party to take legal possession of and title to land or a dwelling simply by using the land or living in the dwelling without the owner's permission.

Possession period

Possession must be hostile, actual, exclusive, open and notorious, and continuous for 15 years.

Valid claim criteria

Virginia requires the would-be adverse possessor to meet strict legal requirements and show clear and convincing evidence to prove a claim of adverse possession. The legal holder of the property's title is presumed to be the owner until or unless the claimant can prove otherwise.

A claim of adverse possession in Virginia requires the claimant's possession to be all of the following:

- hostile (against the right of the property owner and without permission)
- actual (exercising control over the property)
- exclusive (possession by only the trespasser);
- open and notorious (using the property and not hiding the occupancy)
- continuous (for 15 years).

The claimant does not have to pay property taxes to make an adverse possession claim.

==

SNAPSHOT REVIEW: UNIT ONE

REAL ESTATE LAW AND REGULATIONS

REAL ESTATE LAW AND REGULATIONS
The Real Estate Board
- Virginia Real Estate Board (REB) regulatory board certifies and licenses individuals
- Enforces, amends, and promulgates rules and regulations
- DPOR directs and supervises

Structure and functions
- 9 members- 2 citizens, 7 with real estate broker/salesperson licenses for 5 consecutive years
- Governor appoints
- 4-year staggered terms
- Limitations- arbitrating disputes; establishing commission rates/splits; standardizing listing agreements, sales contracts, real estate forms

Powers
- Administering, enforcing Chapter 21 regulations of the Virginia Code
- Real estate licensure & renewal requirements
- License fees
- adopting regulations- licensure educational requirements
- waiving education/experience requirements
- issuing, renewing real estate licenses
- activities unlicensed independent contractors permitted to perform
- administering Virginia real estate transaction recovery fund
- enforcing Virginia Fair Housing law, conducting investigations, penalties on violators
- imposing discipline & sanctions for license law violations
- investigating allegations of unlicensed individuals performing real estate activities, issuing cease and desist orders, imposing civil penalties, reporting individual to commonwealth attorney
- obtaining & examining licensee's documents, books, records related

IMPROPER DEALINGS & PROHIBITED ACTS
- offering property for sale/lease without knowledge/consent of owner/owner's representative
- offering property for sale/lease terms not authorized by property owner/owner's representative
- placing sign on property without property owner/owner's representative consent
- advertising property for sale, rent, lease without real estate firm name
- entering into brokerage relationship that does not include termination date/means to determine termination

DISCIPLINARY PROCEDURES

Complaints
- written
- Department receives within 3 years of act
- Regulatory Programs and Compliances Section reviews complaint
- ADR could mediate
- Formal hearings in accordance with Administrative Process Act of the Code of Virginia

Sanctions

- REB can impose disciplinary actions- remedial education, fine up to $1,000, license suspension/revocation
- REB cannot require refunds, deficiency corrections, personal remedies

LICENSED ACTIVITIES

- buying, selling, exchanging, leasing, renting
- showing property/holding open houses
- listings, title, financing, closing, contracts, brokerage agreements, legal documents
- discussing, explaining, interpreting, negotiating contract, listing, lease agreement, property management agreement
- negotiating/agreeing on commission, commission split, management fee, referral fee

Activities not requiring a license

- clerical duties, answering phones, electronic media, information shown on listing, appointments
- submit listings to MLS, keys made for listings, signs on properties, repairs directed by licensee
- approved promotional materials
- prepare contract forms for licensee and supervising broker's approval, assemble closing documents, act as a courier service
- obtain public information from governmental entities
- record/deposit earnest money deposits, security deposits, advance rents
- follow up on loan commitments
- compute commission checks
- monitor license/personnel files
- receive compensation at predetermined rate not contingent on real estate transaction
- perform activities for which license not required

REPORTING TO THE BOARD

- Current name & physical address
- Report changes within 30 calendar days
- Report professional names
- Return license to Board within 10 calendar days of status change
- Return broker license to Board within 3 business days

VIRGINIA RESIDENTIAL PROPERTY DISCLOSURE ACT

- Governs information property owners must disclose
- Residential property 1-4 units transferred by sale, exchange, land sales contract, lease with option to buy
- Exemptions: administration of estate, eminent domain, first sale of property other than foreclosure, divorce, etc.

PROPERTY DISCLOSURES

- Sellers provide Residential Property Disclosure Statement
- Septic systems to be disclosed
- Repetitive claims with National Flood Insurance Program must be disclosed
- Megan's Law- publicize registered sex offender information
- Stigmatized properties do not need disclosures (murder, felony, reputed haunting, communicable disease)
- HOA/POA disclosures
- Environmental- defective drywall, building/zoning violations, lead-based paint, Chesapeake Bay Preservation Act

SERVICEMEMBERS CIVIL RELIEF ACT
- Support active military members with rental agreements, prepaid rent, security deposits, evictions, mortgage interest rates, mortgage foreclosures, credit card interest rates, etc

VIRGINIA RESIDENTIAL LANDLORD AND TENANT ACT

- Protects landlord/tenant rights/obligations
- Covers single-family housing, apartments, motels, hotels, manufactured homes, public/federally subsidized housing
- Landlord provides tenant with written report of pre-existing damages
- Tenant to responsibly maintain dwelling

VIRGINIA COMMON INTEREST COMMUNITY ACT

- Common Interest Communities designed by developers
- Public offering statement includes community/amenity description; declaration & bylaws; management contract; easements; liens; buyer's right to cancel disposition within timeframe.
- 11 governor appointed members in CIC Board
- CIC managers provide services to CIC
- CIC Ombudsman give information to association members

VIRGINIA PROPERTY OWNER'S ASSOCIATION ACT

- Regulates associations that manage real estate developments with CC&Rs
- Property owners to disclose if development is subject to POA and provide association resale certificate

VIRGINIA CONDOMINUM ACT AND REGULATIONS

- CC&RS to set use, appearance, maintenance, restrictions, management of property
- Unit owner rights include access to all association records, voting on association matters, board meeting/proceeding notifications, serving on board

VIRGINIA REAL ESTATE COOPERATIVE ACT

- Administered by CIC Board
- Governs residential co-ops
- Each co-op member is shareholder of cooperative community, not unit owner
- Similar requirements as CICs- annual budget, management, common elements, meetings, insurance, etc.
- POS before selling co-op interest
- Purchaser can cancel contract within 10 days of signing

VIRGINIA RESALE DISCLOSURE ACT

- Combines elements of the Virginia Condominium Act, the Property Owners' Association Act, and the Virginia Real Estate Cooperative Act
- Mandates use of a standardized resale certificate for all sales in common interest communities
- Allows buyers to cancel the contract for sale within any named timeframe

VIRGINIA TIME SHARE ACT

- Requirements for creating/selling time-shares
- Developer to record time-share instrument in clerk's office
- POS similar to POS of CIC; filed with CIC Board
- POS delivered to prospective buyer
- Purchaser can cancel contract within 5 days of certificate

VIRGINIA UNDERGROUND UTILITY DAMAGE PREVENTION ACT

- Protect underground storage/conveyance of water, sewage, telecommunications, electric energy, cable television, oil, petroleum products, gas, or other substances
- Pipes, sewers, combination storm/sanitary sewer systems, conduits, cables, valves, lines, wires, manholes, attachments, portions of poles below ground

VIRGINIA HOMESTEAD

- Protect against loss of primary residence in drastic economic conditions
- Single family homes, condominiums, mobile/manufactured homes used primary residence
- Exemption amounts vary from $5,000-$20,000

VIRGINIA JOINT TENANCY

- 2+ people own property as a single person
- Joint tenancy automatically established without survivorship
- Time, title, interest, and possession create joint tenancy

VIRGINIA REAL PROPERTY TAXATION

- Property taxes fund local government's operations/services
- Annual tax due dates vary by county
- Unpaid property taxes become liens
- Property sold by public auction if assessed value below $100,000 and taxes delinquent on December 31 one year after due date
- Special assessment taxes collected to fund specific improvements for specific areas
- Tax exemptions- Commonwealth owners, non-profit cemetery, religious use, veteran with 100% disability, etc.
- Taxpayer Bill of Rights- rights, privacy, dignity, property of taxpayers during tax assessment, collection, and enforcement processes

TRANSACTION TAXES

- Transfer taxes, recordation taxes when property is sold by deed
- Transfer tax- excise tax when property's title transferred from seller to buyer
- Recordation tax- when deed submitted for recording, buyer pays two deed recordation taxes to state and county/city

VIRGINIA HOUSING AUTHORITY

- Help residents find affordable housing
- Funds from capital markets not taxes
- Mortgages for first-time buyers, financing for apartment communities and neighborhood revitalization efforts, free homebuyer classes, assistance for elderly/disabled in making homes accommodating, down payment and closing cost assistance, housing counseling
- Virginia Housing Trust Fund- early-stage financing for development/rehabilitation of affordable housing development

ADVERSE POSSESSION

- Take legal possession title to land/dwelling by using/living on land/dwelling without permission
- Possession is hostile, actual, exclusive, open, notorious, and continuous for 15 years

Check Your Understanding Quiz:

Unit One: Real Estate Law and Regulations

Carefully read each question then provide your best answer based on what you learned in this unit. Then check your answers against the Answer Key which immediately follows the quiz questions.

1. Which of the following activities does not require a license?

    a. Leasing a property
    b. Submitting listings to MLS
    c. Negotiating a contract
    d. Holding an open house

2. Which statute requires law enforcement authorities to make information about registered sex offenders available to the public?

    a. Megan's Law
    b. Public Information Act
    c. Buyer Beware Law
    d. Criminal Offender Act

3. Developers design _____ for community living.

    a. subdivision plat maps
    b. common area boundaries
    c. multi-unit conference centers
    d. Common Interest Communities

4. Which statute mandates the requirements for creating and selling time-shares?

    a. Cooperative Community Law
    b. The Virginia Time-Share Act
    c. The Virginia Condominium Act
    d. Shared Rental Property Law

5. Adverse possession must be hostile, actual, and continuous for _____.

    a. 21 years.
    b. 6 months.
    c. 18 months.
    d. 15 years.

6. Virginia requires certain time, title, interest and _____ conditions be satisfied in order to create a joint tenancy.

   a. possession
   b. hostility
   c. entitlement
   d. equality

7. The Real Estate Board falls under the organizational purview of the _____.

   a. DPOR.
   b. NAR.
   c. VAR.
   d. VOB.

8. Complaints against licensees must be in writing and received by the Department within _____ of the alleged act.

   a. 6 months
   b. 3 years
   c. 12 months
   d. 7 years

9. Which party pays the grantor tax?

   a. Buyer
   b. Tenant
   c. Seller
   d. Landlord

10. Which of the following liens are prioritized over all other liens?

   a. Mechanic's liens
   b. Tax liens
   c. HOA liens
   d. Bank liens

11. Properties owned by seniors who are _____ years of age and older may be exempt from taxation.

   a. 65
   b. 55
   c. 75
   d. 80

12. What must the developer provide the purchaser when a home is sold in a common interest community?

    a. The developer's budget
    b. The bylaws
    c. The HOA documents
    d. A public offering statement

13. Which statute addresses the effects of land use planning and development on water quality?

    a. Civil Relief Act
    b. Virginia Residential Act
    c. Chesapeake Bay Preservation Act
    d. Virginia Land Use Act

14. Which of the following is one of the REB's general powers?

    a. Standardizing listing agreements
    b. Determining license fees
    c. Establishing commission rates
    d. Arbitrating disputes between brokers

15. The Disclosures Statement makes no warranties as to _____.

    a. historic district ordinances.
    b. aircraft noise.
    c. present septic systems.
    d. HOA memberships.

16. Which of the following parties offers assistance to association members regarding their rights in relation to their associations?

    a. CIC manager
    b. Real estate board
    c. Director of communities
    d. CIC Ombudsman

17. Which of the following statutes protects underground conveyance of telecommunications?

    a. The Telecommunications Protection Act
    b. The Virginia Conveyance Act
    c. The Virginia Underground Utility Damage Prevention Act
    d. The Virginia Homestead Act

18. What statute(s) help homeowners shield portions of their home equity against creditors?

    a. Homeowner Protection Act
    b. Virginia homestead laws
    c. Survivorship Act
    d. Joint tenancy laws

19. If a property's assessed value is _____ or less, the property may be sold by public auction to pay delinquent taxes.

    a. $100,000
    b. $250,000
    c. $200,000
    d. $350,000

20. If a street is being widened in a particular neighborhood, who will be charged with a special assessment tax?

    a. Everyone in that county
    b. Only the renters in that neighborhood
    c. Everyone in that city
    d. Only the homeowners in that neighborhood

21. Which of the following activities does not require a real estate license?

    a. Computing commission checks
    b. Showing homes
    c. Leasing property
    d. Negotiating referral fees

22. Which of the following is NOT something the REB does?

    a. Establish real estate renewal requirements
    b. Arbitrate disputes between salespersons and brokers
    c. Waive education requirements
    d. Administer regulations under Chapter 21

23. How long do members of the REB serve for?

    a. 7 years
    b. 4 years
    c. 1 year
    d. 5 years

24. How many of the members in the REB are citizen members?

    a. Seven
    b. Five
    c. Two
    d. Nine

25. Which statute was created to support active military members with rental agreement issues?

    a. SCRA
    b. VRLTA
    c. ADA
    d. UETA

26. Which of the following is a tenant obligation?

    a. Supplying running hot and cold water at all times
    b. Providing locks for the dwelling
    c. Maintaining major systems in good working order
    d. Removing all waste from the dwelling in appropriate receptacles

27. Which of the following is a landlord obligation?

    a. Maintaining the dwelling free of insects
    b. Providing certification that all smoke alarms are in working order
    c. Complying with building health and safety codes
    d. Being reasonably responsible to prevent any personal injury

28. Which of the following is an accurate statement with respect to a buyer's right to cancel the sales contract?

    a. A buyer may cancel within five days of signing the contract.
    b. A buyer may cancel within seven days of receiving the HOA documents.
    c. A buyer may cancel within any agreed upon number of days.
    d. A buyer may not cancel the contract.

29. Which statute mandates the requirements for creating and selling time-shares?

    a. Virginia Time-Share Act
    b. POS Act
    c. Co-op Act
    d. Community Property Act

30. When ownership is established as a _____, a deceased owner's share can be passed on to other owners without going through the probate process.

    a. legacy tenancy
    b. tenancy without survivorship
    c. passing tenancy
    d. joint tenancy with survivorship

31. Which legislative act allows buyers in common interest communities to negotiate their recission period?

    a. Virginia Resale Disclosure Act
    b. Virginia Resale Certificate Act
    c. Virginia Sales Contract Act
    d. Virginia Homeowners' Association Act

==

UNIT 2:

AGENCY LAW

Unit Two Learning Objectives: When the student has completed this unit he or she will be able to:

- Describe the various forms of agency relationship allowed by Virginia law, and how each relationship varies in form and duties.
- Summarize relationship disclosure requirements by type of relationship imposed.

Creating the brokerage relationship

Intent. If a customer's intent is to enter into a real estate transaction with the help of a licensee's professional judgment and advice, then based on that intent, the customer has entered into a brokerage relationship with the licensee. For example, if the customer requests the licensee to show her homes just so she can see typical features of homes in the area, then there is no such intent. However, if the customer requests the licensee to show her homes that meet her criteria so she may put an offer in on one of them, then her intent is to enter into a brokerage transaction.

Written agreement. At the point where this relationship has been created, Virginia requires a written brokerage agreement because the acts the licensee will perform for the customer will go beyond the definition of ministerial acts. Keep in mind that it is this intent and not compensation or use of a common source information company (explained later in this unit) that creates the relationship and requires the agreement. While compensation is typically included in the relationship agreement, compensation alone does not create the relationship.

Before the customer makes the relationship official by signing the agreement, the licensee is required to:

- determine that the customer is not already in a brokerage agreement with another licensee
- explain the type of brokerage relationship the licensee is proposing
- discuss and agree to the broker's compensation
- disclose whether the broker will be sharing the compensation with another broker who may have a brokerage relationship with another party to the transaction
- disclose any broker relationship the licensee has with another party to the same transaction

These requirements must be met at the earliest practical time but at least prior to the licensee performing any specific real estate assistance for the customer/client.

Commencement and termination

A brokerage relationship begins when a customer's intent creates the relationship by engaging a licensee. The relationship typically continues until the services agreed to in the brokerage agreement have been completed. For example, the agreement may terminate when a property sale closes. However, the relationship may also terminate for any of the following reasons:

- expiration on date specified in the agreement
- termination on any date mutually agreed to by the parties to the transaction
- agreement default by any party to the transaction
- licensee's withdrawal from the relationship if the client refuses to consent to a disclosed dual agency or dual representation
- death or incapacity of either party
- condemnation or destruction of the property (sellers and landlords)
- bankruptcy of either party
- revocation of the broker's license

To ensure that the Real Estate Board's broker and salesperson licensees comply with **§ 54.1-2137. Commencement and termination of brokerage relationships**, the Board directs licensees to review the following information.

The following are relevant excerpts from the *Code of Virginia*:

§ 54.1-2137. Commencement and termination of brokerage relationships.

B. Brokerage agreements shall be in writing and shall:
1. Have a definite termination date; however, if a brokerage agreement does not specify a definite termination date, the brokerage agreement shall terminate 90 days after the date of the brokerage agreement;
2. State the amount of the brokerage fees and how and when such fees are to be paid;
3. State the services to be rendered by the licensee;
4. Include such other terms of the brokerage relationship as have been agreed to by the client and the licensee; and
5. In the case of brokerage agreements entered into in conjunction with the client's consent to a dual representation, the disclosures set out in subsection A of § 54.1-2139.

§ 54.1-2137. Commencement and termination of brokerage relationships.
A. The brokerage relationships set forth in this article shall commence at the time that a client engages a licensee and shall continue until (i) completion of performance in accordance with the brokerage agreement or (ii) the earlier of (a) any date of expiration agreed upon by the parties as part of the brokerage agreement or in any amendments thereto, (b) any mutually agreed upon termination of the brokerage agreement, (c) a default by any party under the terms of the brokerage agreement, or (d) a termination as set forth in subsection F of § 54.1-2139.

§ 54.1-2130. Definitions.
As used in this article: ...
"Brokerage agreement" means the written agreement creating a brokerage relationship between a client and a licensee. The brokerage agreement shall state whether the real estate licensee will represent the client as an agent or an independent contractor.
"Brokerage relationship" means the contractual relationship between a client and a real estate licensee who has been engaged by such client for the purpose of procuring a seller, buyer, option, tenant, or landlord ready, able, and willing to sell, buy, option, exchange or

rent real estate on behalf of a client.

"Client" means a person who has entered into a brokerage relationship with a licensee.

"Customer" means a person who has not entered into a brokerage relationship with a licensee but for whom a licensee performs ministerial acts in a real estate transaction. Unless a licensee enters into a brokerage relationship with such person, it shall be presumed that such person is a customer of the licensee rather than a client.

"Ministerial acts" means those routine acts which a licensee can perform for a person which do not involve discretion or the exercise of the licensee's own judgment.

The Code of Virginia requires a written brokerage agreement when a brokerage relationship, as defined in § 54.1-2130, is created. When a customer becomes a client is based upon the party's intent. A licensee needs to use his judgment based upon a customer's words and actions to make a determination as to when the intent to enter into a brokerage relationship is established and therefore, requires a brokerage agreement. Is the party looking for the licensee to provide advice and counsel requiring the licensee to exercise his judgment or discretion for the purpose of procuring a seller, buyer, option, tenant, or landlord ready, able, and willing to sell, buy, option, exchange or rent real estate? If so, this would require a written brokerage agreement as these acts don't fall within the definition of ministerial acts. Has the party engaged the licensee for the purpose of procuring a seller, buyer, option, tenant or landlord ready, able and willing to sell, buy, option, exchange, or rent real estate? If yes, then a brokerage relationship is established and this requires a written brokerage agreement.

Below are some examples of situations which require the licensee to use his judgment to determine the party's intent:

• Many acts may be ministerial or could require a written brokerage agreement depending on the party making the request and his intent. For example, showing a house may be ministerial if the licensee takes the party to see what the typical features are in homes in the market area or to gather information on the market or area. However, if the party asks the licensee to show him real estate because his intent is to have the licensee procure someone who is ready, able and willing to sell, buy, option, exchange, or rent real estate then a brokerage relationship exists requiring a written brokerage agreement.

o Another example relates to a request for a multiple listing service (MLS) search. If a party requests a licensee to provide MLS search results without the intent to engage the licensee for the purpose of procuring a seller, buyer, option, tenant or landlord ready, able and willing to sell, buy, option, exchange, or rent real estate then a written brokerage agreement is not necessary. However, if a party requests MLS search results having the intent to engage the licensee for the purpose of procuring a seller, buyer, option, tenant or landlord ready, able and willing to sell, buy, option, exchange, or rent real estate then a written brokerage agreement is necessary.

• If a party asks the licensee for general information about items such as tax rates, HOA dues, schools or typical features of property in the area, these acts appear to be ministerial. However, if the party asks these questions about specific property because his intent is to have the licensee procure someone who is ready, able and willing to sell, buy, option, exchange, or rent real estate, or if he asks the licensee to provide the licensee's opinion as to those features or properties that have those features, then a brokerage relationship exists requiring a written brokerage agreement.

• Many licensees may perform marketing activities in order to induce a party to engage them for the purpose of procuring a seller, buyer, option, tenant, or landlord ready, able, and willing to sell, buy, option, exchange or rent real estate. For instance, if a party asks the licensee to provide him with a valuation or analysis of real estate or an MLS search for informational purposes and does not yet intend to engage the licensee to procure a buyer or seller for the real estate, a written brokerage agreement is not necessary. However, if at the time the party asks the licensee to provide the valuation and the party intends to use the valuation or analysis of the real estate for the purpose of having that licensee procure a buyer for the real estate, then a written brokerage agreement is needed.

o As a further example, a licensee may provide marketing materials and a competitive market analysis to a prospective seller who is interviewing for the purpose of retaining a licensee to sell their property, without the necessity of a written brokerage agreement.

The party's intent can change during the performance of ministerial acts by the licensee. The licensee needs to be aware of when the intent of the party changes from that of customer to client, and get the party to sign a written brokerage agreement before performing any nonministerial acts for that party. It is important for brokers to have policies in place to guide their licensees, based upon the firm's business practices, in determining when a written brokerage agreement is required and procedures for obtaining such agreements.

Types of relationships permitted

Virginia allows for three types of brokerage relationship:

- standard agency, which includes dual standard agency and designated standard agency, if properly disclosed
- limited service representation
- independent contractor representation

STANDARD AGENCY

Standard agency is a brokerage relationship wherein the licensee represents a seller, buyer, landlord, or tenant as a client in the relationship and owes the client specific duties or obligations as covered in an upcoming section. In addition to allowing representation of a single transaction party, standard agency allows for dual agency and designated agency.

Dual standard agency

A Virginia licensee is allowed to represent both parties to a real estate transaction (seller and buyer or landlord and tenant). The licensee is required to disclose the dual relationship and its consequences to both parties, to obtain informed written consent from both parties, and have both parties sign the disclosure notice. Once signed, the disclosure is to be given to all parties to the transaction prior to the actual commencement of the transaction.

The licensee may be either a dual agent or a dual representative, based on the brokerage agreement. A dual agent has an agency relationship under the brokerage agreements with the clients. A dual representative has an independent contractor relationship under the brokerage agreements with the clients.

The licensee representing both parties has a limited ability to represent either party fully and exclusively. The licensee must maintain information confidentiality, such as not telling the buyer client that the seller client will accept a lower price for the property or telling the seller client that the buyer client will pay a higher price.

Designated standard agency

Virginia law allows a principal or supervising broker to designate different affiliated licensees to represent different clients in the same transaction. For example, the broker may designate one salesperson to represent the seller and another salesperson to represent the buyer in the same transaction.

As long as neither designated licensee is representing more than one party in the same transaction, the designations do not constitute a dual agency or representation. However, while the licensees are not engaged in a dual agency, their supervising broker is considered a dual agent or representative as both clients are represented by the same brokerage. Unlike the dual relationship, these designated licensees represent only the interest of their respective clients and so may represent those interests fully.

Just as with a dual agency, designated agency/representation requires disclosure and informed written consent from both parties. The disclosure may be provided in combination with other disclosures or information. If the disclosure is not a separate document, it must be conspicuous and printed in underlined bold all capital lettering or in a separate box.

The disclosure form includes the broker's name and firm, parties being represented (seller and buyer or landlord and tenant), the designated licensee's name, the client being represented by that designated licensee (seller, buyer, landlord, tenant), the type of representation (standard agent, limited service agent, independent contractor), and the following statement:

The undersigned understand that the foregoing dual agent or representative may not disclose to either client or such client's designated agent or representative any information that has been given to the dual agent or representative by the other client within the confidence and trust of the brokerage relationship except for that information which is otherwise required or permitted by Article 3 (§ 54.1-2130 et seq.) of Chapter 21 of Title 54.1 of the Code of Virginia to be disclosed.

Designated licensees may not disclose their client's personal or financial information or any other confidential information to anyone other than their broker unless the disclosure is required by law or the client consents in writing to its disclosure.

Dual relationship disclosure form

The disclosure form includes the clients being represented (seller, buyer, landlord, tenant), the type of representation (standard agent, limited service agent, independent contractor), and the consequences of this type of relationship. The same form is used for two existing clients in the transaction and for one existing client and one new client in the transact6ion.

The form provides the following disclosures of conditions to take effect on commencement of the dual agency:

- The dual agent or dual representative may not disclose to either client any information that has been given to the dual agent or representative by the other client within the confidence and trust of the brokerage relationship.
- The licensee cannot advise either party as to the terms to offer or accept any offer or counteroffer, even though the licensee may have done so with one party prior to the commencement of the dual relationship.
- The licensee cannot advise the buyer client as to the suitability of the property, its condition (other than to make any disclosures as required by law), or advise either party as to what property repairs to make or request.
- The licensee cannot advise either party in any dispute related to the transaction.
- The licensee may be acting without knowing the client's needs, knowledge of the market, or capabilities in dealing with real estate transactions.
- Either party may engage another licensee at additional cost to represent his or her respective interests.

LIMITED SERVICE REPRESENTATION

Virginia law requires a licensee who represents a client in an agency relationship in a residential real estate transaction to act as either a standard agent or a limited service agent. A standard agent's obligations and duties to the client are mandated by statute. On the other hand, because a limited service agent may be an independent contractor, the agent is not bound to provide the obligations and duties mandated by statute. Instead, this agent's obligations and duties are contractual and limited to those the client and agent agree to at the time the written brokerage agreement is created.

A limited service agent can represent a seller, a buyer, or both; or a landlord, a tenant, or both. Regardless of whom the licensee represents, there must be a written brokerage agreement between agent and client, with written informed consent to the relationship from the client or clients.

Whether the limited service relationship is with a single client or both clients, the client or clients must be informed about the relationship, consent to the relationship, and sign the relationship disclosure form. A limited service brokerage agreement must disclose that the licensee is acting as a limited service agent. It must also provide a list of the specific services the licensee will provide to the client or clients and include a list of which specific standard agent duties the limited service representative will not perform.

These disclosures must be conspicuous and printed in either bold or capital underlined lettering or in a separate box. The disclosure must include or comply with the following verbiage:

By entering into this brokerage agreement, the undersigned do hereby acknowledge their informed consent to the limited service representation by the licensee and do further acknowledge that neither the other party to the transaction nor any real estate licensee representing the other party is under any legal obligation to assist the undersigned with the performance of any duties and responsibilities of the undersigned not performed by the limited service representative.

The limited service agent must provide all required disclosures to the client at the time the brokerage agreement is created. These disclosures include the rights and obligations of the client under the Virginia Residential Property Disclosure Act, the right of a condominium buyer to receive the condominium resale certificate, or of a POA buyer to receive the association resale certificate.

BROKERAGE AGREEMENTS

By definition, a brokerage agreement is the written agreement creating a brokerage relationship between a client and a licensee. The agreement is to state whether the licensee will represent the client as an agent or an independent contractor.

Requirements

The agreement must also meet the following requirements:

- be in writing
- include a termination date; otherwise, it will terminate after 90 days
- state the amount of brokerage fees as well as how and when the fees are to be paid
- state the services to be provided by the licensee
- include all other terms agreed to by the client and the licensee
- include disclosures required when the client agrees to a dual representation

In the absence of other terms agreed to in writing, the licensee owes the client only the following two duties after the termination of the brokerage agreement:

1) account for all moneys and property related to the relationship
2) keep the client's personal and financial information confidential unless the client consents in writing to the release of the information or unless the law requires the release

Listing agreements

One of the most common brokerage agreements is the listing agreement wherein the licensee represents a property owner selling his or her property. With a listing agreement, the licensee owes his primary responsibilities to the seller.

Because a listing agreement is a brokerage agreement, Virginia listing agreements must be in writing. While the DPOR and the REB have not standardized listing agreements or offered listing agreement forms on their websites, there are other sites that offer fillable and printable versions of the agreement, such as the Virginia Association of REALTORS®.

As discussed in detail in an earlier chapter, there are basically four types of listing agreements for property sales:

- open listing – not an exclusive agreement with one licensee; seller may enter into this agreement with multiple brokers and pay only the broker who finds the buyer; most brokers avoid this type of listing because there is no guarantee of compensation for the work performed
- exclusive agency – allows any broker to sell the property, with the commission paid to the contracted broker only if he or she sells the property; also allows the owner to sell the property and not owe commission to anyone

- exclusive right-to-sell – most commonly-used listing agreement; creates an exclusive relationship between the seller and the broker wherein the contracted broker is paid the commission regardless of who sells the property as long as the property is sold during the listing period
- net listing – illegal in Virginia; seller sets the amount to be received from the sale of the property; broker may sell the property for any amount over the seller's price and keep the difference as compensation; creates a conflict of interest wherein the broker may put his or her own best interest (higher commission) ahead of the client's interest

There are two basic agreements for property leasing representation:

- exclusive right-to-lease – similar to the exclusive right-to-sell; listing broker is paid a commission even if someone else finds a tenant
- buyer and tenant representation agreements – exclusive, exclusive right-to-lease, or open, with the same conditions for compensation as in the sale agreements

Most listing agreements include the following:

- seller's disclosure of no other current listing agreements
- selling price
- items to be conveyed with the property
- terms of the agreement
- broker's compensation
- termination/expiration date and conditions (required)
- duties owed by the broker and by the client
- required disclosures regarding the property
- fair housing statement
- disclosure of dual or designated agency relationship

A sample listing agreement can be found at https://eforms.com/download/2018/10/Virginia-Real-Estate-Listing-Agreement.pdf.

Buyer agency agreements

A buyer agency agreement is a contract between a broker and someone who is looking to purchase a property. Virginia law mandates that licensees must have a buyer agency agreement in place before they can tour properties with a customer or have substantial conversations with a customer about a particular property. The agreement includes the duties the licensee and buyer owe to each other, including the licensee's duty of confidentiality.

A buyer agency agreement typically includes the following:

- agreement's term length
  There is no mandated term length. The typical length is 6 months or one year.
- early agreement termination provision
  This provision outlines the process for terminating the agreement before its stated termination date. The buyer typically owes the licensee a fee if the required notice is not given.

- licensee's compensation
  This includes a retainer fee and the payment for the licensee's services. Not all buyer agreements include a retainer fee, but when they do, the fee is used to compensate the licensee for time and expenses and separates serious buyers from casual lookers.
- The payment to the licensee may be in the form of a commission, typically paid by the listing agent as a percentage of the total commission for the property sale. The payment may also be a flat fee.
- type of representation
  This may be an exclusive representation or a non-exclusive representation. The agreement must state whether dual or designated representation is involved so that proper disclosures can be made.
- licensee's duties to the buyer
  Buyers' licensees not only find properties to tour, but they guide the buyer through the entire purchasing process, research comparable properties, recommend offer amounts and conditions, assist in negotiating the deal, help through the settlement process, and more.
- buyer's duties to the licensee
  Buyers agree to comply with the licensee's reasonable requests to provide necessary information, pay the licensee the agreed-upon compensation, be available for property showings, and so on.

A Virginia Association of REALTORS® exclusive right-to-represent agreement form can be found online at https://eforms.com/images/2020/01/Virginia-Exclusive-Right-To-Represent-Buyer.pdf.

A Virginia Association of REALTORS® non-exclusive right-to-represent agreement form can be found online at https://eforms.com/images/2020/01/Virginia-Non-Exclusive-Buyer-Broker-Agreement.pdf

Common source information companies

A common source information company (CSIC) is a person or business entity that compiles and/or supplies information regarding real estate for sale or lease as well as other related data. A multiple listing service (MLS) is an example of a common source information company. CSICs are not required to hold a real estate license.

A licensee's use of a CSIC does not in itself create a brokerage. For example, a buyer's agent may use a CSIC to look up properties without creating a brokerage relationship with a seller or other licensee. The same holds true for a tenant's agent using a CSIC. That use alone does not create a brokerage relationship with a landlord.

Regarding disclosure, a CSIC may

- require participants or users of their information to disclose the nature of the brokerage relationship with the client and whether the licensee is acting as an independent contractor, a limited service agent, a standard agent, or another role as provided in the brokerage agreement
- assume that a licensee using its services is acting as a standard agent if the licensee does not disclose the brokerage relationship
- provide the licensee's agency relationship information to the company's other participants and to any settlement service it provides, such as title insurance companies, lenders, and settlement agents

Referral agents

Two brokers or brokerages may establish a referral relationship. The parties sign an agreement to recommend clients to each other when one broker seems to be better suited to the client's needs. The referring broker is then paid a fee for the referral, often a percentage of the referred broker's commission on the transaction.

Brokers who engage in referrals must hold a valid real estate license. Often, the two brokers will sign a reciprocal agreement wherein both brokers agree to refer clients to each other for specific situations, typically due to location or jurisdiction. For example, a customer who lives in Virginia may want to purchase a home in Florida, so the customer goes to a broker in Virginia to help find a home. The Virginia broker may then refer the customer to a broker in Florida with whom the broker has a referral agreement.

In addition to individual brokers entering into referral agreements with other individual brokers, referral agencies offer referral services to brokers worldwide by connecting home buyers and sellers with brokers. These agencies employ individuals who hold an active license but are not actively engaged in real estate transactions. Once employed by the agency, the individual's license is changed to referral status and the licensee may not engage in real estate activities outside of the referrals. The agency charges a fee or commission percentage for the referral.

Referral agents are required to complete licensure continuing education each license term.

A Virginia Association of REALTORS® referral agreement form can be found online at

https://virginiarealtors.org/wp-content/uploads/dlm_uploads/2017/04/Virginia-REALTORS-Form-800-Referral-Agreement-2019-07-Fillable.pdf

VIRGINIA AGENCY DISCLOSURE REQUIREMENTS

Relationship disclosures

Disclosure to customers. A licensee who is currently in a brokerage relationship with a client must disclose that relationship to any customer who is not represented by this licensee or another licensee and who has had substantive discussions with the licensee about a specific property. The disclosure must be in writing and is to be made at the earliest practical time prior to the licensee providing any real estate services or assistance.

The same brokerage relationship disclosure requirement holds true for leasing transactions and sale transactions. The licensee is required to disclose his or her relationship with another party to the same transaction. The disclosure must be in writing, and, in the case of leasing, included in the lease application or in the lease itself, and made prior to the signing of the lease. No disclosure is required for single or multi-family residential units for leases of two months or less.

Dual or designated agency. A licensee who is in either a dual agency or dual representation relationship with a client must disclose that relationship to any other party to the same transaction. The disclosure must be in writing and be made prior to the licensee entering into a brokerage relationship with the other party. If the other party is a buyer, the disclosure must be provided to and consent obtained from the buyer no later than when an offer to purchase is presented to the licensee who will present it to the seller. If the other party is a seller, the disclosure must be provided to and consent obtained from the seller no later than when the offer is presented to the seller.

Required agency disclosures may be combined with other disclosures or documents as long as the disclosure is conspicuous in underlined, bold capital lettering or within a separate box as shown below. Agency relationship disclosures must be signed by all parties and retained by the broker for three years.

**DISCLOSURE OF BROKERAGE RELATIONSHIP
IN A RESIDENTIAL REAL ESTATE TRANSACTION**

The undersigned do hereby acknowledge disclosure that:

The licensee _____ (name of broker or salesperson) associated with

_____ (Name of Brokerage Firm) represents the following party in a residential real estate transaction:

    ☐ Seller(s)   or   ☐ Buyer(s)

    ☐ Landlord(s) -13m   or   ☐ Tenant(s)

_____   _____
Date   Name

_____   _____
Date   Name

VIRGINIA AGENCY DUTIES

Standard agent duties

To all clients. A licensee who represents a client has the following duties to that client, whether the client is a seller, buyer, landlord, or tenant:

- perform according to the terms of the brokerage agreement

- promote the interests of the client
- assist in drafting and negotiating offers, counteroffers, amendments, and addenda to the real estate contract or lease and establish strategies to accomplish the client's goals
- receive and present written offers and counteroffers in a timely manner to and from the client even when the property is already subject to a contract or lease
- provide reasonable assistance to help the client satisfy his or her contract obligations and to settle the contract or lease
- maintain confidentiality of personal, financial, and other information provided by the client, unless the client consents in writing to the release of information or the law requires the release
- exercise ordinary care
- in a timely manner, account for all money and property received by the licensee in which the client may have an interest
- disclose material facts to the client that are related to the property or the transaction and that are actually known to the licensee
- comply with all provisions of § 54.1-2131–2134, all fair housing statutes and regulations for residential real estate transactions, and other applicable statutes and regulations that do not conflict with § 54.1-2131–2134.
- treat all parties honestly and not knowingly provide them with false information
- disclose the known existence of defective drywall in a residential property to the buyer

To specific client types. A licensee has these further duties, depending on the type of client:

- *to sellers* – disclose all known material adverse facts related to the physical condition of the property to prospective buyers
- *to sellers and landlord s*– conduct marketing activities so as to seek a sale or lease either at the price and terms of the brokerage agreement or with the client's approval; licensee is not obligated to seek additional offers on the property while it is subject to a contract of sale or lease unless included in the brokerage agreement or the contract
- *to buyers* – disclose whether or not the buyer intends to occupy the property as a principal residence; may be disclosed within the purchase contract
- *to buyers and tenants* – seek a property of a type and price and with terms acceptable to the client; licensee is not obligated to seek other properties for the client while the client is a party to a contract to purchase or lease property unless included in the brokerage agreement

To customers. A licensee's duties to customers – those outside of a brokerage relationship with the licensee – are understandably fewer than those to a client. These duties include:

- treat the customer with honesty and do not knowingly provide the customer with false information
- disclose any known material adverse facts related to the property's physical condition
- disclose any known defective drywall on the property
- disclose previous methamphetamine manufacture on the property when the property has not been cleaned according to specific guidelines
- provide all disclosures in writing

- perform ministerial acts to assist the customer unless prohibited by law or a brokerage agreement and without the acts constituting a brokerage agreement between the licensee and the customer
- comply with all provisions of § 54.1-2131–2134, all fair housing statutes and regulations for residential real estate transactions, and other applicable statutes and regulations that do not conflict with § 54.1-2131–2134
- *not a duty, but allowed* – show alternative properties to prospective buyers or tenants

Unrepresented parties

When a licensee who represents a party in a transaction encounters someone who is not represented by any licensee regarding the potential transaction, the licensee must immediately disclose to the unrepresented party, in writing, the licensee's relationship with the represented party.

After disclosure, the licensee may perform ministerial duties for the unrepresented party but must avoid performing services that would constitute a brokerage relationship with the unrepresented party without first disclosing the requirements of a dual relationship and obtaining written consent from both parties. Otherwise, an illegal undisclosed dual agency may result. The licensee must retain the signed relationship disclosure for three years.

Statutory duties

Violations. The Virginia Administrative Code defines the statutory duties of representation by deeming the following actions and failures to perform required duties as illegal misrepresentations or omissions:

- bait and switch advertising wherein the licensee offers property for sale or rent at a different price than the licensee intends to accept
- a standard agent's failure to disclose to a prospective buyer or renter in a timely manner all known material adverse facts about the condition of the subject property
- a licensee's failure to provide every written offer, counteroffer, and rejection to buy, lease, or option to the buyer and seller in a timely manner
- an agent's failure to disclose all material facts related to the subject property or the transaction to the agent's client thereby failing to provide ordinary care to the client
- a dual representative licensee's failure to maintain confidentiality between the two represented clients in the same transaction
- a licensee's failure to include complete terms and conditions of the transaction, including leases, property management agreements, or offers to purchase
- a licensee's failure to identify all those holding deposits for any application, lease, or offer to purchase
- a licensee knowingly making false statements or reports or willfully misstating the value of a land, property, or security
- a licensee knowingly making any material misrepresentation
- a licensee making a false promise through other agents, salespersons, advertising, or any other means

LISTING AGREEMENT ANALYSIS EXAMPLE

Herman Thompson of Fast Sell Realty just aced his listing appointment with Andrew Stevens on 12/05/2021 so he is rushing home to write the listing agreement. Andrew currently lives on 123 Main Street Richmond, VA 23173. Andrew is adamant about taking his new refrigerator with him to his next house, but he is willing to leave his washer and dryer for the next buyer.

Use the above information to fill out the first page of the listing agreement. What information is missing? Where can Herman find that information?

VIRGINIA REAL ESTATE LISTING AGREEMENT

I. The Parties. This Real Estate Listing Agreement ("Agreement") made on December 5th , 20 21 , is between:

Seller: Andrew Stevens ("Seller") with a mailing address of 123 Main Street , City of Richmond , State of Virginia

AND

Agency: Herman Thompson ("Broker") of Fast Sell Realty ("Agency") with a mailing address of _____, City of _____, State of _____. Collectively, the Seller and Agency shall be referred to as the "Parties".

If for any reason the Broker is not able to fulfill their duties under the terms and conditions of this Agreement, another agent from the Agency may be appointed during the term of this Agreement.

II. Real Property. The real property, that is the subject of this Agreement, is located at the street address of 123 Main Street Richmond, VA 23173

    a.) **Legal Description**.
        Tax Map/Lot: _____/_____
        Deed Book/Page: _____/_____
        Other: _____
    b.) **Fixtures**. The Seller agrees that all fixtures shall be included as part of the sale
        EXCEPT: refrigerator
    c.) **Personal Property**. The Seller agrees that ONLY the following personal property shall be included as part of the sale: washer and dryer

The aforementioned real property, personal property, and included fixtures shall be hereinafter referred to as the "Property".

Answer: Herman should know the address of his brokerage but he can find that with a quick internet search. The legal description portion of the listing agreement can be found in the property tax records online. Once Herman fills that out the first page of the agreement will be complete and he can get it initialled by the seller.

===

SNAPSHOT REVIEW: UNIT TWO

AGENCY LAW

CREATING THE BROKERAGE RELATIONSHIP

- Customer intent to enter real estate transaction with licensee's help
- Written brokerage agreement required

COMMENCEMENT AND TERMINATION

- Brokerage relationship begins with customer intent
- Agreement terminates when services completed (property closes, etc.)

TYPES OF RELATIONSHIPS PERMITTED

- Standard agency (dual standard agency & designated standard agency)
- Limited service representation
- Independent contract representation

STANDARD AGENCY

- Licensee represents seller, buyer, landlord, tenant & owes the client specific duties

Dual standard agency

- Licensee representing both parties (seller/buyer or landlord/tenant)
- Disclosure, written consent from parties required
- Dual agent- agency relationship under brokerage agreements with clients
- Dual representative- independent contractor relationship under brokerage agreements with the clients
- Licensee must maintain confidentiality

Designated standard agency

- Principal/supervising broker designate different affiliated licensees to represent different clients in transaction
- Supervising broker is dual agent/representative
- Disclosure, written consent from parties required

Dual relationship disclosure form

- Clients represented (seller, buyer, landlord, tenant), representation (standard, limited service, independent contractor), consequences of relationship

LIMITED SERVICE REPRESENTATION

- Licensee in agency relationship act as standard or limited service agent
- Standard agent's obligations mandated by statute
- Independent contractor not bound by obligations mandated by statute; contractual duties
- Represent seller/ buyer or both; landlord/tenant or both

- Written brokerage agreement

BROKERAGE AGREEMENTS

- Written agreement creating brokerage relationship between client and licensee
- States if licensee act as agent/independent contractor

Requirements

- Written; termination date; brokerage fees; services; agreed terms; disclosures

Listing agreements

- Licensee represents property owner selling property
- Licensee owes primary responsibilities to seller
- Written
- Types for sales- open; exclusive agency; exclusive right-to-sell; net listing
- Types for leases- exclusive right-to-lease; buyer/tenant representation agreements

Buyer agency agreements

- Contract between broker and buyer
- Includes- term length, early agreement termination, compensation, representation type, licensee duties, buyer duties

Common source information companies

- Person/business entity compiles/supplies real estate information
- MLS is example
- License not required
- Agent using CSIC does not create brokerage relationship

Referral agents

- Agreement to recommend clients to broker
- Referring broker gets fee- often percentage of referred broker's commission
- Both brokers must have valid real estate license

VIRGINIA AGENCY DISCLOSURE REQUIREMENTS

Relationship disclosures

- Licensee in brokerage relationship must disclose in writing relationship to any customer not represented by licensee
- Licensee in dual agency/representation relationship must disclose in writing relationship to any party in the same transaction

VIRGINIA AGENCY DUTIES

Standard agent duties

- Licensee duties to clients- perform according to brokerage agreement; promote client interests; assist in drafting/negotiating offers; receive/present written offers; maintain confidentiality, etc
- Licensee duties to customers- honesty; disclose known material adverse facts; ministerial acts, etc.

Unrepresented parties

- When licensee who represents party in transaction encounters unrepresented person regarding the transaction, licensee must disclose in writing the licensee's relationship
- Licensee may perform ministerial duties for unrepresented party but avoid services constituting brokerage relationship with unrepresented party without disclosing requirements of dual relationship and obtaining written consent from both parties

Statutory duties

- Violations- bait and switch advertising; failing to disclose material adverse facts; failure to provide every written offer; knowingly making material representation, etc.

Check Your Understanding Quiz:

Unit Two: Agency Law

Carefully read each question then provide your best answer based on what you learned in this unit. Then check your answers against the Answer Key which immediately follows the quiz questions.

1. The brokerage agreement states whether the licensee will represent the client as an agent or a(n) _____.

    a. dual agent.
    b. broker.
    c. independent contractor.
    d. salesperson.

2. A multiple listing service (MLS) is an example of a _____.

    a. CSIC.
    b. MIC.
    c. LSC.
    d. HOA.

3. Which agency type allows a licensee to represent both parties to a real estate transaction?

    a. Standard agency
    b. Designated standard agency
    c. Dual standard agency
    d. Joint agency

4. Which of the following can trigger a brokerage relationship?

    a. A customer attending an open house and asking licensee about neighboring homes.
    b. A licensee signing a customer up for MLS emails.
    c. A customer wanting to see the typical home features in an area.
    d. A customer asking a licensee to show her homes that meet her criteria so she can submit an offer.

5. Which listing agreement allows a seller to work with multiple brokers and only pay the broker who finds the buyer?

    a. Exclusive agency
    b. Open listing
    c. Multiple agency
    d. Net listing

6. A supervising broker may designate one salesperson to represent the seller, and another salesperson to represent the buyer in the same transaction. What is this type of agency called?

   a. Designated standard agency
   b. Dual relationship
   c. Identical brokerage agency
   d. Standard agency

7. Which listing agreement is illegal in Virginia?

   a. Net listing
   b. Exclusive right-to-sell
   c. Exclusive agency
   d. Open listing

8. Which of the following is a duty a licensee owes to clients (rather than customers)?

   a. Showing alternative properties to prospective buyers
   b. Disclosing previous methamphetamine manufacture on the property
   c. Disclosing whether or not the buyer intends to occupy the property as a principal residence
   d. Seeking other properties while client is a party to a contract to purchase

9. In which listing agreement type does the seller set the amount to be received from the sale of the property?

   a. Open listing
   b. Net listing
   c. Exclusive agency
   d. Exclusive right-to-sell

10. Which of the following is a buyer's duty to the licensee?

    a. Finding properties to tour
    b. Researching comparable properties
    c. Being available for property showings
    d. Assisting in negotiating the deal

11. What should a broker have in place before touring properties with a customer?

    a. A buyer agency agreement
    b. A listing agreement
    c. A customer relationship agreement
    d. Nothing needs to be in place before the first tour

12. Emily's friend is moving from Virginia to Atlanta and is planning to buy a house there. Emily calls a few real estate agents and finds the perfect one for her friend. What happens next?

    a. Emily can now represent her friend in Georgia despite not being licensed there.
    b. Emily can sign a referral agreement with the other agent to ensure she gets paid a fee at closing.
    c. Emily gets the full commission on the sale of the home.
    d. Emily cannot receive a referral fee because she is not licensed in Georgia.

13. Mark lists a property for $50,000 below what he plans to accept because he wants to attract attention to his listing. What is this type of advertising called?

    a. Buyer beware advertising
    b. Caveat emptor
    c. Bait and switch
    d. Fool's gold advertising

14. Limited service agents are _____.

    a. bound to provide the obligations mandated by statute.
    b. required to provide certain duties enforced by the city.
    c. bound by the same duties a standard agent is bound by.
    d. limited to the duties agreed upon at the time the written brokerage agreement is created.

15. Kaitlin is in a dual agency relationship with the sellers and the potential buyers. The prospective buyers ask Kaitlin for advice on what offer the sellers are likely to accept. What should Kaitlin do?

    a. Kaitlin has to advise the terms that will benefit the sellers.
    b. Kaitlin cannot advise what terms to offer.
    c. Kaitlin has to protect the buyers and advise terms that are beneficial to them.
    d. Kaitlin owes her loyalty to whomever she started working with first.

===

UNIT 3:

ESCROW REQUIREMENTS

Unit Three Learning Objectives: When the student has completed this unit, he or she will be able to:

- Characterize salient regulations governing the operation of brokerage companies, including those relating to branches, escrow procedures, recordkeeping, and trade names.
- Discuss the closing process from start to finish.

ESCROW ACCOUNTS

Account requirements

Escrow funds. Virginia law requires brokers to maintain escrow accounts only if the broker holds money or documents belonging to others in relation to real estate transactions. If the money or documents are held by a third party, the broker is not required to maintain escrow accounts. The monies or documents are typically held until the transaction closes or cancels. Monies may include down payments, earnest money deposits, money received related to final settlements, application deposits, rental payments, rental security deposits, money advanced for expenses related to transaction closings, and any other funds received by the broker to be held until required to be disbursed.

Account maintenance. If a broker does maintain escrow accounts, he or she is held responsible for the accounts and is required to have signatory authority on all of the accounts. The accounts are to be maintained in a federally insured depository unless all principals to the transaction have agreed otherwise in writing.

The accounts must be designated and labeled as "escrow" accounts. Each deposit, check, or bank statement is also to be labeled as "escrow." Earnest monies, rental deposits, and other monies received by the broker must be deposited into the appropriate escrow account by the end of the fifth business banking day following ratification of the related contract unless all principals to the transaction agree otherwise in writing.

Interest. Escrow accounts are not required to be interest bearing. However, if the broker uses an interest-bearing account, he or she must include a disclosure to the principals within the purchase or lease contract. The disclosure must include how the interest will be disbursed.

Deposits

Lease transactions. Unless otherwise agreed in writing, all prepaid rent and deposits paid by a tenant must be deposited into an escrow account by the end of the fifth business banking day following receipt of the funds. The money is to stay in the account in accordance to the lease.

Withdrawals and disbursements

Purchase transactions. Unless otherwise agreed in writing by all principals to the transaction, no licensee is entitled to any part of the escrow funds until the transaction closes.

Fund sufficiency. No funds may be disbursed from an escrow account unless the account balance is sufficient to cover the amount of funds to be disbursed.

Failed transactions. If the transaction does not close, the escrow funds are to stay in the account until one of the following happens:

- all principals to the transaction agree in writing how the funds are to be disbursed
- a court orders the disbursement
- the funds are interpleaded for the appropriate court to decide
- the broker releases the funds in accordance with the terms of the purchase contract that established the earnest money deposit

The broker is not required to determine the recipient of the earnest money deposit and cannot be held liable to any of the involved parties.

Notice of disbursement. The broker may send a notice to the principal who is not receiving any of the escrow funds regarding the **release** of funds and giving the principal 15 calendar days to submit a written protest to the disbursement. Unless a specific method of notice delivery is included in the contract, the broker may hand deliver, mail with proof of mailing, use electronic means with proof of delivery, or use overnight delivery by a delivery service to get the disbursement notice to all parties to the transaction.

Foreclosures. If the broker is holding escrow funds for a property and the property is subject to a foreclosure sale, the principal broker may file an interpleader action to handle the disbursement of escrow funds. If the purchase contract on the property includes provisions for **broker** to return the good faith deposit to a principal in the transaction upon termination of the contract, the foreclosure is deemed a termination of the contract. The broker may then return the escrow funds to the buyer without obtaining consent from or providing notice to the other parties.

Misuse of funds

Commingling. Depositing private or business funds into an escrow account that holds monies belonging to others is commingling and is illegal. The same holds true for depositing monies belonging to others into a private or business account. By law, commingling also occurs when "escrow funds are used to purchase a certificate of deposit, the pledging or hypothecation of such certificate, or the absence of the original certificate from the direct control of the principal broker." (18 VAC 135-20-180)

Sometimes, money deposited into an escrow account will ultimately belong to the licensee. Those deposits must be identified in the account records as designated for the licensee. Even though money ultimately belonging to the licensee may be in the same account as money belonging to others, this is not considered commingling as long as the funds are periodically withdrawn at intervals of not more than every six months. Additionally, these funds must be identifiable at all times. These funds may not be paid directly to the licensee but, rather, are to be paid to the firm who then pays the licensee when the funds are due to the licensee.

Conversion. Conversion is the act of misappropriating escrow funds for the broker's business or personal use. More serious than mere commingling, conversion is effectively an act of theft: using monies which do not belong to the broker. If the broker uses any escrow funds belonging to others for his or her own purposes, the broker is committing conversion. Conversion carries serious consequences, including license revocation.

Protection of escrow

At times, the REB may have reason to believe that a broker is not able to adequately protect the interests of the principals in a transaction or that the broker's actions threaten their interests.

In such situations, the REB will file a petition with a court of record that has equity jurisdiction over the broker and any escrow funds held by the broker so the court can temporarily prohibit further activity by the broker. The court will take action to conserve, protect, and disburse the subject funds and may appoint a receiver. The receiver's expenses and fees are to be paid by the broker.

If the broker is unable to pay, the Board will decide if the payment can be made by the Transaction Recovery Fund or by the Board. The Board's decision must be made within 30 days of the Board's receipt of the receiver's invoices. If the Board determines the broker was not at fault and did not violate any provision of the law or administrative regulations, then the payment will be made by the Board.

Transaction records

Brokers must retain all business records for 3 years from the date of execution. These records include each brokerage agreement, each disclosure and consent to dual agency or dual representation, each disclosure and consent to designated agency or designated representation, and each disclosure of a brokerage relationship to an unrepresented party.

Records to be retained for 3 years also include any disclosure relative to fully executed purchase contracts, a complete and legible copy of each executed contract of sale, any executed release from contract, any executed lease agreement, any executed property management agreement, and each settlement statement related to a real estate transaction that are in the broker's control or possession unless prohibited by law.

Brokers must maintain a complete record of financial transactions that were conducted under the broker's authority. The records may be maintained electronically and/or in paper form but must be maintained in the broker's place of business or a branch office within Virginia.

Escrow records

The broker is to maintain a bookkeeping or recordkeeping system that accurately and clearly discloses full compliance with the related regulations within the Virginia Administrative Code. The records are to show from whom money was received; the date of receipt; the place of deposit; the date of deposit; and, after the transaction has been completed, the final disposition of the funds.

Escrow records are to be retained for 3 years from the date of closing or ratification if the transaction fails to close.

Inspections and audits

From time to time, the REB may wish to conduct an inspection or audit of the brokerage and/or financial records. If the REB requests any documents, books, or records of real estate transactions in which the licensee or broker was involved, those items must be produced within 10 days of the Board's request.

ESCROW AND THE CLOSING PROCESS

Closing process

The closing process consists of buyer and seller verifying that each has fulfilled the terms of the sale contract. If they have, then the mortgage loan, if any, is closed, all expenses are apportioned and paid, the consideration is exchanged for the title, final documents are signed, and arrangements are made to record the transaction according to local laws.

Exhibit 3.1 The Closing Process

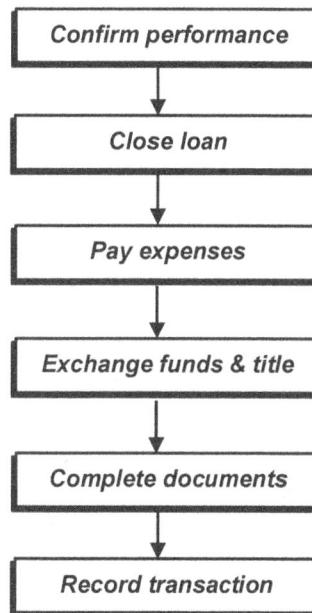

```
┌─────────────────────────┐
│   Confirm performance   │
└─────────────────────────┘
            │
            ▼
┌─────────────────────────┐
│       Close loan        │
└─────────────────────────┘
            │
            ▼
┌─────────────────────────┐
│      Pay expenses       │
└─────────────────────────┘
            │
            ▼
┌─────────────────────────┐
│  Exchange funds & title │
└─────────────────────────┘
            │
            ▼
┌─────────────────────────┐
│    Complete documents   │
└─────────────────────────┘
            │
            ▼
┌─────────────────────────┐
│    Record transaction   │
└─────────────────────────┘
```

Transfer of title and purchase funds

The seller must produce evidence of marketable title, such as a commitment for title insurance by a title insurer. Before making a title commitment, a title company performs a title search to discover any liens, encumbrances, restrictions, conditions, or easements attaching to the title.

If there are any encumbrances or liens that damage the title, the seller is expected to remove these prior to the date specified in the contract. The most common title cloud is an unpaid lien.

The seller may also be asked to execute an affidavit of title stating that, since the date of the original title search, the seller has incurred no new liens, judgments, unpaid bills for repairs or improvements, no unrecorded deeds or contracts, no bankruptcies or divorces that would affect title, or any other defects the seller is aware of.

The purchaser, purchaser's lender, or title company may require a survey to verify the location and size of the property. The survey also identifies any easements, encroachments, or flood plain hazard.

The buyer should inspect the property to make certain that the property is in the condition in which the seller states that it is, and that any repairs or other required actions have been performed. A final inspection, called a **buyer's walk-through**, should be conducted as close to the closing date as possible.

If the seller's mortgage lien(s) are to be satisfied at closing, the lender will provide a **payoff statement**, also called an **offset statement**, specifying the amount of unpaid principal and any interest due as of the closing date, plus fees that will be due the lender and any credits or penalties that may apply. The holder of a note secured by a trust deed will provide a similar statement, called a **beneficiary statement**, to show any unpaid balance. Even if the buyer is assuming the seller's mortgage loan, the buyer will want to know the exact amount of the unpaid balance as of the closing date. Finally, the seller produces and/or deposits with the escrow agent the deed that conveys the property to the buyer.

Transfer of purchase funds. The buyer usually produces and/or deposits with the escrow agent the following:
- earnest money
- loan funds and documents
- any other cash needed to complete the purchase

Escrow procedures

If the closing occurs "in escrow" rather than face-to-face, the principal parties deposit funds and documents with the appointed escrow agent, and the escrow agent disburses funds and releases documents to the appropriate parties when all the conditions of the escrow have been met. If for any reason the transaction cannot be completed, for instance if the buyer refuses the title as it is offered, or the buyer fails to produce the necessary cash, the escrow instructions usually provide a mechanism for reconveying title to the seller and funds to the buyer. In such a case, both parties return to their original status as if no sale had occurred.

Lender closing requirements

A lender is concerned about the quality of the collateral a borrower is providing in return for the mortgage loan. The collateral would be endangered by defects in the title, by liens that would take precedence over the mortgage lien, such as a tax lien, and by physical damage to the property which is not repaired. Consequently, the lender typically requires a survey; a property inspection; hazard insurance; a title insurance policy; a reserve account for taxes and insurance; and possibly, private mortgage insurance. In some cases the lender may also require a *certificate of occupancy* verifying that any new construction performed complies with local building codes.

MORTGAGE ESCROWS- RESPA LIMITS ON WITHHOLDING

Section 10 of RESPA limits the amounts lenders can require borrowers to place in escrow for purposes of paying taxes, hazard insurance, and other property-related expenses. The limitation applies to the initial deposits as well as deposits made over the course of the loan's term.

Interactive Exercises

Unit 3: Escrow Requirements

3.1) "WHAT IF" SITUATION EXAMPLE: Handling escrow disbursement disputes.

Alex is a buyer's agent and his buyer currently has a home under contract. A few days ago, he deposited $5,000 into an escrow account but after going over all of the inspection reports, the buyer decides he is no longer interested in the home. He wants a refund of his escrow deposit and to look for a new home.

What advice can Alex offer his client?

_____

_____

_____

_____

_____

_____

_____

_____

_____

SNAPSHOT REVIEW: UNIT THREE

ESCROW REQUIREMENTS

ESCROW ACCOUNTS

Account requirements
- Brokers maintain escrow accounts if broker holds money/documents
- Brokers with escrow accounts must have signatory authority on all accounts
- Accounts must be in federally insured depository
- Interest bearing is not requirement

Deposits
- Prepaid rent/deposits deposited in escrow account by fifth business banking day

Withdrawals and disbursements
- Licensee not entitled to escrow until transaction closes
- Broker not required to determine recipient of earnest money
- If broker holding escrow funds for foreclosure property, broker file interpleader action for disbursement

Misuse of funds
- Commingling- depositing private/business funds into escrow account with money belonging to others; depositing others' money into private/business account; illegal
- Conversion- misappropriating escrow funds for broker's business/personal use

Protection of escrow
- REB file petition with court to temporarily prohibit further activity by broker
- Court to conserve, protect, disburse funds
- Transaction Recovery Fund might step in to pay

Transaction records
- Brokers retain business records for 3 years

Escrow records
- Broker maintain bookkeeping/recordkeeping system from whom money received, date of receipt, place of deposit, date of deposit, final disposition
- Kept for 3 years

Inspections and audits
- Brokerage has 10 days to comply with REB's requests of documents

ESCROW AND THE CLOSING PROCESS

Closing process
- Confirm performance, close loan, pay expenses, exchange funds & title, complete documents, record transaction

Transfer of title and purchase funds
- Seller expected to remove damages to title prior to date specified in contract
- Purchaser/lender/title company may require survey
- Buyer's walk-through conducted close to closing date
- Buyer produces/deposits earnest money, loan funds, cash to close

Escrow procedures
- "in escrow" closing- principal parties deposit funds, documents with escrow agent

- Escrow agent disburses funds & releases documents to appropriate parties when conditions met.

Lender closing requirements

- Survey, inspection, hazard insurance, title insurance policy. reserve account for taxes/insurance, private mortgage insurance.
- New construction needs *certificate of occupancy*

MORTGAGE ESCROWS- RESPA LIMITS ON WITHHOLDING

- Section 10 of RESPA limits amounts lenders can require to place in escrow

==

Check Your Understanding Quiz:

Unit Three: Escrow Requirements

Carefully read each question then provide your best answer based on what you learned in this unit. Then check your answers against the Answer Key which immediately follows the quiz questions.

1. Depositing private or business funds into an escrow account that holds monies belonging to others is called _____.

    a. conversion.
    b. transitioning.
    c. commingling.
    d. mixing.

2. Which of the following is the last step in the closing process?

    a. Confirming performance
    b. Recording the transaction
    c. Exchanging funds
    d. Paying expenses

3. Which statute limits the amount lenders can require borrowers to place in escrow?

    a. RESPA
    b. Escrow Deposit Act
    c. MLS
    d. Borrower Closing Costs Act

4. All prepaid rent must be deposited into an escrow account by the end of the _____.

    a. fifth business banking day.
    b. third calendar day.
    c. fourth business day.
    d. seventh business banking day.

5. How long must brokers retain business records for?

    a. For 7 years
    b. For 12 months from the closing date
    c. For 10 years from the day funds were released
    d. For 3 years from the date of execution

6. Who conducts audits of financial records for a brokerage?

   a. Virginia Treasury Fund
   b. Real Estate Board
   c. Housing Authority
   d. RESPA

7. Misappropriating escrow funds for the broker's business use is called _____.

   a. transferring.
   b. conversion.
   c. auditing.
   d. commingling.

8. Which of the following is NOT a proper use of escrow funds?

   a. Paying taxes
   b. Paying hazard insurance
   c. Paying the principal
   d. Escrow funds can be used for anything.

9. What is another name for an offset statement?

   a. Payoff statement
   b. Beneficiary statement
   c. Walk-through statement
   d. Closing statement

10. What is the first step in the closing process?

    a. Closing the loan
    b. Paying expenses
    c. Recording the transaction
    d. Confirming performance

11. When do buyers typically conduct the buyer's walk-through?

    a. Within 3 days of going under contract
    b. As close to the closing date as possible
    c. Within 7 days after going under contract
    d. 5 days after the inspection

12. When can escrow funds be returned to a buyer without obtaining consent from the other parties?

    a. When a forbearance terminates a contract
    b. When the buyer backs out after the inspection period
    c. When a foreclosure terminates a contract
    d. Written consent from all parties is always required for escrow disbursement.

13. Before making a _____, a title company performs a title search to discover any liens, encumbrances, restrictions, conditions, or easements attaching to the title.

    a. title commitment
    b. purchase contract
    c. loan commitment
    d. closing disclosure

14. The holder of a note secured by a trust deed will provide a _____ to show any unpaid balance due at closing.

    a. earnest money statement
    b. beneficiary statement
    c. closing disclosure
    d. loan balance statement

15. What is the most common title cloud?

    a. A missed mortgage payment
    b. Unpaid taxes
    c. A drainage easement
    d. An unpaid lien

===

UNIT 4:

REAL ESTATE FINANCE

Unit Four Learning Objectives: When the student has completed this unit he or she will be able to:

- Understand the mechanics of a mortgage loan including the components of a loan, qualification and the loan closing process.
- Summarize the various finance related laws.
- Discuss the primary and secondary mortgage markets and the roles of FNMA, GNMA, and FHLMC.
- Understand the types of loans available.
- Discussing the role TILA/RESPA play in financial advertising.

ESSENTIAL MECHANICS OF THE MORTGAGE LOAN

It is common to use borrowed money to purchase real estate. When a borrower gives a note promising to repay the borrowed money and executes a mortgage on the real estate for which the money is being borrowed as security, the financing method is called mortgage financing. The term "mortgage financing" also applies to real estate loans secured by a deed of trust. The process of securing a loan by pledging a property without giving up ownership of the property is called **hypothecation**.

States differ in their interpretation of who owns mortgaged property. Those that regard the mortgage as a lien held by the mortgagee (lender) against the property owned by the mortgagor (borrower) are called **lien-theory** states. Those that regard the mortgage document as a conveyance of ownership from the mortgagor to the mortgagee are called **title-theory** states. Some states interpret ownership of mortgaged property from a point of view that combines aspects of both title and lien theory.

A valid mortgage or trust deed financing arrangement requires

- a *note* as evidence of the debt
- the *mortgage or trust deed* as evidence of the collateral pledge

Note. In addition to executing a mortgage or trust deed, the borrower signs a promissory note for the amount borrowed. The amount of the loan is typically the difference between the purchase price and the down payment. A promissory note creates a personal liability for the borrower to repay the loan.

Mortgage. A mortgage is a legal document stating the pledge of the borrower (the **mortgagor**) to the lender (the **mortgagee**). The mortgage document pledges the borrower's ownership interest in the real estate in question as collateral against performance of the debt obligation.

The flow of funds and obligations in a mortgage transaction is as follows:

Exhibit 4.1 Flow of a Mortgage Transaction

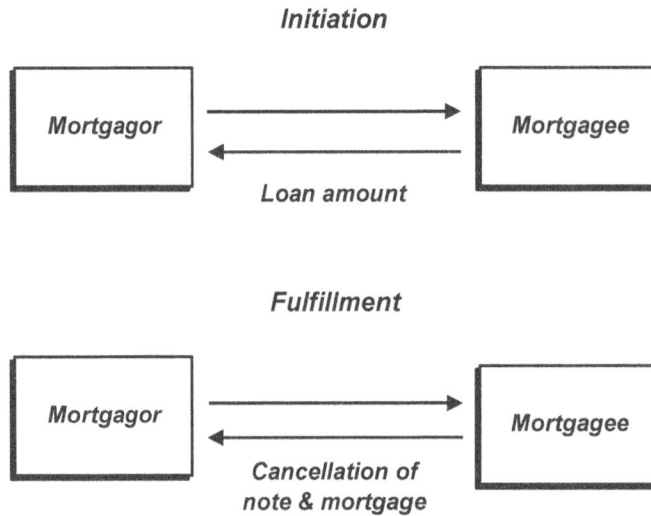

Initiation

Mortgagor → Mortgagee

Loan amount

Fulfillment

Mortgagor → Mortgagee

Cancellation of note & mortgage

The deed of trust. A deed of trust conveys title to the property in question from the borrower (**trustor**) to a **trustee** as security for the loan. The trustee is a third party fiduciary to the trust. While the loan is in place, the trustee holds the title on behalf of the lender, who is the **beneficiary** of the trust. On repayment of the loan, the borrower receives the title from the trustee in the form of a deed of reconveyance.

The flow of funds and obligations in a trust deed transaction is as follows:

Exhibit 4.2 Flow of a Trust Deed Transaction

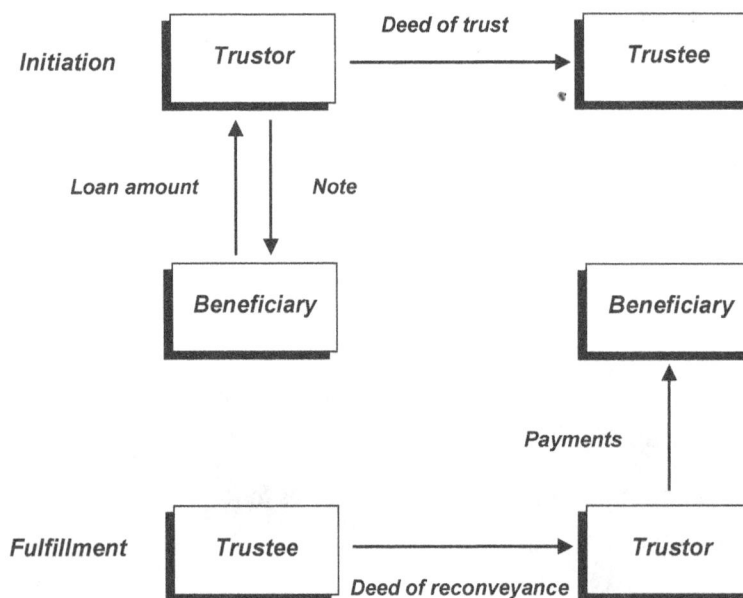

Initiation

Trustor — Deed of trust → Trustee

Loan amount / Note

Beneficiary

Beneficiary

Payments

Fulfillment

Trustee → Trustor

Deed of reconveyance

70

Financial components

The financial components of a mortgage loan include:

- principal
- interest and interest rate
- points
- term
- payments

Principal. The capital amount borrowed, on which interest payments are calculated, is the original loan **principal**. In an amortizing loan, part of the principal is repaid periodically along with interest, so that the principal balance decreases over the life of the loan. At any point during the life of a mortgage loan, the remaining unpaid principal is called the **loan balance**, or **remaining balance**.

Interest and interest rate. Interest is a charge for the use of the lender's money. Interest may be paid in *advance* at the beginning of the payment period, or in *arrears* at the end of the payment period, according to the terms of the note. Mortgage interest is most commonly paid in arrears. The **interest rate** is a percentage applied to the principal to determine the amount of interest due. The rate may be *fixed* for the term of the loan, or it may be *variable*, according to the terms of the note. A loan with a fixed interest rate is called a fixed-rate loan; a loan with a variable interest rate is commonly called an adjustable rate loan.

Because the interest rate on a mortgage loan does not reflect the full cost of the loan to the borrower, federal law requires a lender on a residential property to compute and disclose an **Annual Percentage Rate (APR)** that includes other finance charges in addition to the basic interest rate in the calculation.

Many states have laws against **usury**, which is the charging of excessive interest rates on loans. Such states have a maximum rate that is either a flat rate or a variable rate tied to an index such as the prime lending rate.

Points. From the point of view of a lender or investor, the amount loaned in a mortgage loan is the lender's capital investment, and the interest paid by the borrower is the return earned by the invested capital. It is often the case that a lender needs to earn a greater return than the interest rate alone provides. For example, a lender may require additional yield on a low-interest VA loan which has an interest rate maximum. In such a case, the lender charges up-front **discount points** to make up the difference between the interest rate on the loan and the required return. This effectively raises the yield of the loan to the lender.

A discount point is *one percent of the loan amount*. Thus, one point on a $100,000 loan equals $1,000. The lender charges this as *pre-paid interest* at closing by funding only the face amount of the loan minus the discount points. The borrower, however, must repay the full loan amount, along with interest calculated on the full amount.

The value of one discount point to a lender is usually estimated to be equivalent to raising the interest rate on the loan by 1/8%. Thus, a lender has to charge eight points to raise the yield by 1%. If a lender needs to earn 7% on a loan offered at 6.5%, the number of points necessary would be figured as follows:

$$7.0\% - 6.5\% = .5\%$$

$$.5\% \times 8 \text{ (points per 1\%)} = 4 \text{ points}$$

On a loan of $100,000, the 4 points would cost the borrower:

$$100,000 \times .04 = \$4,000.$$

The borrower would effectively receive from the lender $96,000, and owe principal and interest based on $100,000. For tax reasons, it is usually advisable for the borrower to receive the full loan amount from the lender and pay the points in a check which is separate from that used for other closing costs. As pre-paid interest, points paid in this way may be deductible on the borrower's income tax return for the year of the purchase. The borrower should seek the advice of a tax consultant concerning this matter.

Term. The loan term is the period of time over which the loan must be repaid. A "30-year loan" is a loan whose balance must be fully paid off at the end of thirty years. A "five-year balloon loan" is a loan whose balance must be paid off at the end of five years, although its payments may be calculated on a term of another length, such as fifteen or thirty years. Such a loan is also sometimes described as a 30-year loan with a five-year "call."

Payments. The loan term, loan amount, and interest rate combine to determine the periodic payment amount. When these three quantities are known, it is possible to identify the periodic payment from a mortgage table or with a financial calculator. Mortgage payments are usually made on a monthly basis. On an amortizing loan, a portion of the payment goes to repay the loan balance in advance, and a portion goes to payment of interest in arrears.

For example, Mary and Jerry King borrow $400,000 to finance the purchase of a home. The loan has a term of thirty years at an interest rate of 5% and is amortizing. The monthly payment for this loan will be $2,147. For the first payment at the end of the month, the Kings owe interest on $400,000 for the monthly period. At 5%, this amounts to $1,666.67. Since their payment is $2,147 and the interest charge is $1,666.67, the difference, which is $480.33, is applied to an advance payment of principal. The following month, the Kings will pay interest on the new, smaller loan balance of $399,519.67 ($400,000.00 – 480.33).

If a borrower pays more than the scheduled payment amount, the excess is credited to repayment of the principal, which is reduced by the amount of the excess payment. The required minimum payment amount remains constant for the life of the loan, but the loan term can be reduced by this means, thereby also reducing the total amount of interest paid over the life of the loan.

FINANCIAL QUALIFICATION

Income qualification

Lenders want to be assured that the borrower has adequate means to make all necessary periodic payments on the loan in addition to other housing expenses and debts such as credit card payments and car payments. Most lenders use two ratios to estimate an applicant's ability to fulfill a loan obligation: an *income ratio,* or *housing ratio*, and a *debt ratio*, or *housing plus debt ratio.* They also consider the stability of an applicant's income. Please note that the income and debt ratios in the discussion below do not necessarily reflect the latest ratios used by FHA, VA, or other lenders. Check for updates on the websites of those agencies.

Income ratio. The income ratio, or housing expense ratio, establishes borrowing capacity by limiting the percent of gross income a borrower may spend on housing costs. Housing costs include principal, interest, taxes, and homeowner's insurance, and may include monthly assessments, mortgage insurance, and utilities. The income ratio formula is:

Income Ratio

$$\frac{monthly\ housing\ expense}{monthly\ GROSS\ income} = income\ ratio$$

To identify the maximum monthly housing expense an income ratio allows, modify the formula as follows:

monthly gross income x income ratio = monthly housing expense

Most conventional lenders require that this ratio be *no greater than 25-28%*. In other words, a borrower's total housing expenses cannot exceed 28% of gross income. For an FHA-backed loan, the ratio is 31%. VA-guaranteed loans do not use this qualifying ratio.

For example, if a couple has combined monthly gross income of $12,000, and a lender's maximum income ratio is 28%, the couple's monthly housing expense cannot exceed $3,360:

$12,000 x 28% = $3,360

Debt ratio. The debt ratio considers all of the monthly obligations of the income ratio *plus any additional monthly payments the applicant must make for other debts*. The lender will look specifically at minimum monthly payments due on revolving credit debts and other consumer loans. The debt ratio formula is:

Debt Ratio

$$\frac{monthly\ housing\ expense + monthly\ debt\ obligations}{monthly\ GROSS\ income} = debt\ ratio$$

To identify the housing expenses plus debt a debt ratio allows, modify the formula as follows:

monthly gross income x debt ratio = monthly housing expense + monthly debt obligations

Most conventional lenders require that this debt ratio be *no greater than 36%*. For an FHA-backed loan, the debt ratio may not exceed 43%. The VA uses 41% and a variable "residual income" calculation. The FHA and VA include in the debt figure any obligation costing more than $100 per month and any debt with a remaining term exceeding six months.

Using the 36% debt ratio, the couple whose monthly income is $12,000 will be allowed to have monthly housing and debt obligations of $4,320:

$12,000 gross income x 36% = $4,320 expenses and debt

VA-guaranteed loans also require a borrower to meet certain qualifications based on net income after paying federal, state, and social security taxes, housing maintenance and utilities expenses. Such **residual income requirements** vary by family size, loan amount, and geographical region.

Income stability. A lender looks beyond income and debt ratios to assess an applicant's income stability. Important factors are:

- how long the applicant has been employed at the present job
- how frequently and for what reasons the applicant has changed jobs in the past
- how likely secondary income such as bonuses and overtime is to continue on a regular basis
- how educational level, training and skills, age, and type of occupation may affect the continuation of the present income level in the future.

Cash qualification and loan to value

A lender will usually lend only a portion of the property's value. The relationship of the loan amount to the property value, expressed as a percentage, is called the **loan-to-value ratio, or LTV**. If the lender's loan to value ratio is 80%, the lender will lend only $80,000 on a home appraised at $100,000. The difference between what the lender will lend and what the borrower must pay for the property is the amount the borrower must provide in cash as a down payment.

Since a lender lends only part of the purchase price of a property according to the lender's loan-to-value ratio, a lender will verify that a borrower has the cash resources to make the required down payment. If some of a borrower's cash for the down payment comes as a gift from a relative or friend, a lender may require a **gift letter** from the donor stating the amount of the gift and lack of any requirement to repay the gift. On the other hand, if someone is lending an applicant a portion of the down payment with a provision for repayment, a lender will consider this another debt obligation and adjust the debt ratio accordingly. This can lower the amount a lender is willing to lend.

Loan commitment

When a lender's underwriters have qualified an applicant and the lender has decided to offer the loan, the lender gives the applicant a written notice of the agreement to lend under specific terms. This written promise is the **loan commitment**. The commitment may take a number of common forms, including *a firm commitment, a lock-in commitment, a conditional commitment, and a take-out commitment.*

A **firm commitment** is a straight forward offer to make a specific loan at a specific interest rate for a specific term. This kind of commitment is the one most commonly offered to home buyers.

A **"lock-in" commitment** is an offer to lend a specific amount for a specific term at a specific interest rate, *but the interest rate is subject to an expiration date*, for instance, sixty days. This guarantees that the lender will not raise the interest rate during the application and closing periods. The borrower may have to pay points or some other charge for the lock-in.

A **conditional commitment** offers to make a loan if certain provisions are met. This kind of commitment generally applies to construction loans. A typical condition for funding the loan is completion of a development phase.

A **take-out commitment** offers to make a loan that will "take out" another lender's loan, i.e., pay it off and replace it. The take-out loan is most often used to retire a construction loan. The take-out lender agrees to pay off the short-term construction loan by issuing a long-term permanent loan.

Loan closing

Closing of a mortgage loan normally occurs with the closing of the real estate transaction. At the real estate closing, the lender typically has deposited the funded amount with an escrow agent, along with instructions for disbursing the funds. The borrower deposits necessary funds with the escrow agent, executes final documents, and receives signed copies of all relevant documents.

Title to the mortgaged property is transferred and recorded according to legal procedures in effect at the time of closing. The borrower receives a package containing copies of all documents relevant to the transaction.

FAIR FINANCING LAWS

ECOA

Equal Credit Opportunity Act prohibits discrimination in extending credit based on race, color, religion, national origin, sex, marital status, age, or dependency upon public assistance. A creditor may not make any statements to discourage an applicant on the basis of such discrimination or ask any questions of an applicant concerning these discriminatory items. A real estate licensee who assists a seller in qualifying a potential buyer may fall within the reach of this prohibition. A lender must also inform a rejected applicant in writing of reasons for denial within 30 days. A creditor who fails to comply is liable for punitive and actual damages.

Fair Credit Reporting Act

The FCRA ensures that all credit reporting agencies provide accurate information to the consumer. This statute lists every entity that can have access to the credit report. Thanks to the FCRA, consumers have a right to see their credit score and credit report.

TILA/RESPA

Effective October 3, 2015, a TILA/RESPA Integrated Disclosure Rule (TRID) integrates the disclosure requirements of RESPA and Truth-in-Lending, replacing the old Good Faith Estimate form and HUD-1 Uniform Settlement Statement a new Loan Estimate form and Closing Disclosure form, respectively.

The **Real Estate Settlement Procedures Act** (RESPA) is a consumer protection statute enacted in 1974. Its purpose is to clarify settlement costs and to eliminate kickbacks and fees that increase settlement costs. RESPA specifies certain closing procedures when a purchase:

- involves a residential property, including one- to four-family residences, cooperatives and condominiums;
- involves a first or second mortgage lien; and
- is being financed by a "federally-related" mortgage loan, which includes loans made by a federally-insured lender; loans insured or guaranteed by the VA or FHA, loans administered by HUD, and loans intended to be sold to FNMA, FHLMC, or GNMA.

RESPA regulations do not apply to transactions being otherwise financed except in the case of an assumption in which the terms of the assumed loan are modified or the lender's charges for the assumption are greater than $50.

RESPA is directed at lenders and settlement companies, but licensees should be familiar with requirements and changes. The Dodd-Frank Act of 2010 granted rule-making authority under RESPA to the Consumer Financial Protection Bureau (CFPB) and generally granted the CFPB authority to supervise and enforce compliance with RESPA and its implementing regulations.

In 2013, the CFPB made substantive and technical changes to the existing regulations. Substantive changes included modifying the servicing transfer notice requirements and implementing new procedures and notice requirements related to borrowers' error resolution requests and information requests. The amendments also included new provisions related to escrow payments, force-placed insurance, general servicing policies, procedures, and requirements, early intervention, continuity of contact, loss mitigation and the relation of RESPA's servicing provisions to State law.

RESPA is a federal law which aims to *standardize settlement practices and ensure that buyers understand settlement costs*. RESPA applies to purchases of residential real estate (one- to four-family homes) to be financed by "federally related" first mortgage loans. Federally related loans include:

- VA- and FHA-backed loans
- other government-backed or -assisted loans
- loans that are intended to be sold to FNMA, FHLMC, GNMA, or other government-controlled secondary market institutions
- loans made by lenders who originate more than one million dollars per year in residential loans.

In addition to imposing settlement procedures, RESPA provisions prohibit lenders from paying kickbacks and unearned fees to parties who may have helped the lender obtain the borrower's business. This would include, for example, a fee paid to a real estate agent for referring a borrower to the lender.

To assist in informing and educating borrowers, RESPA requires that lenders provide a loan applicant with a **loan information booklet** and a **loan estimate**. The booklet, produced by the Consumer Financial Protection Bureau, explains RESPA provisions, general settlement costs, and the required **Closing Disclosure** form. The lender must provide the estimate of closing costs within three days following the borrower's application.

Disclosures. The Consumer Financial Protection Bureau (CFPB) requires lenders to use two specific forms to disclose settlement costs to the buyer. A lender must provide a Loan Estimate (H-24) within three days of receiving the loan application and allow the buyer to see the Closing Disclosure (H-25) three days before loan consummation. A lender must also provide a buyer with a copy of the information booklet, "Your Home Loan Toolkit," concerning mortgage loan, closing costs and closing procedures. The disclosures specify:

- settlement charges
- title charges
- recording and transfer fees
- reserve deposits required
- tax and insurance escrow deposits required
- any other fees or charges
- total closing costs

The disclosure forms vary, depending on loan type. The costs in the Closing Disclosure must match those in the Loan Estimate within certain standards.

Violations. RESPA stipulates that the parties to certain purchase transactions must be given accurate information reflecting their closing costs. It also prohibits certain business practices that are not considered to be in the consumer's best interest.

The licensee's risks regarding RESPA primarily relate to:

- failing to ensure that the consumer is informed about his or her rights under the law
- giving or receiving an illegal kickback.

RESPA currently requires lenders to:

- give a copy of a Consumer Financial Protection Bureau loan information booklet to the applicant. The booklet explains RESPA provisions, general settlement costs, and the required **Closing Disclosure** form. The lender must provide the estimate of closing costs within three business days following the borrower's application.
- give the applicant a Loan Estimate (Form H-24) of expected closing costs within three business days of receiving the application. Actual closing costs may not vary from the estimate beyond certain limits.
- give the buyer the Closing Disclosure (Form H-25) specifying costs to be paid by buyer and seller at closing three business days before consummation.
- give the **buyer** the opportunity to review the final settlement statement *one business day prior to closing.*

RESPA specifically ***prohibits*** any fee or kickback paid to a party for a service when the party has not actually rendered the service. For example, it is prohibited for an insurance company to pay a real estate agent or a lender for referring a client.

Fees for referring clients to the following services are strictly forbidden:

- title services (search, insurance)
- appraisals
- inspections
- surveys
- loan issue
- credit report
- attorney services

The sharing of commissions and the payment of referral fees among cooperating brokers and multiple-listing services are not RESPA violations.

SAFE Act

Secure and Fair Enforcement for Mortgage Licensing Act was established to create a national standard for residential mortgage loan originators to be licensed and registered.

PRIMARY & SECONDARY MORTGAGE MARKET

Primary market

The primary mortgage market consists of lenders who originate mortgage loans directly to borrowers. Primary mortgage market lenders include:

- savings and loans
- commercial banks
- mutual savings banks
- life insurance companies
- mortgage bankers
- credit unions

Mortgage brokers are also part of the primary mortgage market, even though they do not lend to customers directly. Rather, they are instrumental in procuring borrowers for primary mortgage lenders.

The primary lender assumes the initial risk of the long-term investment in the mortgage loan. Primary lenders sometimes also **service** the loan until it is paid off. Servicing loans entails collecting the borrower's periodic payments, maintaining and disbursing funds in escrow accounts for taxes and insurance, supervising the borrower's performance, and releasing the mortgage on repayment. In many cases, primary lenders employ mortgage servicing companies, which service loans for a fee.

Portfolio lenders. A primary mortgage market lender may or may not sell its loans into the secondary market. Many lenders originate loans for the purpose of retaining the investments in their own loan *portfolio*. These loans are referred to as *portfolio loans*, and lenders originating loans for their own portfolio are called *portfolio lenders*. Portfolio lenders are less restricted by the standards and forms imposed on other lenders by secondary market organizations. In retaining their portfolio loans, portfolio lenders may vary underwriting criteria and hold independent standards for down payment requirements and the condition of the collateral.

Secondary market

Lenders, investors and government agencies that buy loans already originated by someone else, or originate loans indirectly through someone else, constitute the **secondary mortgage market**.

Secondary mortgage market organizations include:

- Federal National Mortgage Association (FNMA, or Fannie Mae)
- Federal Home Loan Mortgage Corporation (FHLMC, or Freddie Mac)
- Government National Mortgage Association (GNMA, or Ginnie Mae)
- investment firms that assemble loans into packages and sell securities based on the pooled mortgages
- life insurance companies
- pension funds
- primary market institutions who also invest as secondary lenders

Secondary mortgage market organizations buy pools of mortgages from primary lenders and sell securities backed by these pooled mortgages to investors. By selling securities, the secondary market brings investor money into the mortgage market. By purchasing loans from primary lenders, the secondary market returns funds to the primary lenders, thereby enabling the primary lender to originate more mortgage loans.

Primary lenders make a profit on the sale of loans to the secondary market. The secondary market acquires a profitable long-term investment without having to underwrite, originate, and service the loans. Secondary market organizations customarily hire primary lenders or loan servicing companies to service mortgage pools.

Secondary market loan requirements. The secondary market only buys loans that meet established requirements for quality of collateral, borrower and documentation. Since many primary lenders intend to sell their loans to the secondary market, the qualification standards of the secondary market limit and effectively regulate the kind of loans the primary lender will originate.

Roles of FNMA; GNMA; FHLMC

As major players in the secondary market, the Federal National Mortgage Association (FNMA, "Fannie Mae"), Government National Mortgage Association (GNMA, "Ginnie Mae), and Federal Home Loan Mortgage Corporation (FHLMC, "Freddie Mac") tend to set the standards for the primary market.

Federal National Mortgage Association, or Fannie Mae. Fannie Mae is a government-sponsored enterprise, originally organized as a privately-owned corporation. As a secondary market player, it:

- buys conventional, FHA-backed and VA-backed loans
- gives banks mortgage-backed securities in exchange for blocks of mortgages
- offers lenders firm loan purchase commitments, provided they conform to Fannie Mae's lending standards
- sells bonds and mortgage-backed securities
- guarantees payment of interest and principal on mortgage-backed securities

Government National Mortgage Association, or Ginnie Mae. Ginnie Mae is a division of the Department of Housing and Urban Development. Its purpose is to administer special assistance programs and to help Fannie Mae in its secondary market activities. Specifically, GNMA

- guarantees payment on FNMA high-risk, low-yield mortgages and absorbs the difference in yield between the mortgages and market rates
- guarantees privately generated securities backed by pools of VA-and FHA-guaranteed loans

Federal Home Loan Mortgage Corporation, or Freddie Mac. Freddie Mac is a government-sponsored enterprise, originally chartered as an corporation in 1970. As a secondary market player, FHLMC buys mortgages and pools them, selling bonds backed by the mortgages in the open market. Freddie Mac guarantees performance on FHLMC mortgages.

A federal conservator, the Federal Housing Finance Authority (FHFA), now operates Fannie Mae and Freddie Mac as conservator with the U.S. Treasury a majority owner of both organizations.

TYPES OF LOANS

Conventional loans

A conventional mortgage loan is a permanent long-term loan that is not FHA-insured or VA-guaranteed. Market rates usually determine the interest rate on the loan. Because of the lack of insurance or guarantee by a government agency, the risk to a lender is greater for a conventional loan than for a non-conventional loan. This risk is usually reflected in higher interest rates and stricter requirements for the down payment and the borrower's income qualification. At the same time, conventional loans allow greater flexibility in fees, rates, and terms than do insured and guaranteed loans.

The primary sources of conventional loans are banks and savings and loan associations. Other conventional lenders include credit unions, life insurance companies, pension funds, mortgage bankers, and private individuals. Various types of lenders specialize in mortgage lending for specific purposes and type of borrower, such as commercial, construction, or single-family residential loans.

FHA-insured loans

The Federal Housing Administration (FHA) is an agency of the Department of Housing and Urban Development (HUD). It does not lend money, but *insures* permanent long-term loans made by others. The lender must be approved by the FHA, and the borrower must meet certain FHA qualifications. In addition, the property used to secure the loan must meet FHA standards. The FHA insures that the lender will not suffer significant loss in the case of borrower default. To provide this security, FHA provides insurance and charges the borrower an insurance premium. FHA loans typically have a higher loan-to-value ratio than conventional loans, enabling a borrower to make a smaller down payment.

The basic FHA-insured loan program is the **Title II, Section 203(b)** program for loans on one- to four-family residential properties. Among the features of this program are the following.

FHA mortgage insurance. The FHA determines how much mortgage insurance must be provided and charges the borrower an appropriate mortgage insurance premium (MIP). The initial premium is payable at closing or is added to the borrower's loan balance and financed. Further annual premiums are charged monthly. The amount of the premium varies according to the loan term and the applicable loan-to-value ratio.

Borrower default. The FHA reimburses the lender for losses due to default by the borrower, including costs of foreclosure.

Appraisal. The property must be appraised by an FHA-approved appraiser. The property must also meet the FHA's standards for type and quality of construction, neighborhood quality, and other features.

Maximum loan amount. The FHA has set maximum loan amounts for over 80 regions. Borrowers within a region are limited to the loan ceiling amount in effect for the region. In addition, the maximum loan amount is restricted by the loan-to-value ratios in effect. The maximum FHA-backed loan a borrower can obtain will be the lesser of the regional ceiling amount or the amount dictated by the loan-to-value standard. Calculations are based on the lesser of sale price or appraised value.

Down payment requirement. The minimum down payment for an FHA-backed loan is based on the lower of the appraised value or the sales price. The present requirement for single-family residential loans is 3.5%.

Maximum loan term. Thirty years is the maximum length of the repayment period.

Prepayment privilege. The borrower has the right to pay off the loan at any time without penalty, provided the lender is given prior notice. The lender may charge up to 30 days' interest if the borrower provides less than 30 days' notice.

Assumability. FHA-backed loans on owner-occupied properties are assumable if the buyer is qualified. Lenders and borrowers should check with FHA for current requirements.

Interest rate. The lender and borrower negotiate the interest rate on an FHA- backed loan without any involvement by FHA.

Points, fees and costs. The lender may charge discount points, a loan origination fee, and other such charges. These may be paid by buyer or seller. However, if the seller pays more than a specified percentage of the costs normally paid by a buyer, the FHA may regard these as sales concessions and lower the sales price on which the loan insurance amount is based.

In addition to Section 203(b) loan programs, FHA offers insurance coverage for other loan products. These include:

- home improvement loans
- subsidized loans for low- and middle-income families
- loans for condominiums
- loans for multi-family projects
- graduated-payment loans
- adjustable-rate loans

VA-guaranteed loans

The Veterans Administration (Department of Veterans Affairs) offers *loan guarantees to qualified veterans*. The VA, like the FHA, does not lend money except in certain areas where other financing is not generally available. Instead, the VA partially guarantees permanent long-term loans originated by VA-approved lenders on properties that meet VA standards. The VA's guarantee enables lenders to issue loans with higher loan-to-value ratios than would otherwise be possible. The interest rate on a VA-guaranteed loan is usually lower than one on a conventional loan. The borrower does not pay any premium for the loan guarantee, but does pay a VA funding fee at closing.

Borrower default. The VA reimburses the lender for losses up to the guaranteed amount if foreclosure sale proceeds fail to cover the loan balance.

Appraisal. The property must be appraised by a VA-approved appraiser. The VA issues a *Certificate of Reasonable Value* which creates a maximum value on which the VA-guaranteed portion of the loan will be based. The property must meet certain VA specifications.

Down payment requirement. The VA usually requires no down payment, although the lender may require one.

Maximum loan amount. The VA does not cap the loan amount, but it does limit the liability it can assume, which usually influences the amount an institution will lend. The amount a qualified veteran with full entitlement can borrow without making a downpayment determines the practical loan limits. This amount varies by county. The basic entitlement available to each eligible veteran is $36,000. Lenders will generally lend a maximum of 4 times that amount without a down payment if the veteran is fully qualified and the property appraises for the asking price.

A veteran must apply for a *Certificate of Eligibility* to find out how much the VA will guarantee in a particular situation.

Maximum loan term. The maximum loan term for one- to four-family residences is 30 years. For loans secured by farms, the maximum loan term is 40 years.

Prepayment privilege. The loan may be paid off early without penalty.

Assumability. VA loans are assumable with lender approval. Usually, the person assuming the loan must have VA eligibility, and the assumption may have to be approved by the VA.

Interest rate. Lender and borrower negotiate the interest rate for all VA-insured loans.

Points, fees and costs. The lender may charge discount points, origination fees, and other reasonable costs. These may be paid by seller (with some limits) or buyer but may not be financed. The VA funding fee, however, may be included in the loan amount. The funding fee is a percentage of the loan amount which varies based on the type of loan, military category, whether the loan is a first-time loan, and whether there is a down payment.

Other VA programs. In addition to insuring loans to veterans, the VA may insure loans for lenders who set up a special account with the VA. The VA may also actually lend money directly when an eligible veteran cannot find other mortgage money locally.

Seller financing

The seller may provide some or all of the financing for the buyer's purchase. Some of the most common methods of seller financing are purchase money mortgages, including the wraparound, and the contract for deed.

Purchase money mortgage. With a purchase money mortgage, the borrower gives a mortgage and note to the seller to finance some or all of the purchase price of the property. The seller in this case is said to "take back" a note, or to "carry paper," on the property. Purchase money mortgages may be either senior or junior liens.

Wraparound. In a wraparound loan arrangement, the seller receives a junior mortgage from the buyer, and uses the buyer's payments to make the payments on the original first mortgage. A wraparound enables the buyer to obtain financing

with a minimum cash investment. It also potentially enables the seller to profit from any difference between a lower interest rate on the senior loan and a higher rate on the wraparound loan. A wraparound is possible only if the senior mortgagee allows it.

Contract for deed. Under a contract for deed arrangement, the seller retains title and the buyer receives possession and equitable title while making payments under the terms of the contract. The seller conveys title when the contract has been fully performed.

Home equity loan

The ostensible purpose of this type of loan is to obtain funds for home improvement. Structurally, the home equity loan is a junior mortgage secured by the homeowner's equity. For some lenders, the maximum home equity loan amount is based on the difference between the property's appraised value and the maximum loan-to-value ratio the lender allows on the property, inclusive of all existing mortgage loans. Thus, if a home is appraised at $500,000 and the lender's maximum LTV is 80%, the lender will lend a total of $400,000. If the owner's existing mortgage balance is $325,000, the owner would qualify for a $75,000 home equity loan.

Reverse annuity

In a reverse annuity mortgage, a homeowner pledges the equity in the home as security for a loan which is paid out in regular monthly amounts over the term of the loan. The homeowner, in effect, is able to convert the equity to cash without losing ownership and possession.

VIRGINIA HOUSING DEVELOPMENT AUTHORITY

Virginia Housing, formerly known as the Virginia Housing Development Authority, was created by the General Assembly in 1972 to help the state's residents obtain affordable, quality housing. The organization is self-supporting and does not receive funding from taxes. Instead, its funds come from capital markets.

Virginia Housing works with local governments, community service organizations, lenders, real estate professionals, developers, and others to provide housing services to those in need. These services include mortgages for first-time buyers, financing for apartment communities and neighborhood revitalization efforts, free homebuyer classes, assistance for the elderly and disabled in making their homes more accommodating for them, down payment and closing cost assistance, as well as housing counseling. They also provide grants for rental housing modifications for the disabled, Granting Freedom funds to help disabled veterans modify their homes for better accessibility, and voucher programs to help low-income families and those who may be homeless.

FINANCE ADVERTISING REGULATIONS

Mortgage lenders have to be cautious of a few regulations when advertising. They must be sure to include their NMLS identification number and the name of the mortgage lender/broker. If they are advertising a specific mortgage interest rate, they have to disclose that the rate might change. Mortgage lenders also have to be honest and avoid making misleading statements about obtaining a mortgage loan. (10VAC5-160-60)

TILA/RESPA INTEGRATED DISCLOSURE RULE

Forms and procedures

As mentioned earlier, the TILA/RESPA Integrated Disclosures (TRID) rule is currently in effect. These changes introduce new mandatory forms and procedures to replace the old ones, as follows.

- Lenders must give the consumer a copy of the **booklet**, "Your Home Loan Toolkit" **at the time** of loan application.
- Lenders must deliver or mail the **Loan Estimate** (Form H-24) to the consumer **no later than the third business day** after receiving a loan application. (A "business day" in this context is any day on which the lender's offices are open for business. An "application" exists when the consumer has given the lender or mortgage broker six pieces of information: name; income; Social Security number; property address; estimated value of property; loan amount sought).

- Lenders must provide the **Closing Disclosure** (Form H-25) to the consumer **at least three business days** before consummation of the loan. (A "business day" in this context is any calendar day except a Sunday or the day on which a legal public holiday is observed. "Consummation" refers to the day on which the borrower becomes indebted to the creditor; this may or may not correspond to the day of closing the transaction.)

Good faith estimate

Creditors are responsible for ensuring that the figures stated in the Loan Estimate are made in good faith and consistent with the best information reasonably available to the creditor at the time they are disclosed.

Good faith is measured by calculating the difference between the estimated charges originally provided in the Loan Estimate and the actual charges paid by or imposed on the consumer in the Closing Disclosure.

Generally, if the charge paid by or imposed on the consumer exceeds the amount originally disclosed on the Loan Estimate it is not in good faith, regardless of whether the creditor later discovers a technical error, miscalculation, or underestimation of a charge, although there are exceptions.

Types of charges

For certain costs or terms, creditors are permitted to charge consumers more than the amount disclosed on the Loan Estimate without any tolerance limitation.

These charges are:

- prepaid interest; property insurance premiums; amounts placed into an escrow, impound, reserve or similar account

- charges for services required by the creditor if the creditor permits the consumer to shop and the consumer selects a third-party service provider not on the creditor's written list of service providers
- charges paid to third-party service providers for services not required by the creditor (may be paid to affiliates of the creditor

However, creditors may only charge consumers more than the amount disclosed when the original estimated charge, or lack of an estimated charge for a particular service, was based on the best information reasonably available to the creditor at the time the disclosure was provided.

Charges for third-party services and recording fees paid by or imposed on the consumer are grouped together and subject to a 10% cumulative tolerance ("10% tolerance" charges). This means the creditor may charge the consumer more than the amount disclosed on the Loan Estimate for any of these charges so long as the total sum of the charges added together does not exceed the sum of all such charges disclosed on the Loan Estimate by more than 10%.

For all other charges ("zero tolerance" charges), creditors are not permitted to charge consumers more than the amount disclosed on the Loan Estimate under any circumstances other than changed circumstances that permit a revised Loan Estimate.

If the amounts paid by the consumer at closing exceed the amounts disclosed on the Loan Estimate beyond the applicable tolerance threshold, the creditor must refund the excess to the consumer no later than 60 calendar days after consummation.

==

SNAPSHOT REVIEW: UNIT FOUR

REAL ESTATE FINANCE

ESSENTIAL MECHANICS OF THE MORTGAGE LOAN

- Borrower gives note promising to repay borrowed money; executes mortgage on real estate for which money is being borrowed as security
- Lien-theory states- mortgage is lien held by mortgagee (lender) against property owned by mortgagor (borrower)
- Title-theory states- mortgage document is conveyance of ownership from mortgagor to mortgagee
- Valid mortgage requires note, mortgage/trust deed

Financial components

- Principal; interest/interest rate; points; term; payments

Income qualification

- Income/housing expense ratio
- Debt/housing plus debt ratio-
- Income stability

Cash qualification and loan to value

- LTV- loan amount to property value; percentage
- Lender verifies borrower has cash for required down payment

Loan commitment

- Written promise lender will offer loan
- Conditional commitment- offers to make loan if provisions met

Loan closing

- Lender deposits funded amount with escrow agent
- Borrower deposits necessary funds with escrow agents, executes final documents
- Title transferred and recorded

FAIR FINANCING LAWS

ECOA

- Prohibits discrimination in extending credit based on race, color, religion, national origin, sex, marital status, age, or dependency upon public assistance

Fair Credit Reporting Act

- Ensures credit reporting agencies provide accurate information to consumer

TILA/RESPA

- TILA/RESPA Integrated Disclosure Rule (TRID) integrates disclosure requirements of RESPA and Truth-in-Lending
- Clarifies settlement costs; eliminates kickbacks and fees increasing settlement costs
- RESPA prohibits kickback paid for service when party has not rendered service

SAFE Act

- Creates national standard for residential mortgage loan originators to be licensed/registered

PRIMARY & SECONDARY MORTGAGE MARKET

Primary market

- lenders who originate mortgage loans directly to borrowers
- Savings/loans; commercial banks; mutual savings banks; life insurance companies; mortgage bankers; credit unions

- Mortgage brokers
- Can sell loans to secondary market

Secondary market

- Lenders, investors, government agencies buy loans originated by someone else; originate loans indirectly through someone else
- FNMA; FHLMC; GNMA; investment firms that sell securities; life insurance companies; pension funds; primary market institutions investing as secondary lenders
- Qualifications limit loans primary lenders originate

Roles of FNMA, GNMA, FHLMC

- FNMA, GNMA, FHLMC set standards for primary market
- FNMA buys conventional, FHA, VA loans, etc.
- GNMA is division of HUD; guarantees payment on FNMA high-risk low-yield mortgages; guarantees privately generated securities backed by VA/FHA loans
- FHLMC guarantees FHLMC mortgages

TYPES OF LOANS

Conventional loans

- Not FHA-insured or VA-guaranteed
- Higher interest rates
- Stricter requirements for down payment
- Flexibility in fees, rates, terms
- Source- banks, savings, loan associations, credit unions, life insurance companies, pension funds, mortgage bankers, private individuals

FHA-insured loans

- Property to meet FHA standards
- Higher loan-to-value ratio than conventional loans

VA-guaranteed loans

- VA offers loan guarantees to qualified veterans
- Interest rate usually lower than conventional loan
- VA funding fee at closing

Seller financing

- Seller provide some/all financing
- Purchase money mortgages; wraparound; contract for deed

Home equity loan

- Obtain funds for home improvement
- Junior mortgage secured by homeowner's equity

Reverse annuity

- Homeowner pledges home equity as security for loan paid out monthly over term of loan
- Convert equity to cash without losing ownership

VIRGINIA HOUSING DEVELOPMENT AUTHORITY

- help state's residents obtain affordable, quality housing

FINANCE ADVERTISING REGULATIONS

- Mortgage lenders to include NMLS ID number, mortgage lender/broker name
- Lenders to disclose rate might change

TILA/RESPA INTEGRATED DISCLOSURE RULE

Forms and procedures

- Lenders give consumer "Your Home Loan Toolkit" booklet
- Lenders deliver loan estimate no later than third business day after loan application
- Lender provide closing disclosure three business days before closing

Good faith estimate

- Loan estimate figures made in good faith, consistent with best information available to creditor

Types of charges

- For certain costs, creditors permitted to charge consumers more than amount disclosed on Loan Estimate without tolerance limitation
- Prepaid interest; property insurance premiums; amounts placed into escrow, impound, reserve

===

Check Your Understanding Quiz:

Unit Four: Real Estate Finance

Carefully read each question then provide your best answer based on what you learned in this unit. Then check your answers against the Answer Key which immediately follows the quiz questions.

1. The process of securing a loan by pledging property, without giving up ownership of the property, is called _____.

   a. trading.
   b. bartering.
   c. conveyance.
   d. hypothecation.

2. The financial components of a mortgage loan include principal, points, term, payments and _____.

   a. usury.
   b. interest rate.
   c. credit score.
   d. escrow.

3. What is another name for housing expense ratio?

   a. Income ratio
   b. Gross income
   c. Cash flow ratio
   d. Payment obligation

4. The relationship of the loan amount to the property value is called _____.

   a. DTI
   b. CVT
   c. LTV
   d. LPI

5. Andrew's lender offers to make a loan if certain provisions are met. What type of loan commitment is this?

   a. Firm commitment
   b. Lock-in commitment
   c. Take-out commitment
   d. Conditional commitment

6. Which statute eliminates kickbacks and protects consumers?

    a. RESPA
    b. Fair housing law
    c. Fair Commissions Act
    d. Equal Opportunity Act

7. In a _____ state, the mortgage is a lien held by the mortgagee against the property owned by the mortgagor.

    a. lender-friendly
    b. lien-theory
    c. consumer-friendly
    d. title-theory

8. What is a loan with variable interest rate called?

    a. Fixed-rate loan
    b. Step-rate loan
    c. Customizable loan
    d. Adjustable rate loan

9. Gina applies for a mortgage loan and she gets a quote for a $250,000 loan, paid off in 10 years, with an interest rate of 3%. The quote is valid and in effect for 60 days after which the offer expires. What type of loan commitment is this?

    a. A "lock-in" commitment
    b. A conditional commitment
    c. A take-out commitment
    d. A firm commitment

10. Which statute prohibits discrimination in extending credit based on race, color, and religion?

    a. TILA
    b. Fair Credit Reporting Act
    c. ECOA
    d. Consumer Financial Protection Act

UNIT 5:

FAIR HOUSING, ADA AND CIVIL RIGHTS

Unit Five Learning Objectives: When the student has completed this unit he or she will be able to:

- Define and describe the principal forms of illegal discrimination
- Identify what parties are exempt from the fair housing prohibitions
- Describe how fair housing violations are enforced
- Summarize the key provisions of the Americans with Disabilities Act

PURPOSE OF FAIR HOUSING

Federal and state governments have enacted laws prohibiting discrimination in the national housing market. The aim of these fair housing laws, or equal opportunity housing laws, is to give all people in the country an equal opportunity to live wherever they wish, provided they can afford to do so, without impediments of discrimination in the purchase, sale, rental, or financing of the property.

PROTECTED CLASSES

The protected classes under Title VIII of the Civil Rights Act (known as the Fair Housing Act) as amended are:

- race
- color
- religion
- national origin
- sex
- familial status
- handicapped status

The Federal Civil Rights Act does not directly cover Sexual Orientation or Sexual Identity as protected classes; however, the U.S. Supreme Court recently ruled the LGBT community is protected under the protected class of sex.

The Fairhaven Program

In 2020, NAR launched a new program on its website called Fairhaven. This program takes the agent through several different scenarios and asks them how they would handle it. It then gives feedback on the agent's responses. The program takes 60 to 90 minutes to complete. NAR recommended all agents complete the program. It is also recommended that an agent does the program multiple times, answering different ways to see how and why certain situations are illegal.

Agents must know how to answer specific questions or react to certain situations, since they can be charged and fined if they mishandle a question or problem.

Title VIII exemptions

The Fair Housing Act provides for exemptions under a few specific circumstances. These are:

- sale by the owner of a single-family home if:
  - the owner owns no more than three single-family homes, and
  - the owner or family member was the last resident, and
  - the house is sold without the use of a real estate licensee, and
  - no discriminatory ads are used
- rental of housing of four units or less if the owner resides in one of the units
- rental of rooms in a private home if owner or family member resides there or intends to live there after an absence of no more than twelve months
- local, state, or federal maximum occupancy standards
- religious organizations and not-for-profit groups in conjunction with religious organizations, if not run commercially
- rental of rooms in housing for persons of one sex
- housing for seniors

DEFINITIONS

Demographic information

Demographic information is data gathered on customers or clients. It may include information such as age, sex, race, color, or national origin. This information is collected only to assist in operating the brokerage and identifying advertising avenues, not discriminating against anyone in a protected class.

Professional services

The eight professional services a REALTOR® may perform are advertising, buying, auctioning, renting, selling, appraising, leasing, and exchanging.

NAR's protected classes

The NAR Code of Ethics' protected classes includes race, color, religion, sex, handicap, familial status, national origin, sexual orientation, or gender identity.

Public trust

Public Trust refers to misappropriation of client or customer funds or property, discrimination against the protected classes under the Code of Ethics, or fraud.

Duties to the public

The third section of NAR's Code of Ethics covers how REALTORS®® should behave when interacting with the public. Articles 10 to 14 and their Standards of Practices identify specific behavior and guidelines for dealing with the public. This section restates many of the same ideas expressed in Articles 1 through 9; however, it explicitly identifies the duties owed to the member of the public.

FEDERAL FAIR HOUSING LAWS

Fair Housing and Local Zoning. The Fair Housing Act prohibits a broad range of practices that discriminate against individuals on the basis of race, color, religion, sex, national origin, familial status, and disability. The Act does not pre-empt local zoning laws. However, the Act applies to municipalities and other local government entities and prohibits them from making zoning or land use decisions or implementing land use policies that exclude or otherwise discriminate against protected persons, including individuals with disabilities.

Civil Rights Act of 1866

The original fair housing statute, the Civil Rights Act of 1866, prohibits discrimination in housing *based on race.* The prohibition relates to selling, renting, inheriting, and conveying real estate.

Executive Order 11063. While the Civil Rights Act of 1866 prohibited discrimination, it was only marginally enforced. In 1962, the President issued Executive Order 11063 to *prevent discrimination in residential properties financed by FHA and VA loans*. The order facilitated enforcement of fair housing where federal funding was involved.

Civil Rights Act of 1968

Title VIII (Fair Housing Act). Title VIII of the Civil Rights Act of 1968, known today as the Fair Housing Act, prohibits discrimination in housing *based on race, color, religion, or national origin*. The Office of Fair Housing and Equal

Opportunity (FHEO) administers and enforces Title VIII under the supervision

of the Department of Housing and Urban Development (HUD).

Forms of discrimination

The Fair Housing Act explicitly prohibits illegal discriminatory activities in residential brokerage and financing as detailed by the following.

Discriminatory misrepresentation. An agent may not conceal available properties, represent that they are not for sale or rent, or change the sale terms in order to discriminate. For example, an agent may not inform a minority buyer that the seller has recently decided not to carry back second mortgage financing when the owner has made no such decision.

Discriminatory advertising. An agent may not advertise residential properties in such a way as to restrict their availability to any prospective buyer or tenant.

Providing unequal services. An agent may not alter the nature or quality of brokerage services to any party based on the protected classes of race, color, sex, national origin, religion, familial status, or disability. For example, if an agent typically shows a customer the latest MLS publication, the agent may not refuse to show it to any party. Similarly, if it is customary to show a qualified buyer's prospective properties immediately, an agent may not alter that practice for discriminatory purposes.

Steering. Steering is the practice of directly or indirectly channeling customers toward or away from homes and neighborhoods. Broadly interpreted, steering occurs if an agent indirectly describes an area to encourage or discourage a buyer about such an area's suitability.

For example, an agent tells Buyer A that a neighborhood is beautiful and that desirable families are moving in every week. The next day, the agent tells Buyer B that the same neighborhood is deteriorating and that home values are starting to fall. The agent has steered Buyer B away from the area and Buyer A into it.

Blockbusting. Blockbusting is the practice of inducing owners in an area to sell or rent to avoid an impending change in the ethnic or social makeup of the neighborhood that will cause values to go down.

For example, Agent Smith tells neighborhood owners that several minority families are moving into their neighborhood and that they will be bringing their relatives next year. Smith informs homeowners that several families have already made plans to move in anticipation of a value decline.

Restricting MLS participation. It is considered a discriminatory practice to limit any multiple listing service's involvements based on one's race, religion, national origin, color, sex, familial status, or disability.

Redlining. Redlining is the residential financing practice of refusing to make loans on properties in a particular neighborhood regardless of a mortgagor's qualifications. In effect, the lender draws a red line around an area on the map and denies all financing to applicants within the encircled area, usually based on the neighborhood's socioeconomic makeup.

Specific violations. Specific instances of discriminatory violations in real estate practice include:

- refusing to engage in a real estate transaction with a person
- refusing to make a transaction available
- refusing to receive or transmit an offer
- refusing to negotiate a transaction
- altering the terms, conditions, or privileges in a real estate transaction
- furnishing unequal facilities or services regarding a transaction
- falsely representing that a property is not available for inspection, sale, rental, or lease
- failing to bring a listing to a party's attention
- refusing to permit an individual to inspect a property
- indicating a preference, limitation, or discrimination based on a protected class in any advertising, record, or inquiry
- offering, soliciting, accepting, or using a real estate listing knowing that any discrimination is intended

A recent redlining case to be heard by the U.S. Supreme Court involved pizza delivery to a specific area. Domino's Pizza refused to allow its employees to deliver pizza to a particular neighborhood because their employees were being attacked and robbed. The residents of the area sued Domino's Pizza, stating that this action was a violation of the Fair Housing Law and was an example of redlining.

The Supreme Court agreed with the residents of the neighborhood that this practice was redlining. The Supreme Court told Domino's Pizza they could change policies for delivering to all areas, but they could not refuse to deliver to the specific neighborhood.

Jones v. Mayer

In 1968, the Supreme Court ruled in *Jones v. Mayer* that all discrimination in selling or renting residential property based on race is prohibited under the provisions of the Civil Rights Act of 1866. Thus, while the Federal Fair Housing Act exempts certain kinds of discrimination, anyone who feels victimized by discrimination *based on race* may seek legal recourse under the 1866 law.

Fair Housing poster

In 1972, HUD instituted a requirement that brokers display a standard HUD poster. The poster affirms the broker's compliance with fair housing laws in selling, renting, advertising, and financing residential properties. Failure to display the poster may be construed as discrimination.

Fair Housing Amendments Act of 1988

Amendments to federal fair housing laws prohibit discrimination based on sex and discrimination against handicapped persons and families with children.

Exemptions. Federal fair housing laws do not prohibit age and family status discrimination under the following circumstances:

- in government-designated retirement housing
- in a retirement community if all residents are 62 years of age or older
- in a retirement community if 80 % of the dwellings have one person who is 55 years of age or older, provided there are amenities for elderly residents
- in residential dwellings of four units or less, and single family houses if sold or rented by owners who have no more than three houses

Discrimination by client

Fair housing laws apply to home sellers as well as to agents, with the exception of the exemptions previously cited. If an agent goes along with a client's discriminatory act, the agent is equally liable for violation of fair housing laws. It is thus imperative to avoid complicity with client discrimination. Further, an agent should withdraw from any relationship where client discrimination occurs.

Examples of potential client discrimination are:

- refusing a full-price offer from a party
- removing the property from the market to sidestep a potential purchase by a party
- accepting an offer from one party that is lower than one from another party

Enforcement

Persons who feel they have been discriminated against under federal fair housing laws may file a complaint with the Office of Fair Housing and Equal Opportunity (FHEO) within HUD, or they may file suit in a federal or state court.

Filing an FHEO complaint. Complaints alleging fair housing violations must be filed with the Office of Fair Housing and Equal Opportunity within one year of the violation. HUD then initiates an investigation in conjunction with federal or local enforcement authorities.

If HUD decides that the complaint merits further action, it will attempt to resolve the matter out of court. If efforts to resolve the problem fail, the aggrieved party may file suit in state or federal court.

Filing suit. In addition to or instead of filing a complaint with HUD, a party may file suit in state or federal court within two years of the alleged violation.

Penalties. If discrimination is confirmed in court, the respondent may be enjoined to cease practicing his or her business. For example, a discriminating home builder may be restrained from selling available properties to buyers. Also, the plaintiff may be compensated for damages including humiliation, suffering, and pain. In addition, the injured party may seek equitable relief, including forcing the guilty party to complete a denied action such as selling or renting the property. Finally, the courts may impose civil penalties for first-time or repeat offenders.

VIRGINIA FAIR HOUSING LAWS

Key terms

Assistance animal – an animal that provides assistance to a person with a disability or provides emotional support that alleviates identified symptoms or effects of a person's disability. The animal, typically a dog, is not required to be specifically trained or certified and is not to be considered as a pet.

Disability – a physical or mental impairment that substantially limits the person's major life activities, not to include illegal use or addiction to a controlled substance.

Elderliness – a person 55 years or older.

Familial status – includes pregnant women and individuals under 18 years who live in the household. Does not include housing provided under a state or federal program designed for older persons, housing solely occupied by persons 62 years or older, or housing intended for and occupied by at least one person 55 years or older as long as at least 80% of the units are occupied by at least one person 55 years or older and the policies regarding the age restriction are publicized.

Source of funds – any lawful source providing funds to or on behalf of a housing renter or buyer, to include both governmental and nongovernmental entity programs.

Purposes

The Virginia Fair Housing Law (36-96.1) declares

"It is the policy of the Commonwealth of Virginia to provide for fair housing throughout the Commonwealth, to all its citizens, regardless of

- *race*
- *color*
- *religion*

- *familial status*
- *source of funds*
- *sexual orientation*

96

- *national origin*
- *sex*
- *elderliness*
- *gender identity*
- *military status*
- *disability*

and to that end to prohibit discriminatory practices with respect to residential housing by any person or group of persons, in order that the peace, health, safety, prosperity, and general welfare of all the inhabitants of the Commonwealth may be protected and ensured. This law shall be deemed an exercise of the police power of the Commonwealth of Virginia for the protection of the people of the Commonwealth."

The law makes it illegal to discriminate in residential housing on the basis of any of the above listed classes. The prohibition applies to rental and sales transactions, housing financing and insurance transactions, and housing advertising transactions and specifically to all property managers, owners, landlords, real estate agents, banks, savings institutions, credit unions, insurance companies, mortgage lenders, and appraisers.

Groups not protected under either state or federal fair housing law include students, smokers, and unmarried couples (marital status).

Prohibitions

Virginia statute 36-96.3 prohibits the following housing practices if based on any of the protected classes:

- refusing to sell, rent, or negotiate
- denying a sale or rental
- making a dwelling unavailable for sale or rent to a specific person
- setting different terms, conditions, or privileges of a sale or rental
- publishing or advertising preferences, limitations, or discriminations and/or using words or symbols associated with a particular class
- denying MLS or real estate brokers' organization membership
- including any discriminatory restrictive covenant in the sale or rental of housing
- using steering, blockbusting, or redlining in the sale or rental of housing
- applying one standard to one class of individuals while applying a different standard to another class of individuals
- attempting to record a deed that contains restrictions that violate fair housing
- committing any of the above prohibited when engaged in a real estate transaction with a person with a disability

Reasonable access

State and federal fair housing laws include specific provisions to protect persons with disabilities from housing discrimination. Not only do the prohibitions listed above apply to the disabled, but the law provides for reasonable accommodations to be made or allowed to provide the individual with full enjoyment of the dwelling. A person with a disability must request the accommodations. Qualifying for a reasonable accommodation is based strictly on the person having a disability as defined by law.

Alterations. Accommodations include altering or permitting the individual to alter the dwelling in such ways as widening doorways, installing grab rails in bathrooms, adding ramps at building entrances that are accessible only by stairs, lowering light switches, and so on. Where it is reasonable, landlords may require tenants to restore the interior of the dwelling to its original condition prior to the modifications. A person with a disability may also need parking accommodations by being assigned a parking space close to the building entrance.

Service dogs and assistance animals. Accommodations include the requirement that landlords and homeowner associations make reasonable modifications to rules and policies, such as landlords allowing assistance animals in dwellings and associations allowing large assistance dogs where there is a weight restriction on pets. This accommodation includes allowing service dogs into common area facilities. Service dogs are distinguished from other assistance animals by the special training they require. Service dog handlers may not be charged a pet deposit or other such fee.

The Virginia Consumer Protection Act specifies that doctors and other caregivers may not provide fraudulent documentation which evinces the need for an assistance animal. If a doctor or other caregiver offers bad faith documentation indicating a disability or disability-related need for a service animal, the person harmed by this fraud may sue the provider for damages.

Hoarding. In 2013, the American Psychiatric Association added compulsive hoarding to its list of mental disorders, making it a recognized disability. The APA defined compulsive hoarding as "a type of mental disability and persons with mental disabilities or mental handicaps are a protected class."

Exemptions

The following are exempt from the Virginia Fair Housing Law:

- single-family homes sold or rented by an owner who does not own more than three single-family houses at one time, with additional qualifications (§ 36-96.2 A)
- one- to four-family dwellings where the owner resides in one of the units
- dwellings owned or operated by religious or nonprofit organizations who limit the sale, rental, or occupancy of dwellings to persons of the same religion.
- lodging spaces owned by private membership clubs limited to use by club members, as long as the membership is not restricted based on any of the protected classes
- private, state-owned or supported schools, hospitals, nursing homes, or correctional institutions that restrict occupation of any single-family residence or room or use of restrooms based on sex
- owners renting housing to persons who pose a clear and present danger to others or the housing itself
- owners or managers renting housing to individuals with a criminal background involving harm to persons or property who pose a threat to the health and safety of others
- owners or managers with reasonable occupancy and safety standards for the dwelling
- rental applications requiring the number, ages, sex, and familial relationship of the dwelling's intended occupants
- owners or managing agents of only one 1-4-unit dwelling who deny rental because of the applicant's source of funds

Fair Housing board

Fair Housing Board (FHB). The FHB is responsible, with the Virginia Real Estate Board (REB), for administering and enforcing fair housing laws in Virginia. The FHB investigates complaints of housing discrimination through the Fair Housing Office. Complaints involving real estate licensees are handled by the Virginia Real Estate Board (REB). Both Boards have the power to initiate and receive complaints, conduct investigations, attempt resolution, and issue a charge and refer the complaint to the Attorney General for action. The Boards also have the power to promulgate and amend regulations as necessary.

Fair Housing Office (FHO). The Fair Housing Board investigates discrimination complaints through the Fair Housing Office. The FHO assigns an investigator to gather information about the complaint. The investigator interviews the complainant, the respondent, and any relevant witnesses and reviews documents and records. The Office also attempts reconciliation during the investigative process and provides a report of its findings to the appropriate Board.

Enforcement and penalties

Agencies. As mentioned, fair housing laws in Virginia are enforced by the Real Estate Board (REB) and the Fair Housing Board (FHB). The REB handles complaints against real estate licensees and brokerages, while the FHB handles other complaints.

The Virginia Division of Human Rights serves as counsel to the two boards for allegations of housing discrimination. If an investigation results in a reasonable cause finding and the resulting charges of discrimination are issued by either or both of the Boards, the Division prosecutes the alleged violation through civil actions

Complaints and responses. Fair housing complaints and responses must comply with certain time limits.

- Within one year of the alleged discriminatory act
  - a person complaining of housing discrimination must file a written complaint with the appropriate board.
- Within 10 days of receiving the complaint
  - the board must provide written notice to the complainant acknowledging receipt of the complaint and to the respondent including the specific alleged act of discrimination and the respondent's procedural rights and obligations.
- Within 30 days of receiving the complaint
  - the board must begin investigating the allegation; board may subpoena and interview witnesses and request records or documents related to the investigation.
- Within 100 days of receiving the complaint
  - the board must complete the investigation and prepare a final investigative report (FIR) summarizing the investigation or notify complainant and respondent in writing of why the investigation was not completed on time.
  - the board may encourage the parties to resolve the complaint by reaching a conciliatory agreement. If no conciliation agreement is reached, the investigation continues.
  - the board must determine if there is reasonable cause to conclude that a discriminatory housing practice occurred. If yes, the board may issue a charge. If no, the board must notify the parties within 30 days and dismiss the complaint.

Penalties. The REB may suspend, revoke, or refuse to renew the license of any licensee who has been found guilty of violating fair housing laws.

Civil actions can result in any of the following:

- an award of preventative relief, such as an injunction, restraining order, or other order against the violator
- assessment of a civil penalty against the respondent

- an award of reasonable attorney fees and costs to the prevailing party, to be paid through the liability of the Commonwealth
- an award of any other relief the court deems appropriate, including compensatory damages and punitive damages without limitation imposed by law

ADA

The ADA, which became law in 1990, is a civil rights law that prohibits discrimination against individuals with disabilities in all areas of public life, including employment, education, transportation, and facilities that are open to the general public. The purpose of the law is to make sure that people with disabilities have the same rights and opportunities as everyone else.

The Americans with Disabilities Act Amendments Act (ADAAA) became effective on January 1, 2009. Among other things, the ADAAA clarified that a disability is "a physical or mental impairment that substantially limits one or more major life activities." This definition applies to all titles of the ADA and covers private employers with 15 or more employees, state and local governments, employment agencies, labor unions, agents of the employer, joint management labor committees, and private entities considered places of public accommodation. Examples of the latter include hotels, restaurants, retail stores, doctor's offices, golf courses, private schools, day care centers, health clubs, sports stadiums, and movie theaters.

Titles 1-5

The law consists of five parts, referred to as titles, as follows.

- Title I (Employment) concerns equal employment opportunity. The U.S. Equal Employment Opportunity Commission enforces Title I.
- Title II (State and Local government) concerns nondiscrimination in state and local government services. The U.S. Department of Justice enforces Title II.
- Title III (Public Accommodations) concerns nondiscrimination in public accommodations and commercial facilities. The U.S. Department of Justice enforces Title III.
- Title IV (Telecommunications) concerns accommodations in telecommunications and public service messaging. The Federal Communications Commission enforces Title IV.
- Title V (Miscellaneous) concerns various general situations, including how the ADA affects other laws, insurance providers, and lawyers.

Real estate practitioners are most likely to encounter Titles I and III, and therefore they should become familiar with these. In advising clients, licensees should make it a routine part of their practice to recommend that buyers and sellers and tenants seek qualified legal counsel.

Most people are not familiar enough with ADA Law to realize that the law only covers public, commercial, and governmental buildings; it does not directly cover residential housing. The law states that new home builders should make 5% of new construction accessible but provides no description or standards for accessibility.

Requirements

The act requires landlords in certain circumstances to modify housing and facilities so that disabled persons can access them without hindrance.

The ADA also requires that disabled employees and members of the public be provided access that is equivalent to that provided to those who are not disabled.

- Employers with at least fifteen employees must follow nondiscriminatory employment and hiring practices.
- Reasonable accommodations must be made to enable disabled employees to perform essential functions of their jobs.

- Modifications to the physical components of a building may be necessary to provide the required access to tenants and their customers, such as widening doorways, changing door hardware, changing how doors open, installing ramps, lowering wall-mounted telephones and keypads, supplying Braille signage, and providing auditory signals.
- Existing barriers must be removed when the removal is "readily achievable," that is, when cost is not prohibitive. New construction and remodeling must meet a higher standard.
- If a building or facility does not meet requirements, the landlord must determine whether restructuring or retrofitting or some other kind of accommodation is most practical.

FAIR HOUSING LAWS AND HOARDING INFORMATION: RECENT DECISIONS AND DISCUSSION

The following fair housing case summaries highlight 3 recent Fair Housing law cases and decisions and a presentation of recent developments in hoarding and how fair housing laws impact hoarding. Each synopsis will present an overview of the issue being adjudicated, and the respective outcomes. The cases concern (1) housing discrimination based on color, disability, and source of income; (2) sexual harassment in property rentals. The hoarding discussion will focus on how one might apply to hoarding the concept of reasonable accommodation requirements as imposed by fair housing law.

Case one: Housing discrimination based on color, disability, and source of income

Synopsis: District of Columbia Attorney General in September, 2020 filed suit against seven real estate companies in the District for violating the District's Human Rights Act, specifically for (1) refusing to rent to a prospective tenant based on race and color; (2) for discriminating against a mobility impairment by denying a disability parking space; and (3) for discrimination in housing by denying access based on the tenant's source of income.

Specific circumstances: In the first case involving the refusal to rent, the allegation was that the landlord indicated a preference for white tenants over and above Black tenant prospects. Further, the party had custody over three dependent relatives and was receiving aid via the Housing Choice Voucher program. The discrimination was further pronounced by the landlord's refusal to provide an approval letter the tenant needed to receive specific housing assistance in the complex. This effectively barred the tenant from successfully renting in the property.

In the disability case, a complex offered 3 disability spaces in the parking lot, but had seven tenants with disability parking placards. The complaint alleged that the defendants repeatedly denied requests for disability parking within 200 feet of her rental unit. Instead, management urged the tenant to move to another facility.

In the third case, an online ad contained the discriminatory phrase "no Section 8" tenants. This constitutes an illegal denial of housing access based on one's source of income (housing vouchers).

101

Case two: Sexual harassment in housing rentals (Virginia; October 2020)

Synopsis: In this case, the fair housing complaint alleges a violation by a rental manager who had been making unwelcomed sexual comments and physical advances toward female residents. Specifically, the manager was offering housing benefits in exchange for sexual favors. Additionally, the manager threatened actions against such tenants if they refused to grant sexual favors. Further, the case alleges the manager prohibited residents from entertaining Black guests within their premises.

Specific circumstances: Here, the defendants were fined $330,000 to compensate eight victims injured by the discrimination and harassment. The consent decree further barred the manager from renting properties in the future. Finally the defendants had to each pay $5,000 to "vindicate the public interest."

Case three: Rental agents accused of racial discrimination (October 2020)

Synopsis: This Department of Justice lawsuit alleges discrimination against African-Americans in violation of fair housing law in offering housing units for rent. The suit is the culmination of a series of tests run by the Fair Housing Testing Program to determine whether renting practices were applied uniformly across racially variant groups of prospective renters.

More specifically, the test results affirmed that (1) rental agents told African-American testers about fewer rental units than white testers; (2) white testers were offered rental discounts and inspection opportunities that were not offered to African-American testers, and (3) made more encouraging comments to white testers about available rental units.

Offering variant levels of service in renting properties is a violation of equal access to housing and equal treatment when seeking rental housing regardless of race. In turn, the practice is discriminatory and a violation of federal fair housing law. The lawsuit seeks monetary damages to compensate victims, civil penalties to vindicate the public interest, and a court order barring future discrimination.

HOARDING AND FAIR HOUSING LAW

In 2013, hoarding was declared a clinical disability by the American Psychiatric Association. This conferred fair housing protections for hoarders under fair housing provisions that protect parties with mental or physical impairments. Further, hoarding is a serious concern for housing facilities managers since the health and welfare of all tenants can be adversely impacted.

Reasonable Accommodation process

In the parlance of fair housing law, "reasonable accommodation" (RA) is the request for a waiver of a housing provider's normal policy in order to provide equal access and opportunity to people with disabilities – in this context, hoarders. Since hoarders are deemed to have a physical / mental impairment, the RA can be legally applied to suspend one's normal landlord-tenant policy or procedure in favor of a more exceptional, considerate process that accounts for behavioral conditions that may effectively lie beyond the hoarder's control.

Diagnosing the hoarder

Since housing protections are extendable to hoarders, it is helpful to explore the defining characteristics of a hoarding profile. These include the following:

- difficulty discarding possessions regardless of their value or utility
- visible distress when pressed to throw items of property away
- inability to ensure a safe or hygienic environment
- excessive accumulation of items
- possible excessive accumulation of domesticated animals (animal hoarding)

Additional hoarding traits include loss of use of certain amenities and appliances within the premises owing to excessive clutter and blockage of hallways and doorways; creation of possible fire hazards; and unsafe sanitation systems. One may differentiate hoarding from the more benign traits of messiness and poor housekeeping by the degree of safety gained or lost in occupying the household. In the latter, people in a messy house can still move around freely – in a hoarding environment, rooms are inaccessible and unsafe.

Reacting to the hoarder's tenancy situation

Hoarders living in a rental dwelling have the right to reasonable accommodation from the housing provider – whether they actually make such a request or not. The law requires the housing provider to reasonably accommodate the resident prior to eviction. An RA may take on any number of forms. One common course of action is an extension of time to address compliance with code. Another form of RA is an action plan for the tenant to similarly address the situation. In any case the RA establishes and documents benchmarks for progress and compliance that providers can use to justify future, more severe actions. In most cases, the ultimate objective is to hold off on a quick eviction and substitute that alternative with tenant collaboration involving inputs from the housing provider, mental health professionals, other social organizations, and particularly family members.

Do's and Don'ts in working with hoarder tenants

Courses of action that are not recommended in working with hoarders:

- do not blame or shame the hoarding behavior
- do not remove the clutter yourself
- avoid abrupt or straightforward cleanups that do not involve the hoarder

Recommended courses of action:

- partner with code enforcement personnel and mental health providers
- develop mutually agreed-upon goals and deadlines for changing behavior
- do not initiate eviction prematurely
- involve legal counsel to maintain fair housing compliance
- document interfaces and plans
- maintain follow-up monitoring

Eviction of the hoarder. Regardless of the reasonable accommodation doctrine in fair housing, the law does not condone serious jeopardization of the health, safety and welfare of a jurisdiction's citizenry. Therefore, depending on circumstances, it may become justifiable – indeed necessary – to evict the hoarder. Certainly good documentation and a history of collaboration with the hoarder helps to ensure fair housing compliance while an actual eviction is carried out. Eviction is even more readily an advisable course of action in cases of animal hoarding, animal cruelty, hoarding explosives, or blocking emergency exits and creating fire/safety issues.

Interactive Exercises

Unit 5: Fair Housing, ADA, and Civil Rights

5.1) "WHAT IF" SITUATION EXAMPLE 1: Confronting Fair Housing violations/seller or buyer handling of failing contracts

As Olivia is running her morning MLS searches for clients, she notices that a new listing pops up in her neighborhood. It matches the exact criteria presented to her by her client, Jamie. Jamie falls into one of the protected classes under the Federal Fair Housing Act. Olivia doesn't want him to live in the area. She does not think he will fit in with the other neighbors, so he avoids sending him the listing.

Later on, Jamie notices the listing when he looks online and asks Olivia to see it. Olivia makes up an excuse and says there is already a pending offer. A few days go by, and the home is still marked active, so Jamie calls the listing agent, sees the house, and submits an offer without Olivia's help.

What would you do if you were Jamie?

_____

_____

_____

_____

_____

_____

_____

_____

_____

5.2) "WHAT IF" SITUATION EXAMPLE 2: Fair Housing questions

Mallory has been getting many calls on her current listing with questions about the home, neighborhood, etc. She was used to answering these common questions, but last Wednesday, she got a voicemail from a man named Chase who asked about the neighborhood's demographics. He wanted to know what races lived in the area and whether it was a predominantly white neighborhood. His top priority was living in a suburb that has a high white population.

He also let it be known that he is an all-cash buyer and would submit proof of funds to her as soon as he got home.

How should Mallory approach the situation? What should she say to Chase?

_____

_____

_____

_____

_____

_____

_____

_____

_____

SNAPSHOT REVIEW: UNIT FIVE

FAIR HOUSING, ADA AND CIVIL RIGHTS

FEDERAL FAIR HOUSING LAWS
- Give people equal opportunity to live wherever without discrimination in purchase, sale, rental, financing
- Protected classes- race; color; religion; national origin; sex; familial status; handicapped status

Civil Rights Act of 1866
- Prohibits discrimination (selling, renting, inheriting, and conveying real estate) in housing based on race

Civil Rights Act of 1968
- Prohibits discrimination in housing based on race, color, religion, or national origin

Forms of discrimination
- Discriminatory misrepresentation; discriminatory advertising; providing unequal services; steering; blockbusting; restricting MLS participation; redlining

Jones v. Mayer
- All discrimination in selling/renting residential property based on race is prohibited under Civil Rights Act of 1866

Fair Housing poster
- Brokers to display HUD poster affirming compliance with fair housing laws in selling, renting, advertising, financing residential properties

Fair Housing Amendments Act of 1988
- Prohibit discrimination based on sex; handicapped persons/families with children

Discrimination by client
- If agent goes with client's discriminatory act, agent equally liable for violation of fair housing laws

Enforcement
- Persons discriminated against may file complaint with Office of Fair Housing and Equal Opportunity (FHEO) within HUD, or suit in federal/state court

VIRGINIA FAIR HOUSING LAWS
Key Terms
- Assistance animal; disability; elderliness; familial status; source of funds

Purposes
- Illegal to discriminate on basis of race, color, religion, national origin, sex, familial status, source of funds, sexual orientation, gender identity, military status, elderliness, disability

Prohibitions
- Refusal to sell, rent, negotiate; making dwelling unavailable for sale/rent; setting different terms, conditions, privileges; denying MLS membership; steering, blockbusting, redlining, etc.

Reasonable access
- Protect persons with disabilities from housing discrimination
- Provides reasonable accommodations (i.e. service/assistance animals)

Exemptions
- Single-family homes sold/rented by owner who owns less than three single-family houses at one time

- One- to four-family dwellings where owner resides in one unit
- Owners renting housing to persons who pose clear and present danger to others/housing itself

Fair Housing Board
- Responsible, with Virginia Real Estate Board (REB), for administering/enforcing fair housing laws in Virginia
- FHO assigns investigator to gather information about complaint

Enforcement and penalties
- Enforced by REB (complaints against real estate licensees/brokerages) and FHB (other complaints)
- REB may suspend, revoke, refuse to renew license of licensee guilty of violating fair housing laws

ADA
- Prohibits discrimination against individuals with disabilities in employment, education, transportation, public facilities

Title I
- Equal employment opportunity

Title II
- Nondiscrimination in state/local government services

Title III
- Nondiscrimination in public accommodations/commercial facilities

Title IV
- Accommodations in telecommunications/public service messaging

Title V
- Various general situations (ADA affecting other laws, insurance providers, and lawyers)

Requirements
- Requires landlords to modify housing/facilities so disabled persons can access without hindrance
- Disabled employees/members of public provided access equivalent to those who are not disabled

Check Your Understanding Quiz:

Unit Five: Fair Housing, ADA and Civil Rights

Carefully read each question then provide your best answer based on what you learned in this unit. Then check your answers against the Answer Key which immediately follows the quiz questions.

1.   Which of the following is NOT a protected class under the Fair Housing Act?

   a. Race
   b. Religion
   c. National origin
   d. Sexual identity

2.   What is it called when a licensee directly channels customers away from certain neighborhoods?

   a. Blockbusting
   b. Steering
   c. Redlining
   d. Guiding

3.   NAR recently launched a program to train agents on how to handle sensitive scenarios. What is this program called?

   a. The Fairhaven Program
   b. Title VIII
   c. The Public Relations Program
   d. The Human Rights Course

4.   The Civil Rights Act of 1866 prohibits discrimination in housing based on _____.

   a. gender identity.
   b. sex.
   c. familial status.
   d. race.

5.   Which statute prohibits discrimination against individuals with disabilities?

   a. The Fair Housing Act
   b. Jones v. Mayer Law
   c. The Americans with Disabilities Act
   d. The Fairhaven Act

6. Ella's mortgage lender refuses to make a loan on any properties in her neighborhood. What can he be accused of?

   a. Restricting MLS participation
   b. Redlining
   c. Blockbusting
   d. Bordering

7. Which statute is responsible for preventing discrimination in residential properties financed by FHA and VA loans?

   a. Executive Order 11063
   b. Civil Rights Act of 1866
   c. Federal Fair Housing Act
   d. Government Housing Act

8. What was the name of the Supreme Court case that allowed anyone who felt victimized by discrimination based on race to seek legal recourse?

   a. Lucas v. Nolan
   b. Jones v. Mayer
   c. Andrews v. Swift
   d. Alfred v. Jones

9. The APA has added _____ to its list of mental disorders, making it a recognized disability and a protected class.

   a. OCD
   b. depression
   c. compulsive hoarding
   d. anxiety

10. Section III of the ADA laws touches on nondiscrimination in public accommodations and _____.

    a. commercial facilities
    b. residential properties
    c. parks
    d. non-profit facilities

UNIT 6:

ETHICS AND STANDARDS OF CONDUCT

Unit Six Learning Objectives: When the student has completed this unit he or she will be able to:

- Explain the duties a REALTOR® owes to other REALTORS®
- Define and differentiate between mediation, arbitration, and the Ombudsman program.
- Understand the Code of Ethics.
- Identify the penalties for violating the Code of Ethics.
- Summarize the overriding thesis of the Pathway to Professionalism

REALTORS® CODE OF ETHICS

A set of rules and conduct members must practice in their dealings with others. These standards lay out the values of an organization.

DEFINITIONS

Business ethics. The standards used by a business or company to make decisions and how they treat their Clients, Customers, Vendors, and Employees.

Client. An individual in which we have a fiduciary relationship, such as a Single Agency Relationship.

Code of Ethics. A set of rules and conduct members must practice in their dealings with others. These standards lay out the values of an organization.

Customer. An individual with whom we do not have a fiduciary relationship and owe limited disclosure, such as a Transaction Brokerage Relationship.

Ethics. A system of moral principles, rules, an individual or business uses to determine how they deal with others.

Morals. A person's individual belief of what is right and wrong; religion, culture, and many other factors influence a person's morals.

Preamble. The opening statement of a document reflecting the values or vision of the organization.

Situational Ethics. A person changing their ethical views to fit a specific situation or changing how they react due to a change in circumstance.

Demographic information. Information gathered on customers or clients. May include information such as age, sex, race, color, or national origin. This information is collected only to assist in operating the brokerage and identifying advertising avenues, not discriminating against anyone in a protected class.

Professional services. The eight professional services a REALTOR® may perform are advertising, buying, auctioning, renting, selling, appraising, leasing, and exchanging.

NAR's protected classes. The NAR Code of Ethics' protected classes include race, color, religion, sex, disability, familial status, national origin, sexual orientation, and gender identity.

Duties to the public. The third section of NAR's Code of Ethics covers how REALTORS® should behave when interacting with the public. Articles 10 to 14 and their Standards of Practices identify specific behavior and guidelines for dealing with the public. This section restates many of the same ideas expressed in Articles 1 through 9; however, it explicitly identifies the duties owed to members of the public.

Arbitration. A voluntary process where an independent third party listens to the individuals involved in the dispute and makes a binding decision on who is the winner.

Mediation. A voluntary process where an independent third person helps the parties agree to resolve their dispute. Mediation is considered a win-win option; the idea is that both sides will walk out feeling they got something from the mediation. In 90 days, if no resolution is met, the parties must move on to another dispute resolution method, preferably arbitration.

Ombudsman. A voluntary process where an individual appointed by a local Board of REALTORS® receives assistance to resolve disputes through constructive communication and advocating for consensus and understanding.

Procuring cause. The agent who starts the uninterrupted chain of events leading to the sale or rental of a listing.

Public trust. Public trust refers to misappropriation of client or customer funds or property, discrimination against the protected classes under the Code of Ethics, or fraud.

Duties to REALTORS® The fourth section of NAR's Code of Ethics covers how REALTORS® should behave when interacting with other REALTORS®. Articles 15 to 17 and their Standards of Practices identify specific behavior and guidelines for dealing with other REALTORS®. This section restates many of the same ideas expressed in Articles 1 through 14; however, it explicitly identifies the duties owed to NAR members.

NATIONAL ASSOCIATION OF REALTORS® CODE OF ETHICS

Historical abstract. In the early 1900s, real estate agents were given licenses by county judges, and often they were "peddlers" licenses. The 1900s was a time of land scams and speculation. In 1908, the National Association of REALTORS® (NAR) formed to eliminate the notion of "Caveat emptor" or let the buyer beware. Their goal was to protect the public and promote homeownership in the United States.

In 1913, NAR introduced the Code of Ethics for REALTORS®® to follow in their dealings with their clients, the public, and other REALTORS®. This document has been fluid and ever-changing over the years. Today, REALTORS® have one of the strongest professional Code of Ethics in the United States.

The Code of Ethics also provides standard practices and procedures setting forth how REALTORS® should react in their dealings with specific individuals and others in their field. The Code of Ethics, however, is not law. Rather, the Code of Ethics enhances local, state, or federal laws.

A quote in the Code of Ethics and Arbitration Manual reads, "Because the Code is a living document and real estate is a dynamic business and profession, the law need never be its substitute. So long as the aspiration to better serve the public remails the underlying concept of the code, it must evolve and grow in significance and importance consonant with but independent of the law."

Structure of the Code of Ethics. The Code of Ethics has four parts:

- The Preamble
- Duties to Clients and Customers (Articles 1 – 9)
- Duties to the Public (Articles 10 – 14)
- Duties to REALTORS® (Articles 15 – 17)

The Articles within the Code of Ethics define the broad statements about the licensee's behavior and duties. The **Standards of Practice**, within each Article, give more specific guidance to the licensee. The Standards of Practice support and interpret the Articles.

In resolving ethics complaints, complainants are to cite only the Article(s) violated and not the Standard of Practice. It will be up to the Professional Standards Committee to give the specific Standard of Practice violated in their final report.

It must be noted that the Code of Ethics contains obligations that may exceed those mandated by law. Should a situation arise where the law and Code of Ethics conflict, the obligations of law must always take precedence.

When reading the Preamble and the Code, the word REALTORS® must be read to also include REALTOR-ASSOCIATE®s.

PREAMBLE

"Under all is the land."

This statement is a powerful start to NAR's Code of Ethics. It means that everything we do, are, or aspire to become begins with the land beneath our feet. The quote shows the importance of the role each REALTOR® holds in our society. Real estate impacts everything.

The Preamble of the Code of Ethics serves as a vision statement on how licensees should conduct themselves and represent their profession to the public. The Preamble calls for REALTORS® to "maintain and improve the standards of their calling." It also states that it is the REALTOR®'s responsibility to "act with integrity and honesty."

The NAR Board of Directors later added that licensees should not dishonor the profession or do anything that will hurt the organization's public trust. The altered Preamble reflects the changes in Article 10 of the Code of Ethics (see also Unit 5).

ARTICLE 1

*"When representing a buyer, seller, landlord, tenant, or other client as an agent, REALTORS®
pledge themselves to protect and promote the interests of their client. This obligation to the
client is primary, but it does not relieve REALTORS® of their obligation to treat all parties
honestly. When serving a buyer, seller, landlord, tenant or other party in a non-agency capacity,
REALTORS® remain obligated to treat all parties honestly."*

Central themes. Article 1 of the Code of Ethics promotes honesty as a critical virtue of any licensee. The
16 Standards of Practice within Article 1 describe the different duties a licensee may have and how they
must act in specific situations. The basis of the Standards of Practice is the duties owed to customers
and clients based on agency law. Amendments to SP 1-12 and 1-13, effective June 2025, emphasize that
broker compensation is fully negotiable.

Article 1 Standards of Practice. The central thrust of Article 1 is reflected in its Standards of Practice 1.1
through 1.16. These are as follows:

SP 1.1 – Be careful to abide by the Code when you are representing yourself in a transaction.

SP 1.2 – The Code of Ethics applies to all transactions.

SP 1.3 – Do not mislead the owner as to the real market value of a piece of property.

SP 1.4 – Do not mislead the savings or benefits of utilizing the services of a REALTOR®.

SP 1.5 – No dual agency. An agent cannot have a fiduciary relationship with both parties in a
transaction.

SP 1.6 – Submit all offers and counteroffers promptly.

SP 1.7 – When working as the listing agent, present all offers until closing, unless waived in writing.

SP 1.8 – When working as the buyer's agent, present all offers until contract acceptance, unless waived
in writing.

SP 1.9 – Maintain confidentiality even after termination of a relationship.

SP 1.10 – In property management, the licensee must comply with the management agreement and
ensure their tenants' rights, safety, and health.

SP 1.11 – Use skill, care, and diligence in all transactions.

SP 1.12 – Listing agreements: Advise sellers and landlords of company's cooperation policy and that
broker compensation is fully negotiable and not set by law.

SP 1.13 – Buer-agent agreements: Advise potential clients of company's cooperation policy and that
broker compensation is fully negotiable and not set by law.

SP 1.14 – Appraisal fees must not be based on the market value of the property.

SP 1.15 – Disclose any other offers already presented or any expected offers.

SP 1.16 –Listing brokers and property managers may not enter the under any terms and conditions not
established by the owner.

Article 1 illustration. A broker was preparing a CMA for a listing appointment. The broker knew the seller
was interviewing several other brokers. He decided to increase the property's market value to show the
seller how much more money they could earn from hiring him. The violation in this example is of Article

1, Standard Practice 1.3 and 1.4.

ARTICLE 2

"REALTORS® shall avoid exaggeration, misrepresentation, or concealment of pertinent facts relating to the property or the transaction. REALTORS® shall not, however, be obligated to discover latent defects in the property, to advise on matters outside the scope of their real estate license, or to disclose facts which are confidential under the scope of agency or non-agency relationships as defined by state law."

Central theme. Article 2 of the Code of Ethics discusses the need for transparency in all transactions. While a licensee is not required to seek out defects in the property, they must disclose any defects they know exists. This duty is necessary no matter the type of agency relationship the broker has established.

Article 2 Standards of Practice. Article 2 has five Standards of Practice:

SP 2.1 – A REALTOR® must disclose any latent defects they know about or that are readily observable to a lay-person. They are not required to be experts in fields other than their own.

SP 2.2 – Moved to Standard of Practice 1.12

SP 2.3 – Moved to Standard of Practice 1.13

SP 2.4 – A REALTOR® must not participate in doctoring the numbers on any contract.

SP 2.5 – REALTORS® must not disclose non-material items not pertinent to the transaction.

Article 2 illustration. Susie is showing a potential buyer a house. The MLS stated that the roof was 25 years old and had a few leaks. During the showing, Susie's customer asked about the condition of the roof. Susie stated she was not aware of any problems. Susie has violated Article 2, Standard 2.1.

ARTICLE 3

"REALTORS® shall cooperate with other brokers except when cooperation is not in the client's best interest. The obligation to cooperate does not include the obligation to share commissions, fees, or to otherwise compensate another broker."

Central theme. Article 3 promotes cooperation among brokers unless it is not in their client's best interest. It also addresses compensation negotiation.

Article 3 Standards of Practice. Article 3 has eleven Standards of Practice as follows:

SP 3.1 – REALTORS® must establish terms of cooperation in conjunction with sellers and landlords, including whether compensation is paid or not.

SP 3.2 – Negotiating compensation must not delay or withhold delivery of offers. REALTORS® who change the compensation in a transaction must communicate it to other licensees. Compensation may not unilaterally be changed after an offer has been presented.

SP 3.3 – REALTORS® may change the cooperative compensation.

SP 3.4 – REALTORS® must disclose variable rate commissions.

SP 3.5 – REALTORS® must disclose all pertinent facts before and after the sale.

SP 3.6 - REALTORS® should disclose any current accepted offers.

SP 3.7 – REALTORS® must disclose their status when calling other REALTORS® about a listed property.

SP 3.8 – REALTORS® must not give false information about the availability of property to be shown.

SP 3.9 – Cooperating brokers (and anyone else who is not a listing broker or property manager) must not access or use a listed property in any way other than what is agreed upon by the seller.

SP 3.10 – REALTOR® should share information on listed property and make the property available to other brokers.

SP 3.11 – REALTORS® may not violate Fair Housing laws and refuse to show a piece of property to someone in a protected class.

Article 3 illustration. Janet's seller told her that they did not want to sell their home to anyone who was not white. Janet told potential buyers who were not white that the house was no longer available or was not available to be shown. The violation in this example is of Article 3, Standards of Practice 3.8 and 3.11.

ARTICLE 4

"REALTORS® who have a present ownership interest in property for sale or lease, or contemplated interested to purchase or lease property, must disclose in writing the existence of such interest to all parties to the transaction prior to a party signing any agreement."

Central theme. Article 4 requires REALTORS® to disclose that they have a real estate license when buying or selling property for themselves. If they do not disclose this fact, then they have an unfair advantage over the average consumer. By telling them, the REALTOR® -is giving them a chance to obtain representation in the transaction. Thus, keeping it an arm's length transaction.

Article 4 Standards of Practice. Article 4 has two Standards of Practice as follows:

SP 4.1 – REALTORS® must reveal their own ownership interest, as well as ownership of a family member, their own brokerage firm, or an entity in which they have an interest.

SP 4.2 – REALTORS® must only disclose that they have an interest in a property, but not what that interest is.

ARTICLE 5

"REALTORS® shall not undertake to provide professional services concerning a property or its value where they have a present or contemplated interest unless such interest is specifically disclosed to all affected parties."

Central theme. Article 5 requires REALTORS® to disclose any conflict of interest before providing any professional services. The only time this would be allowed is with the written permission of all parties involved in providing the service.

Article 5 illustration. ABC Realty shares office space with a lender and a title company. They recommend that all their buyers use these companies since they are in the same location, and it allows them to communicate with the lender and title company to ensure the closing goes smoothly. What the REALTOR® did not disclose to their customers is the fact that family members own these companies.

ARTICLE 6

"REALTORS® shall not accept any commission, rebate, or profit on expenditures made for their client, without the client's knowledge and consent.

When recommending real estate products or services (e.g., homeowner's insurance, warranty programs, mortgage financing, title insurance, etc.), REALTORS® shall disclose to the client or customer to whom the recommendation is made any financial benefits or fees, other than real estate referral fees, the REALTOR® or REALTOR®'s firm may receive as a direct result of such recommendation."

Central theme. Article 6 states a REALTOR® may not accept any compensation in the form of a commission, rebate, kickback, etc., without the client's written consent. This requirement includes gifts from home inspectors, appliance companies, plumbers, etc.

Article 6 illustrated. A REALTOR® hired Ace Home Inspection to inspect a home for a buyer. The REALTOR® did not tell the buyer that he received a $50 gift card for the referral. The REALTOR® violates Article 6 of the Code of Ethics.

ARTICLE 7

"In a transaction, REALTORS® shall not accept compensation from more than one party, even if permitted by law, without disclosure to all parties and the informed consent of the REALTOR®'s client or clients."

Central theme. Article 7 states that a REALTOR® cannot accept compensation from more than one person without disclosing the fact to all parties. The REALTOR® should also have that consent in writing.

Article 7 illustrated. A broker has a Buyer's Broker Agreement with a buyer. The agreement states that the broker will get a 3% commission on a home valued at $350,000. The broker finds a home for $300,000 that the buyer likes, and they enter a contract. The broker is getting 3% from the listing broker and then asks the buyer to pay him a 3% commission. The broker tells the buyer he is not getting any commission from the seller's side. This type of action would be a violation of Article 7 of the Code of Conduct. The broker may not receive compensation from more than one party in a transaction unless he has written all the parties' written consent.

ARTICLE 8

"REALTORS® shall keep in a special account in an appropriate financial institution, separated from their own funds, monies coming into their possession in trust for other persons, such as escrows, trust funds, clients' monies, and other like items."

Article 8 central themes. Article 8 addresses escrow funds and how to handle other people's money. A Broker must be careful not to commingle funds. Commingle is mixing their personal money with money held in trust for others. The only time commingling is legal is when a Broker puts up to $1,000 of personal funds for a Sales Escrow Account or $5,000 in a Tenant Escrow Account to stop the possibility of conversion.

ARTICLE 9

> *"REALTORS®, for the protection of all parties, shall assure whenever possible that all agreements related to real estate transactions including, but not limited to, listing and representation agreements, purchase contracts, and leases are in writing in clear and understandable language expressing the specific terms, conditions, obligations, and commitments of the parties. A copy of each agreement shall be furnished to each party to such agreements upon their signing or initialing."*

Central themes. Article 9 states Brokers must ensure all documents related to a real estate transaction be in clear, concise language. The contracts must also clearly represent the terms and conditions of the agreement between the parties.

Article 9 Standards of Practice. Article 9 has 2 Standards of Practice as follows:

SP 9.1 – REALTORS® should use reasonable care to ensure extensions and amendments.

SP 9.2 – REALTORS® should make a reasonable effort to explain and disclose the different parts of a contract and contract relationships to clients whether this is done in person, electronically, or otherwise.

Article 9 illustrated. Broker Jane is working with a buyer in another state. She sends them an electronic contract and indicates where the buyer needs to sign. Jane does not review the Sales and Purchase Agreement with them or go over any of the disclosures. Upon return of the contract, Jane does not send a copy to the buyer. Broker Jane violates Article 9 of the Code of Articles, which requires brokers to explain contracts to clients when done in person, electronically, or otherwise.

ARTICLE 10

> *"REALTORS® shall not deny equal professional services to any person for reasons of race, color, religion, sex, handicap, familial status, national origin, sexual orientation, or gender identity. REALTORS® shall not be parties to any plan or agreement to discriminate against a person or persons on the basis of race, color, religion, sex, disability, familial status, national origin, sexual orientation, or gender identity."*

> *"REALTORS®, in their real estate employment practices, shall not discriminate against any person or persons on the basis of race, color, religion, sex, disability, familial status, national origin, sexual orientation, or gender identity."*

Central theme. Article 10 of the Code of Ethics prohibits REALTORS® from discrimination against the protected classes identified in the Code of Ethics.

Article 10 Standards of Practice. Article 10 has 5 Standards of Practice as follows:

SP 10.1 – REALTORS® may provide necessary demographic information of a neighborhood; however, they cannot provide information about the neighborhood's racial, religious, or ethnic composition. This SP specifically emphasizes a prohibition on steering.

SP 10.2 – REALTORS® may gather demographic information; however, they must be careful how the information is used and distributed.

SP 10.3 – REALTORS® should be cautious with any advertisement that indicates a neighborhood's racial or ethnic makeup or targets one of the protected classes.

SP 10.4 –REALTORS® must follow fair employment practices of employees or independent contractors.

SP 10.5 – REALTORS® may not harass someone in one of the protected classes. Harassment refers to any behavior intended to create a hostile, abusive, or intimidating environment.

Amendments to SP 10.5. After extensive research, the Professional Standards Committee recommended changes that effectively broadened the context of Practice 10.5. In the past, the Code of Ethics only covered REALTORS® activities during a real estate transaction. The applicability of the new Standard of Practice 10.5 covers all activities of a REALTOR®.

Under the changes a REALTOR® can be found guilty of a Code of Ethics violation whether the infraction related to a transaction, or other membership-related context. Presently, any potential breach of Article 10 will be looked at individually to see if it is a violation or if it is someone expressing their First Amendment rights.

The new wording of Article 10, SP 10.5 became:
"REALTORS® must not use harassing speech, hate speech, epithets, or slurs" based upon an individual or group that falls under one of the protected classes."

Further changes were made after a series of meetings in 2025 that considered a more specific definition of "harassment." These came into effect on June 5, 2025, and read as follows:

"REALTORS®, in their capacity as real estate professionals, in association with their real estate businesses, or in their real estate-related activities, shall not harass any person or persons based on race, color, religion, sex, disability, familial status, national origin, sexual orientation, or gender identity."

"As used in this Code of Ethics, harassment is unwelcome behavior directed at an individual or group based on one or more of the above protected characteristics where the purpose or effect of the behavior is to create a hostile, abusive, or intimidating environment which adversely affects their ability to access equal professional services or employment opportunity."

Article 10 illustration. A REALTOR® created an advertisement using models and demographic information about a neighborhood's racial makeup. The purpose was primarily to steer specific individuals to a particular community. This action is a violation of Article 10, Standards of Practice 10.1, 10.2 and 10.3.

ARTICLE 11

"The services which REALTORS® provide to their clients and customers shall conform to the standards of practice and competence which are reasonably expected in the specific real estate disciplines in which they engage; specifically, residential real estate brokerage, real property management, commercial and industrial real estate brokerage, land brokerage, real estate appraisal, real estate counseling, real estate syndication, real estate auction, and international real estate."

"REALTORS® shall not undertake to provide specialized professional services concerning a type of property or service that is outside their field of competence unless they engage the assistance of one who is competent on such types of property or service, or unless the facts are fully disclosed to the client. Any persons engaged to provide such assistance shall be so identified to the client, and their contribution to the assignment should be set forth."

Central theme. REALTORS® should only work within real estate areas in which they have sufficient knowledge to protect their customer or client. One agent can't know everything about all areas of specialization within the industry.

Article 11 Standards of Practice. Article 11 has four Standards of Practice as follows:

SP 11.1 – When preparing an opinion of value on a piece of property, they must know that specific area of real estate and provide detailed information to the customer or client.

SP 11.2 – A REALTOR® should perform only in an area that they have reasonable competence.

SP 11.3 – When providing consulting services or advice, they shall objectively present the material. The fee shall be contingent on the level of difficulty and the market value of the real property.

SP 11.4 – Competency required under Article 11 is based on the services agreed to by the customers or clients and follows the Code of Ethics and state law.

Article 11 illustration. A REALTOR® is asked to prepare an appraisal for a bank on a commercial building's short sale. The agent had no experience in doing an appraisal or in commercial real estate. This agent would be guilty of violating Article 11 Standards of Practice 11.1, 11.2, and 11.4.

ARTICLE 12

"REALTORS® shall be honest and truthful in their real estate communications and shall present a true picture in their advertising, marketing, and other representations. REALTORS® shall ensure that their status as real estate professionals is readily apparent in their advertising, marketing, and other representations and that the recipients of all real estate communications are, or have been, notified that those communications are from a real estate professional."

Central theme. REALTORS® should be honest in all their advertising and marketing.

Article 12 Standards of Practice. Article 12 has 13 Standards of Practice:

SP 12.1 – REALTORS® who advertise something as free must disclose if they will receive any compensation and from whom they are going to receive the payment.

SP 12.2 – Deleted in January 2020.

SP 12.3 – REALTORS® should use care if offering a prize or other compensation for real estate services. They must fully disclose the requirement to receive the compensation.

SP 12.4 – REALTORS® should not advertise a property they are not authorized to market.

SP 12.5 – REALTORS® must be careful not to practice Blind Advertising. The brokerage name must always appear in all advertising.

SP 12.6 – When selling their own property, a REALTOR® must disclose their license status.

SP 12.7 – Only the brokers directly involved in a transaction may advertise that they sold or have a contract on the property with permission from the owner.

SP 12.8 – A REALTORS® website should present current, accurate information, and they should keep the information current.

SP 12.9 – A REALTORS® website shall disclose the brokerage's name and licensure state in a readily apparent manner.

SP 12.10 – REALTORS® must advertise truthfully and give correct information and not deceptive the public in their URLs, websites, or the images they use.

SP 12.11 – REALTORS® who intend to sell consumer information should disclose this wherever they gather the data.

SP 12.12 – REALTORS® shall not use URL or domain names that may mislead the public.

SP 12.13 - REALTORS® are only allowed to use designations, certifications, and other credentials they have earned and have maintained membership.

Article 12 illustration.

A REALTOR® developed a website in which he promoted himself as the top producing agent in his area. He also stated that he had the following designations, Certified International Property Specialist (CIPS) and Graduate Realtor Institute (GRI). He had earned these designations; however, he did not keep up the designations' annual renewal. He also did not put the name of the brokerage on his website. The REALTOR® has violated Article 12 and Standards of Practice 12.5, 12.9, and 12.13.

ARTICLE 13

"REALTORS® shall not engage in activities that constitute the unauthorized practice of law and shall recommend that legal counsel be obtained when the interest of any party to the transaction requires it."

Central theme. REALTORS® must not represent themselves as attorneys nor give legal advice.

Article 13 illustration. While filling out an offer to buy a piece of real property, REALTOR® John was asked by his customer how they should take title to the property. John asked the question without telling his customer that they should seek legal advice. John was practicing law by answering the question and thus in violation of Article 13.

ARTICLE 14

"If charged with unethical practice or asked to present evidence or to cooperate in any other way, in any professional standards proceeding or investigation, REALTORS® shall place all pertinent facts before the proper tribunals of the Member Board or affiliated institute, society, or council in which membership is held and shall take no action to disrupt or obstruct such processes."

Central theme. REALTORS® must assist the Professional Standards Committee in any investigation or hearing. They must always present the truth and not interfere with the process.

Article 14 Standards of Practice. Article 14 has four Standards of Practice:

SP 14.1 – Only one board may hear any case of alleged violations of the Code of Ethics.
SP 14.2 – A REALTOR® should not disclose any information they learned at an ethics hearing.
SP 14.3 – A REALTOR® should not threaten or intimidate a witness or respondent in an ethics case.
SP 14.4 – A REALTOR® should not mislead the investigation into an Ethics case, nor can they file multiple charges based on the same transaction.

Article 14 illustration: Broker Alicia was named in a Code of Ethics violation. She denies the allegations. Trying to get the case canceled, Alicia threatens the person who filed the charges against her and refuses to turn over information to the Professional Standards Committee. Alicia violates Article 14 Standards of Practice 14.3 and 14.4.

ARTICLE 15

" REALTORS® shall not knowingly or recklessly make false or misleading statements about other real estate professionals, their businesses, or their business practices."

Central theme. Article 15 of the Code of Ethics prohibits REALTORS® from making a false or misleading statement about other real estate professionals, their own business, or their business practices.

Article 15 Standards of Practices: Article 15 three Standards of Practices as follows:

SP 15.1 – REALTORS® may not file false or misleading statements about their business.
SP 15.2 – REALTORS® may not make a false or misleading statement about other REALTOR®. This Standard covers the false statements no matter what medium they are presented, i.e., digital, written, in person, etc.
SP 15.3 – REALTORS® publish clarification if they discover a previous statement is false or misleading.

Article 15 Illustration: A REALTOR® told everyone at her office that a competitive brokerage broker was not doing well financially. She even posted these statements on her Facebook page. She was trying to get agents from the other brokerage to join her company. She then boasted about how great her business was doing when in fact, it was struggling. This violation is of Article 15, Standard of Practices 15.1 and 15.2.

ARTICLE 16

" REALTORS® shall not engage in any practice or take any action inconsistent with exclusive representation or exclusive brokerage relationship agreements that other REALTORS® have with clients."

Central theme. REALTORS® must not try to steal away another broker's client. If they know someone is already working with a REALTOR® they must not try and get that client to come to them.

Article 16 Standards of Practice. Article 16 has 20 Standards of Practice as follows:

SP 16.1 – This Standard of Practice serves to set boundaries a REALTOR® should not cross with respect to other practitioners. It is not trying to eliminate aggressive or innovative business practices.

SP 16.2 – A REALTOR® may make general statements about their business and participate in marketing campaigns without infringing on other licensees' client relationships. Standard of Practice 16.2, however, outlines two unethical types of solicitation:
1.) Telephone or personal solicitation of sellers identified by yard signs or through MLS information; and,
2.) Mail or other written solicitation sent to customers or clients of other REALTORS® that are not part of a mass marketing campaign.

SP 16.3 – A REALTOR® may contact a client or customer of another REALTOR® to offer different services than those the client is already under contract. REALTORS® cannot use MLS information to target potential customers.

SP 16.4 & 16.5 – A REALTOR® should not try to steal listings or represented buyers from another agent. The only time a REALTOR® may contact another REALTORS® client is to get specific information not available by the other agent or not listed in the MLS.

SP16.6 – If someone under contract with another REALTOR® contacts a REALTOR® the REALTOR® may discuss how they would work with the customer once their contract is up with the other real estate agent.

SP16.7 – The fact that a customer has worked with a specific REALTOR® in the past does not prohibit another REALTOR® from trying to get hired once any existing contract has expired. People do not have to return to the same REALTOR® for every transaction they complete.

SP 16.8 – The fact that an exclusive agreement existed in the past does not prohibit another REALTOR® from entering into a similar agreement once the first contact expires.

SP 16.9 – Before entering into an agreement with a client, a REALTOR® must ensure that the client is not already in another contract with a different REALTOR®.

SP 16.10 – A buyer's agent should disclose that the agreement exists between them when they begin to negotiate a contract.

SP 16.11 – For unlisted property, REALTORS® must disclose any relationship between themselves and other customers. They should also request and negotiate any desired compensation at the first meeting.

SP 16.12 – All contractual relationships should be disclosed before entering into a Purchase agreement.

SP 16.13 – REALTORS® should communicate to the co-broking REALTOR® and not the customer or client.

SP 16.14 – A REALTOR® may enter into any representation but may not require them to pay compensation if the other party is contracted to pay compensation.

SP 16.15 – All monies and compensation must be paid broker to broker.

SP 16.16 –SP deleted and incorporated into SP 3-2.

SP16.17 – REALTORS® shall not attempt to extend a listing broker's offer of cooperation without the listing broker's consent.

SP 16.18 – A REALTOR® shall not use information obtained from another agent or the MLS to negotiate the client away from the firm.

SP 16.19 – REALTORS® must have the owner's permission before placing signs on the property.

SP 16.20 – When a REALTOR® leaves a brokerage, their listing stays with the brokerage. Agents are not allowed to entice customers to follow them to another agency.

Article 16 Illustration: A REALTOR® is holding an open house. A couple comes in and begins looking around. They start asking the REALTOR® questions and state they want to put an offer in on the house. The agent writes up an offer and presents it to the seller, who accepts it. Only after the offer is accepted does it come out that the buyers have a Buyer's Broker Agreement with another REALTOR®.

The REALTOR® holding the open house should have asked if they were under contract with another REALTOR®. This is a violation of Article 16 under the Code of Ethics.

ARTICLE 17

"In the event of contractual disputes or specific non-contractual disputes as defined in Standard of Practice 17-4 between REALTORS® (principals) associated with different firms, arising out of their relationship as REALTORS®, the REALTORS® shall mediate the dispute if the Board requires its members to mediate. If the dispute is not resolved through mediation, or if mediation is not required, REALTORS® shall submit the dispute to arbitration in accordance with the policies of the Board rather than litigate the matter.

In the event clients of REALTORS® wish to mediate or arbitrate contractual disputes arising out of real estate transactions, REALTORS® shall mediate or arbitrate those disputes in accordance with the policies of the Board, provided the clients agree to be bound by any resulting agreement or award.

The obligation to participate in mediation and arbitration contemplated by this Article includes the obligation of REALTORS® (principals) to cause their firms to mediate and arbitrate and be bound by any resulting agreement or award."

Central theme. REALTORS® should first commit to mediation if there are unsettled disputes. If mediation does not settle the conflicts, then the agents will move to binding arbitration.

Article 17 Standards of Practice: Article 17 has five Standards of Practice:

SP 17.1 – REALTORS® who file litigation and refuse to withdraw in an arbitrable issue will constitute a refusal to arbitrate.

SP 17.2 – Parties to a dispute are not required to commit to mediation, but they are not relieved of the duty to arbitrate by not entering mediation.

SP 17.3 – REALTORS® when acting solely as principals, are not obligated to arbitrate disputes with other REALTORS®.

SP 17.4 – This Standard of Practice lays out specific times when non-contractual disputes are subject to arbitration. Procuring cause disputes fall under this category.

SP 17.5 – The requirement to arbitrate includes disputes between REALTORS® from different states. It also states which association will have jurisdiction over the disputes.

Article 17 illustration. Whenever there is a dispute among REALTORS® or the parties to a real estate transaction, the parties, per our contract, should first go to mediation and then to binding arbitration. REALTORS® should work to keep disputes out of the legal system whenever they are able.

NAR DISPUTE RESOLUTION

Processing complaints

Anyone can file a complaint. It can be REALTOR® vs. REALTOR® or client/customer against REALTOR®. Once filed with a local association of REALTORS®, the complaint is then forwarded to the Grievance Committee to determine if there is a violation of the code of ethics and an arbitrational issue. If the Grievance Committee believes there is sufficient evidence of an Ethics violation, a hearing will be scheduled with the Professional Standards Committee to hear the case and recommend the Board of Directors on outcome and punishment.

If there is a monetary issue, then the matter will be sent to the local Board's Ombudsman program to help the parties decide. If the Ombudsman does not settle the dispute, the parties will be offered the opportunity to enter mediation and then go on to arbitration to resolve the dispute.

Penalties

Possible penalties for violation of the Code of Ethics include:

- Letter of warning;
- Letter of reprimand;
- Education courses;
- Fines not to exceed $15,000;
- Probation for not less than 30 days or more than one year;
- Membership suspension for not less than 30 days or more than one year;
- Expulsion from membership for one to three years; and/or,
- Suspension or termination of MLS rights and privileges.

PATHWAYS TO PROFESSIONALISM

While the Code of Ethics establishes enforceable standards that REALTORS® must follow, it does not set out standards of common courtesy or etiquette that a REALTORS® should use in their dealings with other REALTORS® or the public. This is accomplished with NAR's set of professional courtesy standards called the Pathways to Professionalism.

There are three sections to the Pathways to Professionalism:

1. Respect for the Public
2. Respect for Property
3. Respect for Peers

These Professional courtesies are intended to be used by REALTORS® voluntarily.
They cannot form the basis for a professional standards complaint.

Pathways to Professionalism

Respect for the Public

1. Follow the "Golden Rule": Do unto other as you would have them do unto you.
2. Respond promptly to inquiries and requests for information.
3. Schedule appointments and showings as far in advance as possible.
4. Communicate promptly if you are delayed or must cancel an appointment or showing. If a prospective buyer decides not to view an occupied home, promptly communicate the situation to the listing broker or the occupant.
5. When entering a property ensure that unexpected situations, such as pets, are handled appropriately.
6. Never criticize property in the presence of the occupant.
7. When showing an occupied home, always ring the doorbell or knock—and announce yourself loudly before entering. Knock and announce yourself loudly before entering any closed room.
8. Present a professional appearance.
9. If occupants are home during showings, ask their permission before using the bathroom.
10. Encourage the clients of other brokers to direct questions to their agent or representative.
11. Communicate clearly; ensure specialized language and real estate terminology is understood.
12. Be aware of and respect cultural differences. Show courtesy and respect to everyone.
13. Be aware of—and meet—all deadlines.
14. Promise only what you can deliver—and keep your promises.
15. Do not tell people what you think—tell them what you know.

Respect for Property

1. When showing a property, be responsible for your clients/customers and keep the group together.
2. Make reasonable and timely accommodations to provide access to listed properties.
3. Make reasonable and timely requests to access listed properties.
4. Leave the property as you found it (lights, heating, cooling, drapes, etc.) If you think something is amiss (e.g. vandalism), contact the listing broker immediately.
5. Be considerate of the seller's property. Do not allow anyone to eat, drink, smoke, dispose of trash, use bathing or sleeping facilities, or bring pets. When instructed or appropriate, remove footwear when entering property.
6. Obtain permission from appropriate parties (e.g., listing broker) before photographing, videographing, or streaming the interiors or exteriors of properties, or allowing others to do so.

Respect for Peers

1. Respond to other real estate professionals' communications promptly and courteously.
2. Contact the listing broker if there appears to be a discrepancy in the listing information.
3. Inform anyone accessing the property about important information, (e.g., pets, security systems, video and audio recording equipment).
4. Inform if sellers or listing agent will be present during the showing.
5. Show courtesy, trust, and respect to other real estate professionals.
6. Avoid the inappropriate use of endearments or other denigrating language.
7. Do not prospect at other REALTORS®' open houses or similar events.
8. Secure property and lockbox and/or return keys promptly.
9. Real estate is a reputation business. What you do today may affect your reputation—and business—for years to come.

The above is from the NAR Code of Ethics and Arbitration Manual, Pathways to Professionalism, which can be accessed at: https://www.nar.realtor/code-of-ethics-and-arbitration-manual/pathways-to-professionalism

COMMITMENT TO EXCELLENCE (C2EX)

Commitment to Excellence (C2EX) from the National Association of REALTORS® empowers REALTORS® to evaluate, enhance and showcase their highest professional levels. It's not a course, class, or designation—it's an Endorsement that REALTORS® can promote when serving clients and other REALTORS®.

The NAR Board of Directors has requested that all Board of Directors, committee members, and leadership complete the C2EX program. To date, over 50,000 REALTORS® have completed this program.

Interactive Exercises

SITUATIONAL CASE STUDY:

6.1) Agent John showed Broker Eric's listing to buyer clients, Adam and Eve. The list price in the MLS was $210,000. John contacted Eric to inquire about any offers on the property. Eric told John he had no offers. John then prepared an offer to submit to Eric.

Eric did have an offer for $185,000 cash from Jill and Jack. The seller accepted the offer, not knowing that John's clients submitted a bid for $205,000 with FHA financing and a 5% down payment.

Once John had submitted the offer, he asked Eric for written confirmation that the offer was presented to the seller. Eric never presented the offer, nor were Adam and Eve advised that there was another offer.

When asked, Eric stated that the seller had rejected the offer for a cash deal. Eric decided not to present the offer to the seller because it involved financing and would take longer to close. Eric wanted it to close before the end of the month to win an office selling contest.

DISCUSSION QUESTIONS:

1. How would you have handled the offers if you were Eric?

2. What Articles of the Code of Ethics do you feel were violated?

3. What specific Standards of Practice do you feel were violated?

Interactive Exercises

6.2) A real estate agent is involved in local politics. During the County Commission meeting, the agent made a racist comment to a Black member of the Commission. After the meeting, she went to her social media accounts and made additional derogatory comments against the Commissioner. She also suggested that the county would be better off if the County Commissioner died. Based on this information, discuss this scenario and answer the questions below.

Discussion Questions:

1. Which Article of the Code of Ethics do you feel was violated in this example?

2. What specific Standard of Practice do you feel was violated?

3. How could the situation be handled without violating the Code of Ethics?

Interactive Exercises

SITUATIONAL CASE STUDY:

6.3) Dan, who held an exclusive listing of Joey's property, invited Janet to cooperate with him. Shortly thereafter, Janet received an offer to purchase the property and took it to Dan. Janet asked to be present at the presentation of the offer, and Dan allowed this. Together, they started negotiations with the seller. The next day, Janet called Joey, recommending that Joey accept the offer, which was less than the list price, and Joey agreed. The contract was signed and closed.

Discussion Questions:

1. What Article has is Janet violated?

2. What were Standards of Practice violated?

3. How could the situation be handled without violating the Code of Ethics?

Ethics and Standards of Conduct

REALTORS® CODE OF ETHICS

- Rules members practice in dealings with others

DEFINIITIONS

- Business ethics-business make decisions; treat Clients, Customers, Vendors, Employees
- Client- individual with fiduciary relationship
- Code of Ethics-lay out the values of an organization
- Customer-individual with no fiduciary relationship; limited disclosure
- Ethics- moral principles, rules to determine how to deal with others
- Morals- person's individuals belief of right/wrong; religion; culture
- Preamble- opening statement of document reflecting values/vision of organization
- Situational Ethics-person changing ethical views to fit situation
- Demographic information-Information gathered on customers/clients; age, sex, race, color, national origin. Assist operating brokerage and advertising avenues
- Professional services- advertising, buying, auctioning, renting, selling, appraising, leasing, exchanging.
- NAR's protected classes-race, color, religion, sex, handicap, familial status, national origin, sexual orientation, gender identity
- Public trust-misappropriation of client or customer funds or property; discrimination against the protected classes under the Code of Ethics, or fraud
- Duties to the public-how REALTORS® behave when interacting with public
- Arbitration-voluntary process where independent third party listens to individuals in dispute
- Mediation-voluntary process where third person helps parties agree to resolve dispute
- Ombudsman-voluntary process where individual appointed by local Board of REALTORS®˙ receives assistance to resolve disputes through constructive communication
- Procuring cause-agent who starts uninterrupted chain of events leading to sale/rental of listing
- Duties to REALTORS® ˙how REALTORS® should behave when interacting with other REALTORS®.

NAR'S CODE OF ETHICS

- For REALTORS® to follow in dealings with clients, public, and other REALTORS®

PREAMBLE

- Everything we do, are, or aspire to become, begins with land beneath our feet

ARTICLES 1-17

- Article 1- honesty as critical virtue of any licensee
- Article 2-transparency in all transactions
- Article 3-Cooperation among brokers unless it's not in their client's best interest; emphasizes compensation is negotiable and not set by law
- Article 4- REALTORS® disclose real estate license when buying/selling property for themselves

- Article 5- disclose conflict of interest before providing any professional services
- Article 6- REALTOR® may not accept any compensation in form of commission, rebate, kickback, etc., without client's written consent
- Article 7- REALTOR® cannot accept compensation from more than one person without disclosing to all parties
- Article 8-escrow funds; handling other people's money
- Article 9-brokers ensure documents are written in clear, concise language; all contracts and relationships must be explained fully, whether in person, electronically, or through any other means
- Article 10- prohibits REALTORS® from discrimination against protected classes identified in Code of Ethics
- Article 11-REALTORS® should only work within real estate areas in which they have sufficient knowledge to protect customer/client
- Article 12-honesty in advertising/marketing
- Article 13-REALTORS® must not represent themselves as attorneys nor give legal advice
- Article 14- REALTORS® must assist Professional Standards Committee in investigations
- Article 15-prohibits REALTORS® from false statements about real estate professionals, their own business, business practices
- Article 16- REALTORS® must not steal another broker's client
- Article 17- REALTORS® should commit to mediation if unsettled disputes

NAR DISPUTE RESOLUTION

- Complaint with local association of REALTORS® >Grievance Committee reviews for violation> hearing scheduled with Professional Standards Committee>Ombudsman settles dispute or parties can enter mediation then arbitration

PATHWAYS TO PROFESSIONALISM

- NAR's set of professional courtesy standards
- Respect for the Public; respect for Property; respect for Peers

COMMITMENT TO EXCELLENCE (C2EX)

- Empowers REALTORS® to evaluate, enhance, showcase highest professional levels

Check Your Understanding Quiz:

Unit Six: Ethics and Standards of Conduct

Carefully read each question then provide your best answer based on what you learned in this unit. Then check your answers against the Answer Key which immediately follows the quiz questions.

1. The four parts of the Code of Ethics include the Preamble, duties to Clients and Customers, duties to the Public, and _____.

    a. duties to REALTORS®.
    b. duties to Mortgage Lenders.
    c. duties to Title Agents.
    d. the Conclusion.

2. Article 2 of the Code of Ethics discusses latent defects in a client's property. Which of the following best reflects Article 2's provisions?

    a. REALTORS® are obligated to conduct detailed inspections of both latent and manifest defects.
    b. REALTORS® are not obligated to discover latent defects.
    c. REALTORS® must not disclose defects that violate client confidentiality.
    d. REALTORS® must advise clients on legal matters if they are familiar with such matters.

3. The three sections of Pathways to Professionalism are respect for the Public, respect for Peers, and respect for _____.

    a. REALTORS®
    b. Brokers
    c. Property
    d. Mayors

4. Which of the following is an endorsement that REALTORS® can promote to showcase the highest professional level?

    a. NAR Ethics Standard
    b. Commitment to Excellence
    c. Code of Ethics Achievement
    d. Platinum Service Commitment

5. Article 14 of the Code of Ethics requires REALTORS® to assist the Professional Standards Committee in any investigation or hearing. Which of the following is additionally true as provided by Article 14?

   a. REALTORS® must not practice law without a license
   b. REALTORS® must not misrepresent the condition of a listed property.
   c. REALTORS® may appeal an alleged violation to another board.
   d. REALTORS® must not disclose information ascertained from a hearing.

6. Why was NAR formed in 1908?

   a. To protect the public and promote homeownership
   b. To earn money off of REALTORS®
   c. To promote the notion of "Caveat emptor"
   d. To encourage agents to be professional

7. The agent who starts the uninterrupted chain of events leading to the sale of a listing has _____.

   a. public trust.
   b. procuring cause.
   c. arbitration.
   d. mediation.

8. According to Article 17 of the Code of Ethics, REALTORS® should first commit to _____ if there are unsettled disputes.

   a. arbitration
   b. jury trial
   c. mediation
   d. a NAR panel discussion

9. A REALTOR® posted a blog post about a competing broker who was not doing well financially. What does this violate?

   a. The Preamble of the Code of Ethics
   b. Article 15 of the Code of Ethics
   c. The NAR handbook
   d. The Virginia Real Estate Licensee Act

10. Which portion of the Code of Ethics serves as a vision statement on how licensees should conduct themselves?

    a. Article 1
    b. The Conclusion
    c. Article 18
    d. The Preamble

11. Without the client's knowledge, Charles refers his client to a roofer in order to receive a $150 gift card. Which specific ethical practice of the Code of Ethics does Charles violate?

    a. The prohibition against paid referrals
    b. The prohibition against receiving gift cards, specifically
    c. The prohibition against undisclosed compensation
    d. No violation has been committed.

12. Who can file a complaint to NAR?

    a. Anyone
    b. Only clients
    c. Only customers
    d. Only REALTORs®

13. What is the maximum fine for a Code of Ethics violation?

    a. $1,000
    b. $15,000
    c. $25,000
    d. $50,000

14. Which of the following is a possible penalty for a Code of Ethics violation?

    a. Membership suspension for five days
    b. A $20,000 fine
    c. Membership probation for seven years
    d. Expulsion from membership for one to three years

15. What is the name of a voluntary process where an individual appointed by a local Board of REALTORS® provides assistance to resolve disputes through constructive communication?

    a. Arbitration
    b. Mediation
    c. Ombudsman
    d. Situational ethics

UNIT 7:

RISK MANAGEMENT

Unit Seven Learning Objectives: When the student has completed this unit he or she will be able to:

- Identify numerous ways to capitalize on risk reduction via the adoption of key risk management strategies
- Define and summarize the principal forms of antitrust legislation, including The Sherman Antitrust Act and Clayton Antitrust Act.
- Identify the various insurance options for property owners, managers, and licensees.
- Discuss the potential risks of misrepresenting clients.

RISK MANAGEMENT STRATEGIES

Four well- established strategies for managing risk are:

- Avoidance (elimination)
- Reduction (mitigation, sharing)
- Transference (outsourcing, insuring)
- Retention (acceptance and budgeting)

Not all of these strategies are always possible or available, but a real estate firm or licensee who fails to make a conscious effort to employ one or more of them increases the likelihood of loss from the many potential risks that are always present in the real estate business.

Avoidance

Avoidance includes refraining from an activity that carries risk. One can avoid the risks of being in an automobile accident by not riding in automobiles. Avoiding risks also means missing the opportunity to benefit from the avoided activity. By avoiding automobile travel, one is confined to modes of transportation, such as buses and walking, that do not offer the same high degree of personal freedom and efficiency. Complete avoidance of risk in real estate practice is almost impossible. A broker, for instance, may believe that hiring only experienced affiliates eliminates the risk that affiliates will commit license law violations. However, even experienced practitioners may not know the law, and, sometimes, people break the law deliberately. The risk may be reduced, but it remains.

Reduction

Reduction involves taking steps to reduce the probability or the severity of a potential loss. However, this strategy may result in reducing risk in one area only to increase it in another. A familiar example is a sprinkler system that dispenses water to reduce the risk of fire but at the same time increases the risk of water damage.

In real estate practice, one risk reduction tactic is to share responsibility for making a decision. The agent provides the consumer with expertise, and perhaps some advice, but lets the consumer decide how much to offer. In this way, the agent gets some relief from the risks inherent in the buyer's decision to purchase.

Transference

Transference means passing the risk to another party, by contract or other means. An insurance policy is the common example, but sometimes the wording of a sales or personal services contract can transfer risk without resorting to insurance.

In the real estate business, transference is typically and most successfully accomplished by means of an errors and omissions (E&O) insurance policy, either on the individuals in a firm or on the firm itself. State law may require such insurance.

Retention

Retention of risk means entering into an activity in spite of known risks and taking full responsibility for the consequences. This is, in effect, self-insurance, the only strategy left when risk cannot be reduced or transferred and one has decided not to avoid it because of the desirability of the potential benefits.

RISK MANAGEMENT PROCEDURES

Experience shows that the most practical strategies for risk management in real estate practice are reduction and transference, with procedures focusing on:

- Education
- Disclosure
- Documentation
- Insurance

Education

Education is the first line of defense against risk. When agents are familiar with the forms provided by the office, how and when to complete them and where to send them, the likelihood of errors is reduced. Likewise, agents need to be able to identify and understand common contract elements, complete contract forms developed by attorneys, and evaluate offers received from co-op agents on their listings without committing a license violation or breach of law.

In most states, brokers have a legal obligation to provide training to affiliated licensees. Licensees also have the obligation to seek out appropriate education and training outside the brokerage to ensure that they know how to comply with the law. In addition, licensees must satisfy legal requirements for continuing education, while those who care about personal excellence will seek further education and training to enhance their professional skills.

Disclosure

By ensuring that all parties have the information they are entitled to, proper disclosure reduces the risk that clients and customers will accuse a licensee of misleading or inducing them to make a decision with incomplete information. Further, laws in every state require disclosures of one kind or another.

Disclosure may be made in writing or verbally and may or may not require written acknowledgment from the receiving party.

Required disclosures usually include:

- agency relationships
- property condition
- duties and obligations
- personal interest in the transaction
- personal interest in referrals

Documentation and record keeping

Documentation provides evidence of compliance with laws and regulations. It proves what clients and customers and licensees said and did in a transaction. Some documentation is required by law.

The components of a thoroughly documented paper trail include:

- Policy and procedure manuals
- Standard forms
- Communication records
- Transaction records
- Contracts
- Accounting
- Other important documents

Policy and procedures manual. A written and uniformly enforced company policy lets everyone in the firm know what to expect before problems arise. The policy manual should cover the company's rules in such areas as floor duty privileges, assignment of relocation properties to agents, referrals between agents within the company, and requirements for continuing education, sales meeting participation, and property tours.

The company's procedures manual should spell out how to handle every aspect of the company's business that agents and brokers need to know—from handling consumers' funds and documents, conducting consumer transactions, dealing with MLS-related matters, and placing signage, to all procedures prescribed by state or federal law, especially license, banking and fair housing laws. Adherence to a procedures manual reduces the risk that an individual will inadvertently commit an unlawful act. Whenever changes are made to the policy or procedures manual, each agent should sign the revised manual as evidence that the agent has examined it.

Standard forms. Standard forms save time and protect against the unauthorized practice of law. Since they are most often prepared by lawyers familiar with the market area, they can address contingencies that are common in the area in a manner that reflects the real estate laws of the state. On the other hand, a licensee often needs to adapt a standardized form for a client by assisting with filling in blanks, modifying terms, and attaching addenda. The licensee must always remain aware of the limitations the state has placed on such activities.

Here are a few of the standard forms a brokerage should provide for its agents and affiliates:

- buyer and seller representation agreements, exclusive and nonexclusive
- agreement to show property
- purchase and sale agreement
- agency disclosure form
- property condition disclosure, disclaimer, and exemption form
- lease agreement
- personal interest disclosure form
- referral for service disclosure form
- lead-based paint disclosure form
- special disclosure forms (mold, radon, subsurface sewage system, impact fees/adequate facilities taxes, etc.)
- referral agreement
- independent contractor agreement
- closing checklist

Communication records. Some communications with transaction parties are good and necessary for business. Others are required by law, such as certain disclosures. A transaction checklist is a good tool for managing risk associated with the failure to make required communications to all principals and for keeping track of required communications from co-op agents.

Retaining evidence that information has been communicated is a necessary procedure. Electronic communications should be archived on suitable electronic media. Copies of mailed or faxed communications should be maintained in the transaction folder.

It is always difficult to document telephone or face-to-face conversations, especially with the constant use of cell phones from a variety of locations. It is a good practice to make brief notes at the time and then write them up later for mailing or faxing to the other party. Be sure, however, that you can produce these notes on demand, lest you be accused later of withholding documentation that has been promised.

Maintaining a good record of communications is useful for resolving disagreements where parties dispute what has been said because it allows the agent to produce a dated document that resolves the issue definitively.

Transaction records. State laws require licensees to document transactions. Firms are required to keep written records of all real estate transactions for a number of years (usually three to five) after closing or termination. Required records typically include:

- listing agreements
- offers
- contracts
- closing statements

- agency agreements
- disclosure documents
- correspondence and other communication records
- notes and any other relevant information

Accounting. In addition to other accounting records, there is the requirement to maintain written accounting of escrow funds. For each transaction, property, and principal, escrow records will include:

- depositor
- date of deposit
- date of withdrawal
- payee
- other information deemed pertinent by the real estate commission

Other documents. Additional documents may be required by law or regulation, or should be kept simply as protection in case of disputes and lawsuits. These would include copies of advertising materials, materials used in training agents, records of compliance with continuing education requirements, safety manuals, and anything else that shows how the firm conducts its business and safeguards its staff as well as the rights of consumers.

INSURANCE

Many forms of insurance are available for property owners and managers. Some of these types are also used to manage certain risks of brokers and licensees.

General Liability. General liability insurance provides coverage for risks incurred by a property owner when the public or a licensee enters the owned property (**public liability**). The insurer pays the covered claim and legal fees, costs, and expenses, including medical expenses, resulting from owner negligence or other causes. This type of insurance does not cover **professional liability,** for which an Errors & Omissions policy is necessary.

Errors and Omissions. Professional liability is of two general types:

1. Unprofessional conduct – a claim that one has failed to carry out fiduciary duties and provide an acceptable standard of care
2. Breach of contract – a claim that one has failed to perform services under the terms of a contract in a timely manner

The primary method for transferring the professional liability risks of brokers, managers, and licensees is Errors & Omissions (E&O) insurance. A standard E&O policy provides coverage for "damages resulting from any negligent act, error or omission arising out of Professional Services." A standard policy does NOT cover:

- violations of law
- fraudulent, dishonest, criminal or malicious acts
- mishandling of escrow moneys, earnest money deposits, or security deposits
- antitrust violations
- sexual harassment

- Fair Housing violations
- agent-owned properties
- environmental violations
- failure to detect or disclose environmental conditions, including mold
- acts committed prior to licensure or after termination of active status
- activities as an appraiser if licensing other than a real estate license is required

E&O insurance, in short, covers "mistakes" but not crimes.

Fire and hazard. The risks of property damage caused by fire, wind, hail, smoke, civil disturbance, and other such causes are covered by fire and hazard insurance.

Flood. The risks of property damage caused by floods, heavy rains, snow, drainage failures, and failed public infrastructures such as dams and levies are covered by a specialized flood policy. Regular hazard policies do not include flood coverage.

Other insurance. Other common types of insurance coverage for income and commercial properties include:

- **casualty**—coverage for specific risks, such as theft, vandalism, burglary, illness and accident, machinery damage
- **workers' compensation**—hospital and medical coverage for employees injured in the course of employment, mandated by state laws
- **contents and personal property**—coverage for building contents and personal property when they are not actually on the building premises
- **consequential loss, use, and occupancy**—coverage for the business losses resulting from a disaster, such as loss of rent and other revenue, when the property cannot be used for business
- **surety bond**—coverage against losses resulting from criminal or negligent acts of an employee

PRIMARY AREAS OF RISK

Risks for licensees are present every day in business transactions. Many of these risks carry legal implications as well as possible financial and professional consequences.

Agency
The risks of agency will occur in one of two areas:

- the requirement to inform and disclose
- the requirement to carry out an agency duty

Most states require agency relationships to be in writing and to be disclosed to all parties to a transaction. State law may spell out agency duties, or the duties may be a part of general agency law. In states that do not use agency, there is still the obligation to explain and disclose the nature of the relationship.

Disclosure requirements. A licensee may be acting in a transaction as facilitator, agent, subagent, designated agent, single agent, dual agent, non-agent or in some capacity. Regardless of status, the licensee must follow state disclosure requirements. These are, typically, to:

- disclose status *verbally* to other licensees on initial contact
- disclose status *verbally* to buyer and seller before providing real estate services
- confirm the disclosure *in writing* before signing a listing agreement or presenting a purchase offer (to an unrepresented seller) or before preparing a purchase offer (to an unrepresented buyer)
- get a *signed receipt* indicating the written disclosure has been made

Carrying out the duties of agency also require disclosures of :

- personal interest the agent has in a transaction (such as owner or buyer)
- personal benefit the agent will derive from a service referral
- required property and market information
- information about customers a client is entitled to have

Duties. A licensee who acts for a principal in a real estate transaction is required by law to assume certain responsibilities toward the parties to the transaction. Whether a state applies the fiduciary duties of agency law or specifies its own duties toward clients and consumers, the basic duties remain:

To all parties

- honesty
- fairness
- reasonable care and skill
- disclosures

To clients

- skill
- care
- diligence
- loyalty
- obedience
- confidentiality
- accounting
- full disclosure

The duty to exercise **skill, care and diligence** means that licensees may not be casual or negligent in their actions. Licensee negligence is actionable when principals are harmed by the licensee's failure.

The duty of **loyalty** requires the agent to *put the client's interests above those of everyone else*, including his or her own.

The duty of **obedience** requires the agent to act on the principal's wishes regarding the transaction as long as they do not result in any illegal action. The duty of obedience never overrides the legal obligation of agents to deal fairly and honestly with all parties.

The duty of **confidentiality** requires the agent to hold in confidence any information that would harm the client's interests or bargaining position or anything else the client wishes to keep secret, unless the law requires disclosure. The duty of confidentiality survives the termination of the listing contract.

The duty of **accounting** applies to all funds involved in a real estate transaction. Accounts must be maintained as required by law, and escrow funds are to be handled strictly in accordance with the law.

The duty of **disclosure** applies to both parties to a transaction, although usually with some differences. Proper disclosure to customers primarily concerns agency, property condition, and environmental hazards. To the client, it generally concerns all known facts regarding the property and the transaction, including information about the other transaction party. State laws prescribe what may, must, and must not be disclosed. Licensees must be vigilant to avoid oversights and conflicts of interest that can lead to a disclosure to the wrong party or disclosure of information that is confidential.

Conflicts of interest. Conflicts of interest arise when an agent forgets to put the best interests of a client ahead of those of everyone else. This can happen in situations involving undisclosed dual agencies, broker-owned listings, licensees buying for their own account, vendor referrals, and property management subcontracting of services, among many others. Even ordinary, everyday transactions carry a built-in risk of conflict of interest. Consider the fact that a licensee usually receives no compensation for a failed transaction. Therefore, it is in the licensee's interest to see the transaction completed, even if it may not be in the client's best interest. A negative result from a home inspection or other test has the potential to cause a buyer to back out of a contract. A licensee who has forgotten whose best interest should be primary might be tempted to recommend inspectors who will overlook problems in exchange for receiving

referrals. Licensees must always disclose any self-interest they have in a transaction, and always remember their duties to clients and consumers.

Confidentiality. Licensees have a responsibility to maintain the confidentiality of certain kinds of information they obtain concerning clients and customers. The duty to maintain confidentiality generally survives the termination of a listing agreement into perpetuity. If it seems that revealing confidential information might benefit the client, the licensee should obtain the client's written permission to proceed.

Confidential information generally includes information about a client's motivations in a transaction, financial and personal details, and information specifically designated as confidential by the client. Public information, such as that contained in public records, information that becomes known without the licensee's participation, or that the client reveals to another, is not considered confidential.

State laws often require businesses to provide security for the personal information they obtain about consumers. Security procedures should protect personal information from unauthorized access, destruction, use, modification, or disclosure. Confidential information, when it is not to be retained, must be disposed of in a secure manner.

Penalties. Possible penalties for breach of agency relationships include:

- rescission of transaction
- loss of compensation
- fees and costs

- punitive damages
- ethics discipline
- license discipline

Property disclosures

Property condition. Most states require the seller of a residential property to deliver to the buyer a written disclosure or disclaimer about the property's condition, including any material defects the owner knows about. The disclosure is usually required before any purchase contract is accepted. A second disclosure may be required at closing. The licensee should always obtain the parties' signatures acknowledging receipt of these disclosures.

Depending on the state, the licensee may have no further duty to disclose property condition after properly informing parties of their rights and obligations. However, the licensee may still be subject to legal action for

- deliberately distorting the facts (intentional misrepresentation)
- cheating any party (fraud)
- concealing or failing to disclose adverse facts which the licensee knew about or should have known about (intentional or unintentional misrepresentation)

Lead-based paint and other disclosures. Federal law requires sellers of houses built before 1978 to make a lead-based paint disclosure before accepting an offer to purchase. The licensee must tell the seller about this requirement, give the seller the proper disclosure form, and make sure that the buyer receives it.

Repetitive flood loss risk disclosure. Virginia law now requires sellers to disclose real knowledge of risk to a dwelling unit due to repetitive flooding. This is defined as 2 or more claims made with the National Flood Insurance Program within a 10-year period, starting in 1978. The claims must be greater than $1,000 to require disclosure.

The licensee must also make sure the seller discloses any other circumstances the situation and the law require, which may include:

- wood infestation inspection report
- soil test report
- subsurface sewage disposal system permit disclosure
- impact fees or adequate facilities taxes disclosure
- mold and radon reports or treatments

Mold. This is a fungus that grows under moist conditions and causes allergic reaction for some people. The presence of mold in the home must be disclosed as a latent defect. Flooding and water damage must also be disclosed as both of those can lead to mold growth. Inspections do not always find mold because it often grows inside walls and ductwork. Most molds require removal by a professional.

Chesapeake Bay Preservation Act. The Chesapeake Bay Preservation Act was originally adopted in 1989 and amended in 1991, 2001 and 2012. The concept of the Act is that land can be used and developed to minimize negative impacts on water quality, such as that of the Chesapeake Bay. The Act balances state and local economic interests and water quality improvement and is the only program in Virginia state government that comprehensively addresses the effects of land use planning and development on water quality.

The lands that make up Chesapeake Bay Preservation Areas are those that have the potential to impact water quality most directly. By carefully managing land uses within these areas, local governments help reduce the water quality impacts of nonpoint source pollution and improve the health of the Chesapeake Bay.

Under the Act, each Tidewater locality is required to adopt a program based on the Act. Recognizing local government's responsibility for land use decisions, the Act's regulations are designed to establish a framework for compliance without dictating exactly what local programs must look like.

Listing and selling process

Nature and accuracy of the listing agreement. In most states, a listing agreement is enforceable only if it is in writing. Most states forbid net listings, because they violate the requirement that a valid listing agreement must specify a selling price and the agent's compensation. The licensee, in accordance with the duty of due diligence, must verify the accuracy of the statements in the listing regarding the property, the owner, and the owner's representations. Especially important facts for a broker or agent to verify are:

- the property condition
- ownership status
- the client's authority to act

An agent who does not to act with a reasonable degree of due diligence in these matters may be exposed to liability if it turns out that the property is not as represented or the client cannot perform the contract as promised.

Comparative Market Analysis (CMA). In preparing a Comparative Market Analysis, licensees should guard against using the terms "appraisal" and "value," which are reserved for the use of certified appraisers. Misuse of these terms could lead to a charge of misrepresenting oneself as an appraiser. In discussing listed properties with clients or customers, real estate licensees should be careful to use guarded terms such as "recommended listing price," "recommended purchase price,' and "recommended listing price range."

Agents should make every effort to help the sellers find a reasonable listing price based on the current market. If the CMA leads the seller to list at a price that is too high, the seller may blame the agent when the transaction fails because of an appraisal that comes in below the selling price. To minimize this risk, it is best to be conservative in the CMA and retain documentation that the seller went above the recommended price in spite of the agent's advice.

Estimate of Closing Costs. In preparing an estimate of closing costs for a seller or buyer, there is the risk of forgetting something, leading to an unpleasant surprise when the consumer suddenly faces unexpected costs or conditions. Licensees should use their broker's form, if there is one, and make it clear to the consumer that it is only an estimate of likely costs, not a statement of actual costs. In some states, brokers and agents do not prepare closing cost estimates, leaving that task to the lender.

Advertising. State and federal laws regulate advertising, including the federal Fair Housing laws as they pertain to discriminatory advertising and providing of services. Advertising includes electronic communication, social media/networking, and internet marketing. Usage must be consistent with company image and legal requirements. The license laws of most states list illegal advertising actions subject to discipline such as:

- making any substantial and intentional misrepresentation
- making any promise that might cause a person to enter into a contract or agreement when the promise is one the licensee cannot or will not abide by
- making continued and blatant misrepresentations or false promises through affiliate brokers, other persons, or any advertising medium
- making misleading or untruthful statements in any advertising, including using the term "REALTOR®" when not authorized to do so and using any other trade name, insignia or membership in a real estate organization when the licensee is not a member.

Committing such acts may result in license suspension or revocation.

Authorizations and permissions. Licensees should stay within the bounds of the authority granted by the agency agreement or must not do anything requiring permission without first getting that permission in writing. For instance, permission should be obtained before doing any of the following unless the listing agreement specifically grants the authority:

- post a sign on the property
- remove other signs
- show the property
- hand out the property condition disclosure
- distribute marketing materials
- advertise in various media
- use a multiple listing service
- cooperate with other licensees
- divide the commission or negotiate a commission split
- share final sales data with the MLS
- place a lock box on the property
- appoint subagents
- appoint a designated agent
- change agency status

Scope of expertise. Real estate licensees are not, by nature, financial consultants, accountants, appraisers, soil scientists, well diggers, lawyers, decorators, contractors, builders, plumbers, carpenters, inspectors, prognosticators, and a number of other kinds of expert. However, in today's competitive environment, consumers often demand much more from a licensee than the traditional basic services. An agent who fails to live up to prevailing standards may be held liable for negligence, fraud, or violation of state real estate license laws and regulations. At the same time, agents must be particularly careful about the temptation to misrepresent themselves as experts and offer inappropriate expert advice. Disclaimer and referral are always the best risk control procedures to forestall an accusation of misrepresentation from a consumer who claims to have been harmed by reliance on the licensee's non-existent expertise. The exact nature of the services to be provided should be stated as clearly as possible in the listing agreement.

Contracting process

According to the Statute of Frauds, all contacts for real estate must be in writing to be enforceable. Contracts that contain incorrect information or are inadequately prepared can pose a serious liability for a licensee. To avoid such a situation, it is imperative for the contract to reflect the terms that the parties have agreed upon in the most accurate and honest manner. The agent must also be careful to comply with the letter of the real estate law. Violations can jeopardize the enforceability of a listing or sales contract, in addition to resulting in criminal prosecution.

Common risks and errors in the contracting process include:

- using an illegal form
  A licensee may be punished for using any real estate listing agreement form, sales contract form, or offer to purchase form that lacks a ***definite termination date***.
- failing to state inclusions and exclusions
  The parties should identify as included in or excluded from the transfer any ambiguous items. Unwritten agreements between the parties are a source of later dispute and trouble.
- failing to track the progress of contingency satisfaction
  The time period for completing contingencies such as inspections is specific and limited. Failure to meet or waive a condition may terminate the contract. A "time is of the essence" clause in the standard agreement makes the time period for contingencies critical.
- mistakes in entering data in a form
  All data should be checked and verified: dates, times, amounts, warranties, descriptions, names, representations, promises, procedures, authority, etc. One way to reduce risk in the contracting process is to use a checklist that covers all the contract items.

Unauthorized practice of law. The unintentional practice of law without a license is a great risk in the contracting process, as well as in the representation process. It is illegal for real estate professionals who are not attorneys to draw up contracts for transactions they are not involved in or to charge a separate fee for preparing a contract.

Such licensees may fill in blanks or make deletions on a preprinted contract form prepared by a lawyer. While a licensee may make deletions, additions to a form should be drafted by an attorney. The principals themselves can make changes as long as each change is signed or initialed by all signers. Preprinted riders can often be attached as addenda to a contract without an attorney.

It is also illegal for real estate licensees who are not lawyers to give legal advice or interpret contract language. Licensees, however, may express opinions. For instance, if a licensee believes that a party has grasped the meaning of a contract, it is permissible to say something like, "Though I am not an attorney, in my opinion your understanding of this contract is correct." It would be questionable to make a definitive statement like, "That's correct."

Fair Housing

The risk of violating fair housing laws can be minimized through ongoing education that addresses both the content and the intent of the laws. It is especially necessary for paperwork and documentation to be accurate and concise in a situation where a fair housing issue could arise.

Advertising. The Fair Housing Act forbids real estate advertising that mentions race, color, religion, national origin, sex, handicap, or familial status in any way that suggests preference or discrimination. State laws may add other protected categories, such as creed and age.

Risk can be reduced by the use of street names or other non-biased geographical references when stating where the property is located, and by describing the property rather than the type of persons who might live in or around it. Even if a home appears "ideal for a young family," it is best not to advertise it as such. Such advertising would exclude other groups such as singles, the elderly, and older families.

In advertising the sale or rental of housing covered by the Fair Housing Act, HUD recommends using the Fair Housing Logo or phrase "Equal Housing Opportunity."

Answering questions. When faced with questions that might lead to a *steering* charge or other violation of fair housing laws, it is best for the licensee to limit the response to features of the home and to the process of selling, buying, and listing properties, and refer the questioner to someone else to answer questions about such matters as the demographic make-up of the neighborhood. It is illegal for the licensee to voice an opinion based on race, religion, color, creed, national origin, sex, handicap, elderliness, or familial status. The agent should explain this fact to the buyer and be wary of any situation where the agent's behavior might be construed as discriminatory.

Listing agreements. Before entering into a listing agreement, a licensee should explain that it is necessary to comply with fair housing laws and obtain the potential client's acknowledgment and agreement. The agent should make it clear that the agent will
- reject the use of terms indicating race, religion, creed, color, national origin, sex, handicap, age or familial status to describe prospective buyers.
- terminate the listing if the seller uses race, religion, creed, color, national origin, sex, handicap, age, or familial status in the consideration of an offer.
- inform the broker if the seller makes any attempt to discriminate illegally.

Offers. A seller cannot refuse to sell a property to an individual based on the individual's belonging to a protected class, and if this is attempted, the real estate professional must not be involved. If the seller asks about the color, religion, creed, national origin, ethnicity, age, or familial status of a buyer, the agent must explain that it is illegal to give out such information. The best risk reduction procedure is to treat all buyers and sellers equally, showing no preference for one over another.

Antitrust

Antitrust laws forbid brokers to band together to set a price on their services in listing and selling property. Even being overheard discussing commission rates or being present at such a conversation can lead to charges of *price fixing*.

The law recognizes that some cooperative arrangements between firms – such as joint development projects – may help consumers by allowing these firms to compete more effectively against each other. Even so the government does not prosecute all agreements between companies, but only those that will raise prices for the public or deny the public new and better products.

Sherman Antitrust Act. The *Sherman Antitrust Act* makes illegal all contracts, agreements, and conspiracies among competitors that would unfairly restrict interstate trade by fixing prices, rigging bids, or other means. An unlawful monopoly is created when one company becomes the only supplier of a product or service by getting rid of competition via secret agreements with other companies.

Clayton Act. The *Clayton Act* prohibits mergers or acquisitions that are likely to lessen competition and increase prices to consumers. The Act also prohibits certain other business practices that under certain circumstances may harm competition. Private parties injured by an antitrust violation may sue in federal court for three times their actual damages, plus court costs and attorneys' fees.

Federal Trade Commission Act. The *Federal Trade Commission Act* forbids unfair competition in interstate commerce but establishes no criminal penalties.

Enforcement. Federal antitrust laws are enforced in three main ways:
- the Antitrust Division of the Department of Justice (DOJ) brings criminal and civil enforcement actions
- the FTC brings civil enforcement actions
- private parties bring lawsuits claiming damages

To collect evidence, Department of Justice lawyers often work with the Federal Bureau of Investigation (FBI) on court-authorized searches of a business, monitoring phone calls and employing informants equipped with secret listening devices.

State attorneys general may sue under the Clayton Act on behalf of injured consumers in their states, and groups of consumers often bring lawsuits on their own.

Anyone associated with an organization found guilty of an antitrust violation and determined to have had knowledge of that violation may also suffer legal consequences.

Penalties. Penalties for Violation of Antitrust Laws include:

- fines for individuals and corporations, as well as possible imprisonment.
- Under the Clayton Antitrust Act, parties can sue antitrust violators and recover three times the damages they incurred plus court costs and attorneys' fees.

Rules and regulations

State real estate laws and commissioners' rules and regulations attempt to cover every possible risky situation. Non-compliance poses a direct threat to the legal and financial status of licensee and license in the following general ways:

- license expiration

- license revocation or suspension
- licensee discipline
- suit for damages

License expiration. Licenses expire because licensees neglect to:

- maintain E & O insurance when required
- meet education requirements
- observe correct renewal procedures

License revocation or suspension. Licenses are typically revoked or suspended when a licensee is found guilty of:

- obtaining a license under false pretenses
- committing a "prohibited act"
- neglecting to present every written offer as required
- neglecting to deliver signed copies of accepted offers to transaction parties as required
- failing to make sure that all required terms and conditions are present in a contract to purchase
- handling earnest money and other escrow funds improperly

Licensee discipline. A state real estate commission may assess a civil penalty for violations of a statute, rule, or order. Licensees are disciplined for:

- acting without a license when a license is required
- demanding a referral fee without reasonable cause
- entering into a net listing
- trying to induce another licensee's client to end or change an existing agency contract
- paying a commission to an unlicensed individual or company
- receiving an illegal referral fee, rebate or kickback
- practicing with an expired license

Licensee lawsuits. A licensee may be sued by the Department of Justice, Federal Trade Commission, a state real estate commission, a human rights commission, another licensee or firm, or an individual consumer. Licensees are mainly sued for:

- fair housing violations
- antitrust violations
- license law and other state law violations
- breach of contract
- agency duty violations
- illegal practice of law
- failures to disclose
- customer or client dissatisfaction
- fraud
- theft

Misrepresentation

Misrepresentation may be unintentional or intentional.

Unintentional misrepresentation. This type of misrepresentation occurs when a licensee _unknowingly_ conveys inaccurate information to a consumer concerning a property, financing or agency service. False or inaccurate information that the licensee, as a professional, should have known to be false or inaccurate may be included in the definition. Those found guilty generally have to pay fines and may be disciplined by state real estate regulators and professional organizations.

Risky areas for unintentional misrepresentation include:

- making and reporting measurements
- describing property
- offering opinions about future growth and development of a neighborhood or neighboring property
- making declarative statements about the presence or absence of hazardous materials

The risks of unintentional misrepresentation are reduced if an agent

- learns to measure and calculate areas accurately
- relies on measurements reported by others only with extreme caution and specific disclaimers
- refrains from exaggeration
- avoids stating opinions a consumer might take for expertise

Intentional misrepresentation. Also known as fraud, this kind of misrepresentation occurs when a licensee _knowingly_ conveys false information about a property, financing or service. Fraud is a criminal act that may result in fines and incarceration, in addition to discipline from state regulators and professional organizations.

Recommending providers

There are several risks attending the recommendation of vendors and service providers to a consumer. First, the consumer may not be satisfied with the performance of the recommended party and blame the licensee. Second, in cases where a recommended provider performs illegal acts, there may be legal consequences for the licensee. Third, if a licensee has a business relationship with a recommended vendor or provider and neglects to disclose the fact, there are license violation consequences.

The major risk management technique is to shift the responsibility for choosing a vendor to the consumer. This can be done by refusing to recommend vendors at all; by presenting a broad range of choices and allowing the consumer to select; or by presenting a short list of thoroughly vetted vendors and allowing the consumer to make the decision, always with the disclaimer that **to the best of the licensee's knowledge**, the vendors on the list are competent and honest, but that the consumer is responsible for investigating and making his or her own judgment before hiring or buying.

Financing and closing

In the financing and closing phases of a transaction, a consumer may feel that a licensee has been incompetent or misleading. Licensees have an obligation to inform and educate their clients throughout the transaction process. Surprises and accusations of incompetence or misrepresentation are among possible results of failing to keep the party informed.

Discrimination. Of course, it is important to comply with relevant laws. Licensees must be mindful of the requirements of ECOA and refrain from participating in any manner of discriminatory lending. It is illegal to:

- threaten, coerce, intimidate or interfere with a person who is exercising a fair housing right or assisting another other to exercise that right.
- indicate a limitation or preference based on race, color, national origin, religion, sex, familial status, or handicap in any advertisement or communication. Single-family and owner-occupied housing that is otherwise exempt from the Fair Housing Act is subject to this prohibition against discriminatory advertising.

Progress reporting. All inspections and tests must comply with local and state laws and with the purchase contract. Progress reports should be accurate, timely, in writing, and free of speculation. If a consumer has a question about the meaning of something in an inspection report, the licensee should refer the consumer to the person who wrote the report rather than trying to explain it. This method transfers some of the risk inherent in interpreting the report.

Qualifying buyers. Many transactions fail because a buyer has been improperly qualified before the offer is presented. Using a lender to qualify the buyer saves time and protects the agent against leading a seller to believe a purchaser is fully qualified when this may not be the case. Also, lenders and loan agents are better able to look into the buyer's qualifications than a real estate licensee is. If it becomes necessary to show a property to a potential buyer who has not been qualified by a lender, the licensee can gain some protection by performing an informal qualification and documenting the fact that it was based on the information provided by the buyer. The buyer's signature on this documentation indicates the buyer's acceptance of at least partial responsibility for the qualification.

Lending fees disclosure. The licensee should explain loan fees, charges,

amounts, timing, and responsibilities. Agents can assist in the loan decision by explaining how to compare loans with differing charges and interest rates. The fact that a high origination fee and points may make a loan with a low interest rate unattractive to a borrower is important information for the agent to provide, and providing it may protect the agent against a later complaint that the buyer suffered a loss because of the agent's failure to inform.

Appraisal problems. Delays and appraised value are the typical problem areas. Failure to inform parties about delays can compromise the transaction. An under-appraisal will require the buyer to make a larger down payment or the seller to lower the price. If the property appraises for more than the purchase price, the seller may blame the agent for suggesting the lower price. In such a case, the seller's agent's defense is that the seller agreed to the listing price and that the price was a factor in attracting the buyer to the property.

RESPA Violations. The **Real Estate Settlement Procedures Act (RESPA)** stipulates that the parties to certain purchase transactions must be given accurate information reflecting their closing costs. It also prohibits certain business practices that are not considered to be in the consumer's best interest.

The licensee's risks regarding RESPA primarily relate to

- failing to ensure that the consumer is informed about his or her rights under the law
- giving or receiving an illegal kickback.

RESPA currently requires lenders to:

- give a copy of a Consumer Financial Protection Bureau loan information booklet to the applicant. The booklet explains RESPA provisions, general settlement costs, and the required **Closing Disclosure** form. The lender must provide the estimate of closing costs within three business days following the borrower's application.

- give the applicant a Loan Estimate (Form H-24) of expected closing costs within three business days of receiving the application. Actual closing costs may not vary from the estimate beyond certain limits.

- give the buyer the Closing Disclosure (Form H-25) specifying costs to be paid by buyer and seller at closing three business days before consummation.

- give the **buyer** the opportunity to review the final settlement statement *one business day prior to closing*.

RESPA specifically **prohibits** any fee or kickback paid to a party for a service when the party has not actually rendered the service. For example, it is prohibited for an insurance company to pay a real estate agent or a lender for referring a client.

Fees for referring clients to the following services are strictly forbidden:

- title services (search, insurance)
- appraisals
- inspections
- surveys
- loan issue
- credit report
- attorney services

The sharing of commissions and the payment of referral fees among cooperating brokers and multiple-listing services are not RESPA violations.

Trust fund handling

State laws prescribe how licensees must handle any escrow or earnest money deposits they receive. Those laws usually state that a broker must hold money received in connection with the purchase or lease of real property in a trust fund account. The type of account and financial depository are specified. The broker must record receipt of the money and place that money in the trust account within a specified time period. Usually, the law allows the broker to hold an earnest money check uncashed until the offer is accepted, provided the buyer gives written permission and the seller is informed.

Typical trust fund handling requirements include:

- the broker named as trustee of the account
- a federally-insured bank or recognized depository located in the state
- an account that is not interest-bearing if the financial institution ever requires prior written notice for withdrawals
- maintenance of records in a particular accounting format
- separate records kept for each beneficiary, property, or transaction
- records of funds received and paid out regularly reconciled with bank statements
- withdrawals only by the broker-trustee or other specifically authorized person

Commingling and conversion. Mixing of personal or company funds with client funds is grounds for the revocation or suspension of a real estate license. Depositing client funds in a personal or business account, or using them for any purpose other than the client's business, is also grounds for suspension or revocation of a license. It is important for the broker to remove commissions, fees or other income earned by the broker from a trust account within the period specified by law to avoid committing an act of commingling.

Interactive Exercise

Unit 7: Risk Management

7.1) "WHAT IF" SITUATION EXAMPLE: Mitigating risks when dealing with buyers.

Abigail is a brand-new real estate agent and is hungry for her first deal. She is hosting an open house at a foreclosure property and an investor stops by. They chat briefly and, as he tours the home, he starts asking her for the cost to renovate the kitchen and what the future of the neighborhood looks like. Abigail has no experience pricing renovations but she is very eager to land her first client.

What would you say if you were Abigail?

_____

_____

_____

_____

_____

_____

_____

_____

_____

SNAPSHOT REVIEW: UNIT SEVEN

RISK MANAGEMENT

RISK MANAGEMENT STRATEGIES
- Avoidance (elimination)
- Reduction (mitigation, sharing)
- Transference (outsourcing, insuring)
- Retention (acceptance and budgeting)

RISK MANAGEMENT PROCEDURES
- Education
- Disclosure
- Documentation
- Insurance

PRIMARY AREAS OF RISK
- Agency
- Property disclosures
- Listing, selling
- Contracting
- Fair housing
- Anti-trust
- Rules and regulations
- Misrepresentation
- Recommending providers
- Trust fund handling

Check Your Understanding Quiz:

Unit Seven: Risk Management

Carefully read each question then provide your best answer based on what you learned in this unit. Then check your answers against the Answer Key which immediately follows the quiz questions.

1. Four well-established risk management strategies include avoidance, reduction, transference, and
    _____.

    a. elimination.
    b. mitigation.
    c. retention.
    d. sharing.

2. Which insurance policy is a primary mechanism for transferring the professional liability risks of brokers and licensees?

    a. Errors & Omissions insurance
    b. General liability insurance
    c. Workers' compensation
    d. Consequential loss, use, and occupancy insurance

3. Which of the following duties requires the agent to act on the principal's wishes regarding the transaction?

    a. Confidentiality
    b. Disclosure
    c. Obedience
    d. Skill and diligence

4. An insurance policy is a common example of which risk management strategy?

    a. Retention
    b. Transference
    c. Reduction
    d. Avoidance

5. Which statute forbids brokers to band together to determine a set price on their listing services?

    a. Antitrust law
    b. Clayton Act
    c. Federal Trade Commission Act
    d. Statute of Frauds

6. Federal law requires sellers of houses built before _____ to make a lead-based paint disclosure to potential buyers.

    a. 1988
    b. 1964
    c. 1978
    d. 1950

7. What is the first line of defense against risk?

    a. Education
    b. Diligence
    c. Liability elimination
    d. Avoidance

8. Which type of insurance covers loss of rent due to a fire?

    a. Fire and hazard insurance
    b. Consequential loss, use, and occupancy insurance
    c. Casualty insurance
    d. Surety bond insurance

9. Which keyword should licensees avoid when preparing a CMA?

    a. Market
    b. Analysis
    c. Comparables
    d. Appraisal

10. Ella is buying an off-market home and asks her licensee friend to write a contract for her. The licensee agrees for a fee of $475. What can the licensee be accused of?

    a. Fraud
    b. Misadvertising
    c. Unauthorized practice of law
    d. Price gouging

11. How are federal antitrust laws enforced?

    a. The FTC brings civil enforcement actions
    b. With a $1,000-10,000 fine
    c. With 30 days of incarceration
    d. NAR brings criminal enforcement actions

12. Which of the following actions would be cause for license suspension?

    a. Missing an education requirement
    b. Handling earnest money improperly
    c. Incorrectly renewing a license
    d. Failing to complete continuing education

13. Which licensee duty applies to all funds involved in a real estate transaction?

    a. Confidentiality
    b. Disclosure
    c. Accounting
    d. Diligence

14. Which of the following would be covered by E&O insurance?

    a. Claims that the licensee failed to carry out fiduciary duties
    b. Violations of the law
    c. Antitrust violations
    d. Fair housing violations

15. Which statute requires that parties to certain purchase transactions be given accurate information reflecting their closing costs?

    a. Clayton Act
    b. RESPA
    c. Sherman Antitrust Act
    d. FTCA

UNIT 8:

CONTRACT WRITING

Unit Eight Learning Objectives: When the student has completed this unit, he or she will be able to:

- Discuss the essentials of contract law including validity criteria, electronic contracting, and enforceability.
- Identify primary and secondary contract provisions.
- Understand the differences between varying sales contracts including the option-to-buy contract and residential purchase contract.
- Identify the contracting process.
- Discuss the required disclosures including lead-based paint disclosure and HOA disclosure.
- Recognize the requirements for a leasing contract and the varying lease types.

ESSENTIALS OF CONTRACT LAW

Validity criteria: contracts in general

A contract is valid only if it meets all of the following criteria.

Exhibit 8.1 Contract Validity Requirements

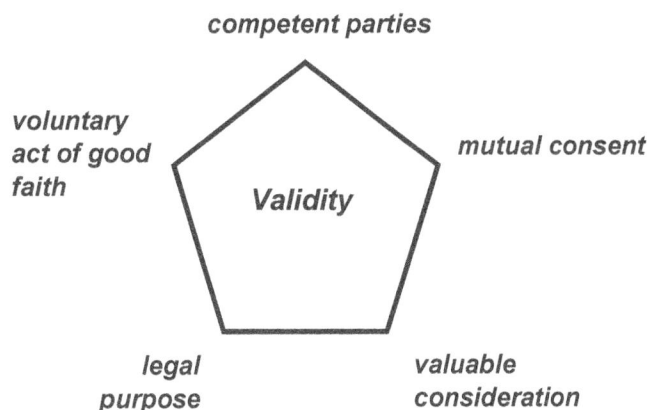

Competent parties. The parties to a contract must have the capacity to contract, and there must be at least two such parties. Thus, the owner of a tenancy for life cannot deed his interest to himself in the form of a fee simple, as this would involve only one party. Capacity to contract is determined by three factors:

- legal age
- mental competency

- legitimate authority

Depending on state law, a contract involving a minor as a party may be either void or voidable. If the law allows a minor to contract, the contract will generally be voidable and the minor can disaffirm the contract.

To be mentally competent, a party must have sufficient understanding of the import and consequences of a contract. Competency in this context is separate and distinct from sanity. Incompetent parties, or parties of "unsound mind," may not enter into enforceable contracts. The incompetency of a party may be ruled by a court of law or by other means. In some areas, convicted felons may be deemed incompetent, depending on the nature of the crime.

During the period of one's incompetency, a court may appoint a guardian who may act on the incompetent party's behalf with court approval.

If the contracting party is representing another person or business entity, the representative must have the *legal authority* to contract. If representing another person, the party must have a bona fide power of attorney. If the contracting party is representing a corporation, the person must have the appropriate power and approval to act, such as would be conferred in a duly executed resolution of the Board of Directors. If the contracting entity is a general partnership, any partner may validly contract for the partnership. In a limited partnership, only general partners may be parties to a contract.

Mutual consent. Mutual consent, also known as *offer and acceptance* and *meeting of the minds,* requires that a contract involve a clear and definite offer and an intentional, unqualified acceptance of the offer. In effect, the parties must agree to the terms without equivocation. A court may nullify a contract where the acceptance of terms by either party was partial, accidental, or vague.

Valuable consideration. A contract must contain a two-way exchange of valuable consideration as compensation for performance by the other party. The exchange of considerations must be two-way. The contract is not valid or enforceable if just one party provides consideration.

Valuable consideration can be something of tangible value, such as money or something a party promises to do or not do. For example, a home builder may promise to build a house for a party as consideration for receiving money from the home buyer. Or, a landowner may agree not to sell a property as consideration for a developer's option money. Also, valuable consideration can be something intangible that a party must give up, such as a homeowner's occupancy of the house in exchange for rent. In effect, consideration is the price one party must pay to obtain performance from the other party.

Valuable consideration may be contrasted with good consideration, or "love and affection," which does not qualify as consideration in a valid contract. Good consideration is something of questionable value, such as a child's love for her mother. Good consideration disqualifies a contract because, while one's love or affection is certainly valuable to the other party, it is not something that is specifically offered in exchange for something else. Good consideration can, however, serve as a nominal consideration in transferring a real property interest as a gift.

In some cases, what is promised as valuable consideration must also be deemed to be *sufficient* consideration. Grossly insufficient consideration, such as $50,000 for a $2 million property, may invalidate a contract on the grounds that the agreement is a gift rather than a contract. In other cases where there is an extreme imbalance in the considerations exchanged, a contract may be invalidated as a violation of good faith bargaining.

Exhibit 8.2 Consideration

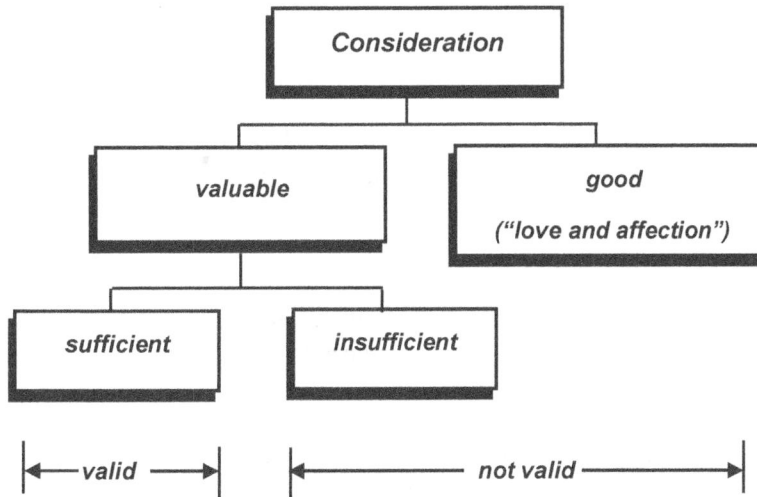

Legal purpose. The content, promise, or intent of a contract must be lawful. A contract that proposes an illegal act is void.

Voluntary, good faith act. The parties must create the contract in good faith as a free and voluntary act. A contract is thus voidable if one party acted under duress, coercion, fraud, or misrepresentation.

For example, if a property seller induces a buyer to purchase a house based on assurances that the roof is new, the buyer may rescind the agreement if the roof turns out to be twenty years old and leaky.

Validity of a conveyance contract

In addition to satisfying the foregoing requirements, a contract that conveys an interest in real estate must:

- be in writing
- contain a legal description of the property
- be signed by one or more of the parties

A lease contract that has a term of one year or less is an exception. Such leases do not have to be in writing to be enforceable.

Electronic contracting (UETA)

Contracting electronically through email and fax greatly facilitates the completion of transactions. Clients, lenders, title agents, inspectors, brokers, and other participants in a transaction can quickly share documentation and information. Electronic contracting is made possible by the Uniform Electronic Transactions Act (UETA) and the Electronic Signatures in Global and National Commerce Act (E-Sign), which are federal laws. UETA, which has been accepted in most states, provides that electronic records and signatures are legal and must be accepted. E-Sign makes contracts, records, and signatures legally enforceable, regardless of medium, even where UETA is not accepted.

Enforceability criteria

Certain contracts that fail to meet the validity requirements are voidable if a damaged party takes appropriate action. The enforcement of voidable contracts, however, is limited by **statutes of limitation.** Certain other contracts which are valid may not be enforceable due to the **statute of frauds.**

Statute of limitations. The statute of limitations restricts the time period for which an injured party in a contract has the right to rescind or disaffirm the contract. A party to a voidable contract must act within the statutory period.

Statute of frauds. The statute of frauds requires that certain contracts *must be in writing* to be enforceable. Real estate contracts that convey an interest in real property fall in this category, with the exception that a lease of one year's duration or less may be oral. All other contracts to buy, sell, exchange, or lease interests in real property must be in writing to be enforceable. In addition, *listing agreements* in most states must be in writing.

The statute of frauds concerns the enforceability of a contract, not its validity. Once the parties to a valid oral contract have executed and performed, even if the contract was unenforceable, a party cannot use the Statute of Frauds to rescind the contract.

Contract creation

Offer and acceptance. The mutual consent required for a valid contract is reached through the process of offer and acceptance: The **offeror** proposes contract terms in an **offer** to the **offeree**. If the offeree accepts all terms without amendment, the offer becomes a contract. The exact point at which the offer becomes a contract is when the offeree gives the offeror notice of the acceptance.

Exhibit 8.3 Offer, Counteroffer and Acceptance

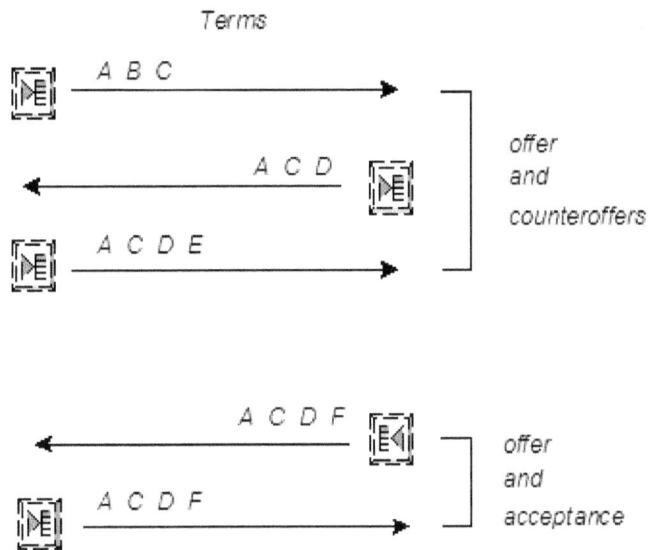

Terms

A B C → offer and counteroffers

A C D ←

A C D E →

A C D F ← offer and acceptance

A C D F →

Offer. An offer expresses the offeror's intention to enter into a contract with an offeree to perform the terms of the agreement in exchange for the offeree's performance. In a real estate sale or lease contract, the offer must clearly contain all intended terms of the contract in writing and be communicated to the offeree.

If an offer contains an expiration date and the phrase "time is of the essence," the offer expires at exactly the time specified. In the absence of a stated time period, the offeree has a "reasonable" time to accept an offer.

Acceptance. An offer gives the offeree the power of accepting. For an acceptance to be valid, the offeree must manifestly and unequivocally accept all terms of the offer without change, and so indicate by signing the offer, preferably with a date of signing. The acceptance must then be communicated to the offeror. If the communication of acceptance is by mail, the offer is considered to be communicated as soon as it is placed in the mail.

Counteroffer. By changing any of the terms of an offer, the offeree creates a counteroffer, and the original offer is void. At this point, the offeree becomes the offeror, and the new offeree gains the right of acceptance. If accepted, the counteroffer becomes a valid contract provided all other requirements are met.

For example, a seller changes the expiration date of a buyer's offer by one day, signs the offer and returns it to the buyer. The single amendment extinguishes the buyer's offer, and the buyer is no longer bound by any agreement. The seller's amended offer is a counteroffer which now gives the buyer the right of acceptance. If the buyer accepts the counteroffer, the counteroffer becomes a binding contract.

Revocation of an offer. An offer may be revoked, or withdrawn, at any time before the offeree has communicated acceptance. The revocation extinguishes the offer and the offeree's right to accept it.

For example, a buyer has offered to purchase a house for the listed price. Three hours later, a family death radically changes the buyer's plans. She immediately calls the seller and revokes the offer, stating she is no longer interested in the house. Since the seller had not communicated acceptance of the offer to the buyer, the offer is legally cancelled.

If the offeree has paid consideration to the offeror to leave an offer open, and the offeror accepts, an option has been created which cancels the offeror's right to revoke the offer over the period of the option.

Termination of an offer. Any of the following actions or circumstances can terminate an offer:

- acceptance: the offeree accepts the offer, converting it to a contract
- rejection: the offeree rejects the offer
- revocation: the offeror withdraws the offer before acceptance
- lapse of time: the offer expires
- counteroffer: the offeree changes the offer
- death or insanity of either party

Contract contingencies

A sale contract often contains contingencies. A contingency is a condition that must be met before the contract is enforceable.

The most common contingency concerns financing. A buyer makes an offer contingent upon securing financing for the property under certain terms on or before a certain date. If unable to secure the specified loan commitment by the deadline, the buyer may cancel the contract and recover the deposit. An appropriate and timely loan commitment eliminates the contingency, and the buyer must proceed with the purchase.

It is possible for both buyers and sellers to abuse contingencies in order to leave themselves a convenient way to cancel without defaulting. To avoid problems, the statement of a contingency should:

- be explicit and clear
- have an expiration date
- expressly require diligence in the effort to fulfill the requirement

A contingency that is too broad, vague, or excessive in duration may invalidate the entire contract on the grounds of insufficiency of mutual agreement.

Default
A sale contract is bilateral, since both parties promise to perform. As a result, either party may default by failing to perform. Note that a party's failure to meet a contingency does not constitute default, but rather entitles the parties to cancel the contract.

Buyer default. If a buyer fails to perform under the terms of a sale contract, the breach entitles the seller to legal recourse for damages. In most cases, the contract itself stipulates the seller's remedies. The usual remedy is forfeiture of the buyer's deposit as **liquidated damages**, provided the deposit is not grossly in excess of the seller's actual damages. It is also customary to provide for the seller and broker to share the liquidated damages.

If the contract does not provide for liquidated damages, the seller may sue for damages, cancellation, or specific performance.

Seller default. If a seller defaults, the buyer may sue for specific performance, damages, or cancellation.

PRIMARY, SECONDARY SALES CONTRACT PROVISIONS

Primary provisions

A typical residential sale contract contains provisions of the following kind.

Parties, consideration, and property. One or more clauses will identify the parties, the property, and the basic consideration, which is the sale of the property in return for a purchase price.

There must be at least two parties to a sale contract: one cannot convey property to oneself. All parties must be identified, be of legal age, and have the capacity to contract.

The property clause also identifies fixtures and personal property included in the sale. Unless expressly excluded, items commonly construed as fixtures are *included* in the sale. Similarly, items commonly considered personal property are *not included* unless expressly included.

Legal description. A legal description must be sufficient for a competent surveyor to identify the property.

Price and terms. A clause states the final price and details how the purchase will occur. Of particular interest to the seller is the buyer's down payment, since the greater the buyer's equity, the more likely the buyer will be able to secure financing. In addition, a large deposit represents a buyer's commitment to complete the sale.

If seller financing is involved, the sale contract sets forth the terms of the arrangement: the amount and type of loan, the rate and term, and how the loan will be paid off.

It is important for all parties to verify that the buyer's earnest money deposit, down payment, loan proceeds, and other promised funds together equal the purchase price stated in the contract.

Loan approval. A financing contingency clause states under what conditions the buyer can cancel the contract without default and receive a refund of the earnest money. If the buyer cannot secure the stated financing by the deadline, the parties may agree to extend the contingency by signing next to the changed dates.

Earnest money deposit. A clause specifies how the buyer will pay the earnest money. It may allow the buyer to pay it in installments. Such an option enables a buyer to hold on to the property briefly while obtaining the additional deposit funds. For example, a buyer who wants to buy a house makes an initial deposit of $200, to be followed in twenty-four hours with an additional $2,000. The sale contract includes the seller's acknowledgment of receipt of the deposit.

Escrow. An escrow clause provides for the custody and disbursement of the earnest money deposit, and releases the escrow agent from certain liabilities in the performance of escrow duties.

Closing and possession dates. The contract states when title will transfer, as well as when the buyer will take physical possession. Customarily, possession occurs on the date when the deed is recorded, unless the buyer has agreed to other arrangements.

The closing clause generally describes what must take place at closing to avoid default. A seller must provide clear and marketable title. A buyer must produce purchase funds. Failure to complete any pre-closing requirements stated in the sale contract is default and grounds for the aggrieved party to seek recourse.

Conveyed interest; type of deed. One or more provisions will state what type of deed the seller will use to convey the property, and what conditions the deed will be subject to. Among common "subject to" conditions are easements, association memberships, encumbrances, mortgages, liens, and special assessments. Typically, the seller conveys a fee simple interest by means of a general warranty deed.

Title evidence. The seller covenants to produce the best possible evidence of property ownership. This is commonly in the form of title insurance.

Closing costs. The contract identifies which closing costs each party will pay. Customarily, the seller pays title and property-related costs, and the buyer pays financing-related costs. Annual costs such as taxes and insurance are prorated between the parties. Note that who pays any particular closing cost is an item for negotiation.

Damage and destruction. A clause stipulates the obligations of the parties in case the property is damaged or destroyed. The parties may negotiate alternatives, including seller's obligation to repair, buyer's obligation to buy if repairs are made, and the option for either party to cancel.

Default. A default clause identifies remedies for default. Generally, a buyer may sue for damages, specific performance, or cancellation. A seller may do likewise or claim the earnest money as liquidated damages.

Broker's representation and commission. The broker's compensation for services rendered in respect to any listing is solely a matter of negotiation between the broker and his or her client, and is not fixed, controlled, recommended, or maintained by any persons not a party to the listing agreement.

Seller's representations. The seller warrants that there will be no liens on the property that cannot be settled and extinguished at closing. In addition, the seller warrants that all representations are true, and if found otherwise, the buyer may cancel the contract and reclaim the deposit.

Secondary provisions

A sale contract may contain numerous additional clauses, depending on the complexity of the transaction. The following are some of the common provisions.

Inspections. The parties agree to inspections and remedial action based on findings.

Virginia Residential Property Disclosure Act. The seller is required to disclose in writing that the seller makes no representations or warranties concerning the physical condition of the property and to sell the property "as-is".

Virginia Resale Disclosure Act. The seller is required to disclose whether or not the property is located within a development controlled by a Property Owners Association Act (POAA) or subject to the Virginia Condominium Act. If the property is located in a common interest community, then the seller is required to provide a resale certificate to the buyer.

Survey. The parties agree to a survey to satisfy financing requirements.

Environmental hazards. The seller notifies the buyer that there may be hazards that could affect the use and value of the property.

Compliance with laws. The seller warrants that there are no undisclosed building code or zoning violations.

Due-on-sale clause. The parties state their understanding that loans that survive the closing may be called due by the lender. Both parties agree to hold the other party harmless for the consequences of an acceleration.

Seller financing disclosure. The parties agree to comply with applicable state and local disclosure laws concerning seller financing.

Rental property; tenants rights. The buyer acknowledges the rights of tenants following closing.

FHA or VA financing condition. A contingency allows the buyer to cancel the contract if the price exceeds FHA or VA estimates of the property's value.

Flood plain; flood insurance. Seller discloses that the property is in a flood plain and that it must carry flood insurance if the buyer uses certain lenders for financing.

Foreign seller withholding. The seller acknowledges that the buyer must withhold 15% of the purchase price at closing if the seller is a foreign person or entity and forward the withheld amount to the Internal Revenue Service. Certain limitations and exemptions apply.

Tax deferred exchange. For income properties only, buyer and seller disclose their intentions to participate in an exchange and agree to cooperate in completing necessary procedures.

Merger of agreements. Buyer and seller state that there are no other agreements

between the parties that are not expressed in the contract.

Notices. The parties agree on how they will give notice to each other and what they will consider to be delivery of notice.

Time is of the essence. The parties agree that they can amend dates and deadlines only if they both give written approval.

Fax transmission. The parties agree to accept facsimile transmission of the offer, provided receipt is acknowledged and original copies of the contract are subsequently delivered.

Survival. The parties continue to be liable for the truthfulness of representations and warranties after the closing.

Dispute resolution. The parties agree to resolve disputes through arbitration as opposed to court proceedings.

C.L.U.E. Report. CLUE (Comprehensive Loss Underwriting Exchange) is a claims history database used by insurance companies in underwriting or rating insurance policies. A CLUE Home Seller's Disclosure Report shows a five-year insurance loss history for a specific property. Among other things, it describes the types of any losses and the amounts paid. Many home buyers now require sellers to provide a CLUE Report (which only the property owner or an insurer can order) as a contingency appended to the purchase offer. A report showing a loss due to water damage and mold, for instance, might lead a buyer to decide against making an offer because of the potential difficulty of getting insurance. A report showing no insurance loss within the previous five years, on the other hand, is an indication that the availability and pricing of homeowner's insurance will not present an obstacle to the purchase transaction, and also that the property has not experienced significant damage or repair during that time period.

Addenda. Addenda to the sale contract become binding components of the overall agreement. The most common addendum is the seller's property condition disclosure. Examples of other addenda are:

agency disclosure	asbestos / hazardous materials
liquidated damages	radon disclosure
flood plain disclosure	tenant's lease

OPTION-TO-BUY CONTRACT

Overview

An option-to-buy is an enforceable contract in which a potential seller, the **optionor**, grants a potential buyer, the **optionee**, the right to purchase a property before a stated time for a stated price and terms. In exchange for the right of option, the optionee pays the optionor valuable consideration.

For example, a buyer wants to purchase a property for $150,000, but needs to sell a boat to raise the down payment. The boat will take two or three months to sell. To accommodate the buyer, the seller offers the buyer an option to purchase the property at any time before midnight on the day that is ninety days from the date of signing the option. The buyer pays the seller $1,000 for the option. If buyer exercises the option, the seller will apply the $1,000 toward the earnest money deposit and subsequent down payment. If the optionee lets the option expire, the seller keeps the $1,000. Both parties agree to the arrangement by completing a sale contract as an addendum to the option, then executing the option agreement itself.

An option-to-buy places the optionee *under no obligation* to purchase the property. However, the seller must perform under the terms of the contract if the buyer exercises the option. An option is thus a *unilateral* agreement. Exercise of the option creates a bilateral sale contract where both parties are bound to perform. An unused option terminates at the expiration date.

An optionee can use an option to prevent the sale of a property to another party while seeking to raise funds for the purchase. A renter with a **lease option-to-buy** can accumulate down payment funds while paying rent to the landlord. For example, an owner may lease a condominium to a tenant with an option to buy. If the tenant takes the option, the landlord agrees to apply $100 of the monthly rent paid prior to the option date toward the purchase price. The tenant pays the landlord the nominal sum of $200 for the option.

Options can also facilitate commercial property acquisition. The option period gives a buyer time to investigate zoning, space planning, building permits, environmental impacts, and other feasibility issues prior to the purchase without losing the property to another party in the meantime.

Contract requirements

To be valid and enforceable, an option-to-buy must:

- include actual, non-refundable consideration
  The option must require the optionee to pay a specific consideration *that is separate from the purchase price*. The consideration cannot be refunded if the option is not exercised. If the option is exercised, the consideration may be applied to the purchase price. If the option is a lease option, portions of the rent may qualify as separate consideration.
- include price and terms of the sale
  The price and terms of the potential transaction must be clearly expressed and cannot change over the option period. It is customary practice for the parties to complete and attach a sale contract to the option as satisfaction of this requirement.
- have an expiration date
  The option must automatically expire at the end of a specific period.
- be in writing
  Since a potential transfer of real estate is involved, most state statutes of fraud require an option to be in writing.
- include a legal description
- meet general contract validity requirements
  The basics include competent parties, the optionor's promise to perform, and the optionor's signature. Note that it is not necessary for the optionee to sign the option.

Common provisions

Beyond the required elements, it is common for an option to include provisions covering:

169

- how to deliver notice of election
  A clause clarifies how to make the option election, exactly when the election must be completed, and any additional terms required such as an earnest money deposit.
- forfeiture terms
  A clause provides that the optionor is entitled to the consideration if the option term expires.
- property and title condition warranties
  The optionor warrants that the property will be maintained in a certain condition, and that title will be marketable and insurable.
- how option consideration will be credited
  A clause states how the optionor will apply the option consideration toward the purchase price.

CONTRACTS FOR DEED

A contract for deed is also called a *land contract*, an *installment sale*, a *conditional sales contract,* and an *agreement for deed*. It is a bilateral agreement between a seller, the **vendor,** and a buyer, the **vendee**, in which the vendor defers receipt of some or all of the purchase price of a property over a specified period of time. During the period, the *vendor retains legal title* and the vendee acquires equitable title. The vendee takes possession of the property, makes stipulated payments of principal and interest to the vendor, and otherwise fulfills obligations as the contract requires. At the end of the period, the buyer pays the vendor the full purchase price and the vendor deeds legal title to the vendee.

Like an option, a contract for deed offers a means for a marginally qualified buyer to acquire property. In essence, the seller acts as lender, allowing the buyer to take possession and pay off the purchase price over time. A buyer may thus avoid conventional down payment and income requirements imposed by institutional lenders. During the contract period, the buyer can work to raise the necessary cash to complete the purchase or to qualify for a conventional mortgage.

A contract for deed serves two primary purposes for a seller. First, it facilitates a sale that might otherwise be impossible. Second, it may give the seller certain tax benefits. Since the seller is not liable for capital gains tax until the purchase price is received, the installment sale lowers the seller's tax liability in the year of the sale.

Interests and rights

Vendor's rights and obligations. During the contract period, the seller may:

- mortgage the property
- sell or assign whatever interests he or she owns in the property to another party
- incur judgment liens against the property

The vendor, however, is bound to the obligations imposed by the contract for deed. In particular, the vendor may not breach the obligation to convey legal title to the vendee upon receipt of the total purchase price. In addition, the vendor remains liable for underlying mortgage loans.

Vendee's rights and obligations. During the contract period, the buyer may occupy, use, enjoy, and profit from the property, subject to the provisions of the written agreement. The vendee must make periodic payments of principal and interest and maintain the property. In addition, a vendee may have to pay property taxes and hazard insurance.

Legal form

Like other conveyance contracts, a contract for deed instrument identifies:

- the principal parties
- the property's legal description
- consideration: specifically what the parties promise to do
- the terms of the sale
- obligations for property maintenance
- default and remedies
- signatures and acknowledgment

The contract specifies the vendee's payments, payment deadlines, when the balance of the purchase price is due, and how the property may be used.

Default and recourse

Seller default. If the seller defaults, such as by failing to deliver the deed, the buyer may sue for specific performance, or for cancellation of the agreement and damages.

Buyer default. States differ in the remedies they prescribe for the seller in case of buyer default. Some states consider the default a breach of contract that may be remedied by cancellation, retention of monies received, and eviction. Others provide foreclosure proceedings as a remedy.

Usage guidelines

Many areas have no standardized contract for deed or any form sanctioned by associations and agencies. Therefore, this kind of conveyance presents certain pitfalls for buyer and seller.

In some states, a breach of the contract for deed is remedied under *local contract law* rather than foreclosure law. The buyer may not have the protections of a redemption period or other buyer-protection laws which accompany formal foreclosure proceedings. The vendor might sue the vendee for breach of contract for the slightest infraction of the contract terms.

A second danger for the vendee is that the vendor has the power and the right to encumber the property in ways that may not be desirable for the buyer. For example, the seller could place a home equity loan on the property, then fail to make periodic payments. The bank could then foreclose on the vendor, thus jeopardizing the vendee's eventual purchase.

For the seller, the principal danger is that the buyer acquires possession in exchange for a minimal down payment. A buyer might damage or even vacate the property, leaving the seller to make repairs and retake possession. Further, since the contract is recorded, the seller must also bear the time and expense of clearing the title.

To minimize risk, principal parties in a contract for deed should observe the following guidelines:

- use an attorney to draft the agreement
- adopt the standard forms, if available
- become familiar with how the contract will be enforced
- utilize professional escrow and title services
- record the transaction properly
- be prepared for the possible effect on existing financing

VIRGINIA SALES CONTRACTS

Statute of Frauds

Remember that the Statute of Frauds requires certain contracts to be in writing to be enforceable. In Virginia, that requirement applies to contracts for the sale of real estate and for the lease of real estate for one year or longer. Even though an oral contract may be valid in some instances, it is not enforceable if it pertains to real estate. Consequently, real estate contracts need to be in writing and signed by both parties to the transaction. When printed, the provisions of the contract must be in 10 point or larger type to be binding upon the buyer.

Preparation of contracts

Under the Code of Virginia (§ 54.1-2101.1), real estate licensees may prepare written contracts for the sale, purchase, option, exchange, or rental of real estate, provided that the contract preparation is incidental to or associated with a real estate transaction. The licensee preparing the contract must be involved in the transaction and may not charge a separate fee for preparing the contract.

The licensee should ensure that all fields on a contract form are completed. If one section does not apply to a particular transaction, then the field should be noted with an N/A.
If the contract has been prepared in English and a party to the transaction needs it translated to another language, the licensee may assist in finding a translator or an electronic translation service without charging a fee for the assistance. The licensee may not be held liable for any errors in the translation.

Residential purchase contract

A residential purchase contract is used for potential buyers to submit an offer to purchase a specific property. The contract includes the buyer's initial terms for the purchase to which the seller must respond. The contract allows the buyer and seller to negotiate the terms of the offer.

The contract form should include the following:

- a statement that it is a legally binding contract
- the identity of all parties to the contract
- an accurate legal description and address of the property
- any personal property also being conveyed such as appliances and furniture
- the purchase price offer and acceptance and how it will be paid, along with deposit payment and disbursement details
- title, title insurance, and closing settlement details

- the closing date
- property condition and inspection options, as well as any needed repairs
- assumption of any current tenant leases
- all required disclosures, including a residential property disclosure statement, lead-based paint disclosure, septic system and defective drywall disclosures, etc.
- any special contingencies required by either party, such as financing, appraisal, sale of buyer's current home contingencies

While there is no mandated contract form for the sale of real estate in Virginia, several fillable and printable contracts can be found online. The latest version of the Virginia REALTORS® Residential Contract of Purchase form is available for Virginia REALTOR® members here - https://virginiarealtors.org/law-ethics/standard-forms-library/residential-contract-purchase/

Attachments and addenda

The contract form is the basis for the contract, but the form alone does not constitute the entire contract. Any contingencies, addenda, and amendments to the contract must also be included with the contract. As discussed in a previous unit, federal and state real estate laws require certain disclosures to be provided to the buyer. Although some of the disclosures may be given to the buyer directly, including them in the contract serves as proof the disclosures were actually provided.

Required disclosures, applicable to the specific transaction and property, include:

- brokerage relationship disclosure
- dual or designated representation disclosure
- limited service representation disclosure
- residential property disclosure
- lead-based paint disclosure
- POAA or Condominium Resale Certificate request
- defective drywall disclosure
- aircraft noise/crash disclosure
- alternative septic system disclosure
- pending building or zoning violations
- on-site methamphetamine manufacture

Contracting procedure

Offer and acceptance. When an individual wishes to purchase a property for sale, the individual's agent should provide a residential purchase contract to the client. The agent may assist the client in filling out the contract form. The form should be completed as previously described with any buyer contingencies included.

The buyer's agent should make sure the buyer understands that the offer will become a legally binding contract if and when the seller accepts the offer. The offer may contain a contingency for review and approval by an attorney.

When the form has been completed, the agent submits it to the seller's agent as an offer to purchase. The seller's agent is required to present the offer to the seller. The offer may be withdrawn at any time before the seller accepts the offer.

Offer and acceptance may come from either the buyer or the seller. The offeree must accept the offer without making any changes whatsoever. A change terminates the offer and creates a new offer or counteroffer. An offeror may revoke an offer for any reason before the communication of acceptance by the offeror.

The seller may accept the offer, reject it completely, or submit a counteroffer that includes any changes the seller wants made. For example, the seller may not accept the offer price and may counteroffer with a different price. Or, the seller may not agree to a buyer's contingency making the purchase contingent on sale of the buyer's current house. Seller and buyer may negotiate until both parties agree to all terms of the contract. Any legal issues that surface during the negotiating process should be resolved by an attorney and not by either licensee.

Document distribution. Once all parties have signed the contract, copies should be distributed to the buyer and the seller. A copy also needs to go to the closing agent. This allows them to get started on the title search for the Opinion of Title or the Abstract of Title.

Earnest money deposits. An agent does want to obtain an earnest money deposit because it provides potential compensation as liquidated damages for the seller if the buyer fails to perform. It also shows that the buyer is serious about buying the property if they are willing to commit to an earnest money deposit.

The sales contract provides the escrow instructions for handling and disbursing escrow funds. The earnest money is placed in the broker's trust account or a third-party's trust or escrow account, such as that of a title company or approved attorney. The deposit money is applied to the sales price at closing and lowers the amount of money the buyer must bring to the closing table.

Trust funds. Virginia law prescribes how licensees must handle any escrow or earnest money deposits they receive. The broker or trust holder is required to place the funds in his or her trust account within the required time periods.

Contingencies. Most sales contracts contain one or more contingencies. A contingency is a condition that must be met within a time frame before the contract can be successfully fulfilled. The most common contingency concerns financing and inspections. A buyer makes an offer contingent on certain terms being met within a specific period of time. For example, a property inspection may need to be completed within ten days of the contract date. If it is completed and problems are found, the buyer can renegotiate the contract or cancel it without penalty. If the inspection is not performed within that time period, the buyer must accept the property as is or default on the contract.

Both buyers and sellers can abuse contingencies to leave themselves a convenient way to cancel without defaulting. To avoid problems, the statement of a contingency should

- be explicit and clear
- have an expiration date

- expressly require diligence in the effort to fulfill the requirements

A contingency that is too broad, vague, or excessive in duration may invalidate the entire contract on the grounds that there is an insufficiency of mutual agreement.

Default. A sale contract is bilateral since both parties promise to perform. As a result, either party may default by failing to perform. Note that a party's failure to meet a contingency does not constitute default but entitles the parties to cancel the contract.

Remedies for default by either party include:

- Liquidated damages to the seller – usually the buyer's earnest money deposit.
- Specific performance by either party – the parties must go through with the sale as agreed in the contract.
- Rescission of contract by either party – the parties are put back to their original positions, and the contract is canceled.
- Compensatory damages – any additional money that either principal has lost. For example, upgrades already completed on the property before the contract default.

Buyer protections

Because Virginia is a caveat emptor state (let the buyer beware), it is important for home buyers to do everything they can to determine the real condition of a home before signing a purchase contract and to take other steps to protect themselves.

Attorney review. The first and most basic protective step, as mentioned earlier, is to have an attorney review the purchase contract before signing and determine that it includes all required disclosures to alert the buyer to existing issues.

Property inspection. The contract should contain a property inspection contingency, and the buyer should have the property inspected for its physical and structural condition, specifically inspecting for the presence of wood-destroying pests, lead-based paint, and other environmental hazards; the existence of defective drywall; the condition of major systems such as electrical and plumbing; water and mold issues in the basement; faulty roof; and so on. The discovery of any such issues can play a critical part in agreeing on the property's purchase price.

Statutory warranty. By Virginia statute, a contract for the sale of a new home contains an implied warranty that

" the dwelling with all of its fixtures is, to the best of the actual knowledge of the vendor or his agents, sufficiently (i) free from structural defects, so as to pass without objection in the trade, and (ii) constructed in a workmanlike manner, so as to pass without objection in the trade." (§ 55.1-357 D)

This implied warranty remains in effect for one year from the earlier of the date of title transfer or the date of possession.

Builder warranties. Most newly constructed homes are covered by builder warranties. These builder warranties cover workmanship, distribution systems, and structural components. The structure is typically covered against defects for 10 years.

The law allows the contract to waive or modify any express or implied warranties and sell the home "as is" provided that the language used to waive or modify is conspicuous as defined by law. Statute also allows for the buyer or buyer's heirs to take legal action against a builder for any breach of the implied warranty.

Home warranties. Buyers can further protect themselves by the purchase of a home warranty. Unlike homeowner's insurance that covers damages to a home and its major systems from fire, flood, and other disasters, home warranties cover repairs or replacements of home systems and appliances.

The seller may even purchase the warranty and offer it to the buyer as part of the sale. Seller-purchased warranties act as incentive and reassurance to a buyer who may be concerned about the condition of appliances and systems. Home warranties typically offer one year of coverage. They may be renewed annually.

Commissions. Salespersons and associate brokers are only to accept monetary payments for real estate services directly from their Principal Broker. The listing broker retains the right to determine the amount of compensation offered to buyer agents or to brokers acting in other agency or nonagency capacities which may be the same or different.

An agent is not allowed to pay any unlicensed person a commission. The only exception to this is if the agent is giving part of their commission to the buyer or the seller. If the agent plans to do this, it must be communicated to all parties before closing.

Property disclosure. The Virginia Residential Property Disclosure Act (§ 55.1-700 et seq. of the Code of Virginia) governs the information property owners must disclose to prospective purchasers of residential real property.

The Act applies only to residential property with one to four dwelling units being transferred by sale, exchange, installment land sales contract, or lease with option to buy, whether or not a real estate licensee is involved.

The following are exempt from disclosure requirements:

- court-ordered or involuntary transfers
    - administration of an estate
    - pursuant to a writ of execution
    - foreclosure sale or deed in lieu of a foreclosure
    - by a bankruptcy trustee
    - eminent domain
    - an assignment for creditors
    - escheats
    - owner's failure to pay taxes
    - a judgment for specific performance

- voluntary transfers
    - from one or more co-owners to other co-owner(s)
    - divorce or property settlement stipulation

- to lineal line relatives
- from government entity or housing authority
- first sale of property other than foreclosure

HOAs. Homeowners' associations (HOAs) and property owners' associations (POAs) are considered common interest communities which are governed by the Virginia Resale Disclosure Act. The act mandates that all sellers must provide buyers with a standardized resale certificate that includes rules and regulations, procedures and mandates, budgets, and other information. They contain all of the benefits and obligations of living in the association.

Sellers within any of these associations must provide this resale certificate to a buyer before the transaction closing. The seller must also disclose in the contract that

- the lot is located within a development that is subject to the Property Owners' Association Act
- the Property Owners' Association Act requires the seller to provide the buyer with an association resale certificate
- the purchaser may cancel the contract within three days after receiving the association resale certificate or being notified that the association resale certificate will not be available
- if the purchaser has received the association resale certificate, the purchaser has a right to request an update of such disclosure packet
- the right to receive the association resale certificate and the right to cancel the contract are waived conclusively if not exercised before settlement

The resale certificate may be delivered to the buyer either in hard copy or electronic format, based on the seller's instructions within the written request for the packet. It must be delivered within 14 calendar days after a written request has been submitted. If hand- or electronically delivered, the request is deemed received on the date of delivery. If sent by U.S. mail, the request is deemed received 6 days after the postmark date.

Exemptions. The following are exempt from HOA or POA disclosure requirements:

- cooperatives & time-shares
- campgrounds
- disposition of a lot by gift
- disposition of a lot pursuant to a court order
- disposition of a lot by foreclosure or deed in lieu of foreclosure
- disposition of a lot by sale at an auction that already includes the resale certificate
- disposition of a lot to a person or entity not acquiring the lot for his or her own residence but who is obligated to comply with the declaration, bylaws, rules and regulations, and architectural guidelines of the association

Selling with an interest. Any agent who is selling their own property or property with which they have an interest in must disclose such a fact upon the "first meaningful contact."

The underlying issue is that an agent has an unfair advantage over the average buyer and seller, given his or her specialized real estate education, knowledge of the process and negotiation skills. This disclosure gives a buyer or seller an opportunity to get representation to theoretically "level the playing field."

Stigmatized properties. Stigmatized properties are those that have experienced an event or condition that may affect the desirability of the property while having no effect on the property's physical condition. Such events or conditions include murder, suicide, a felony; a reputed haunting, or a communicable disease. Virginia does not require inspection, investigation, verification, or disclosure regarding these types of event. A buyer has no cause of action against the seller or licensee for not disclosing any of these events or conditions. However, if the buyer asks a specific question, the seller must answer truthfully.

Sellers who know that **methamphetamine** has been manufactured on the property and that the property has not been cleaned up in accordance with statutory guidelines must disclose that information to potential buyers. The seller must use an REB form for the written disclosure.

Just as with other events that affect the desirability but not the condition of the property, there is no requirement to disclose that the property is or has been occupied by a resident with **HIV or AIDS**.

KEY CONTRACT PROVISIONS OF THE VA SALES CONTRACT

A typical residential sales and purchase contract contains the following primary provisions.

Parties, consideration, and property. One or more clauses will identify the parties, the property, and the consideration.

Parties. There must be at least two parties to the sales contract: the buyer and the seller. All parties must be identified, be of legal age, and have the capacity to contract. Also, if the parties are husband and wife, this is usually identified on the contract.

Property. A legal description sufficient for a competent surveyor to identify the property must be included in the contract. Generally, the postal address and the property appraisal parcel number are also included in the contract.

In addition to the real property location, any personal property that will be transferred with the property needs to be identified. The contract already states what fixtures will transfer with the property. The principal parties are free to add or delete what items are to be included in the sale. Whatever personal property items are staying or not staying with the property should be identified in the contract.

Consideration. Consideration in the contract is the purchase price. Also identified is the amount of earnest money being held. Also, expressly stated will be how the buyer intends to hold title – whether severally (individually), jointly, or as a tenant in common. In addition, the contract will detail what type of deed will be used to effect the transfer. The type of deed basically indicates what assurances the seller is giving as to the marketability of title and whether he or she will defend his or her ownership against any claims against the title being conveyed.

Terms. The selling terms detail how the buyer is going to pay for the property purchase. It will indicate out the type of financing the buyer plans to get, the time frame given for securing the financing, the amount of funding the seller needs, and the interest rate they are willing to accept.

It is important for the agent to include all the acceptable terms in the contract. Failure to put in a maximum interest rate or the exact amount of financing needed could put the buyers in a situation where they must accept bank financing at a higher interest rate than intended.

Loan approval. A financing contingency clause states under what conditions the buyer can cancel the contract without default and receive a refund of the earnest money. If the buyer cannot secure the stated financing by the deadline, the parties may agree to extend the contingency by renegotiating and initializing new deadline dates entered into the contract. However, in the absence of timely renegotiation, not meeting the contract's deadlines makes the contract voidable where the seller can cancel the contract.

Escrow. The escrow clause provides for the custody and disbursement of the earnest money deposit. It also releases the escrow agent from certain liabilities in the performance of legitimate escrow duties.

An earnest money-related clause specifies how the buyer will pay the earnest money and when the deposits will be given to the escrow holder. Occasionally, additional deposits may be due. For example, a buyer who wants to buy a house can make an initial deposit of $200, to be followed in twenty-four hours with an additional $2,000.

Closing and possession dates. The contract states when the title will transfer and when the buyer will take physical possession. Customarily, possession occurs on the date when the deed is signed unless the buyer has agreed to other arrangements. The closing clause generally describes what must take place at closing to avoid default. The seller must provide clear and marketable title. The buyer must produce acceptably liquid purchase funds such as a cashier's check. Failure to complete any pre-closing requirements stated in the sale contract constitutes default and grounds for the aggrieved party to seek recourse.

Conveyed interest and type of deed. One or more provisions will state what kind of deed the seller will use to convey the property and what conditions the deed will be subject to. Among common "subject to" conditions are easements, association memberships, encumbrances, mortgages, liens, and special assessments. Typically, the seller conveys a fee simple interest utilizing a general warranty deed.

Title evidence. The seller agrees to produce the best possible proof of property ownership.

It is important to remember that anything written or added to the contract *supersedes* anything typed or part of the standard contract.

Closing costs. The contract identifies which closing costs each party will pay. Buyer's closing costs are itemized on the RESPA (Real Estate Settlement Procedures Act) required Closing Disclosure and typically include but are not limited to loan fees, recording fees, appraisal costs, any negotiated commissions, taxes and insurance. Seller's fees generally include but are not limited to loan pay-off, taxes owed, excise taxes, negotiated commission fees, and title fees. Buyer closing costs can be offset by negotiated seller paid concessions but those concessions must be mutually negotiated prior to settlement.

Damage and destruction. This clause stipulates the obligations of the parties in case the property is damaged or destroyed prior to closing. The parties may negotiate alternatives, including seller's obligations to repair, buyer's obligations to buy if repairs are made, and the option for either party to cancel.

Seller's representation. Here the seller warrants that there will be no liens on the property that cannot be settled and extinguished at closing. Also, the seller warrants that all representations are accurate, and if found otherwise, the buyer may cancel the contract and reclaim the deposit.

LEASING CONTRACTS

Requirements

State contract laws determine the requirements for a valid lease. These laws generally require the following conditions.

Parties. The principal parties must be legally able to enter into the agreement; i.e., meet certain age, sanity, and other requirements.

Property description. The lease must identify the property by legal description or other locally accepted reference.

Exclusive possession. The landlord must provide an irrevocable right to exclusive possession during the lease term, provided the tenant meets all obligations.

Legal and permitted use. The intended use of the property must be legal. A use that is legal but not permitted does not invalidate the lease but constitutes grounds for default.

Consideration. The lease contract must be accompanied by consideration to the landlord for the rights conveyed. How the consideration is paid does not affect the lease's validity, so long as the parties comply with the terms of the lease.

Offer and acceptance. The parties must accept the lease, and communicate their acceptance to the other party, for the lease to take legal effect.

Signatures. The landlord must sign the lease to convey the leasehold interest. A tenant need not sign the lease, although it is prudent to do so in order to enforce the terms of the lease. Multiple tenants who sign a single lease are jointly and severally responsible for fulfilling lease obligations. Thus, if one renter abandons an apartment, the other renters remain liable for rent.

Oral versus written form. Generally, a *lease for a period exceeding one year cannot be oral but must be in writing to be enforceable* because of the Statute of Frauds. An oral lease or rental agreement is legally construed to be a tenancy at will, having no specified term. Further, an oral lease terminates on the death of either principal party.

Required disclosure in Virginia. Lease agreements are required to include an itemized list of all fees for which a tenant will be charged, including security deposits, rent, and late payment fees.

Lease types

Gross lease. A gross lease, or **full service** lease, requires the landlord to pay the property's operating expenses, including utilities, repairs, and maintenance, while the tenant pays only rent. Rent levels under a gross lease are higher than under a net lease, since the landlord recoups expense outlays in the form of added rent.

Gross leases are common for office and industrial properties. Residential leases are usually gross leases with the exception that the tenants often pay utilities expenses.

Net lease. A net lease requires a tenant to pay for utilities, internal repairs, and a proportionate share of taxes, insurance, and operating expenses in addition to rent. In effect, the landlord "passes through" actual property expenses to the tenant rather than charging a higher rent level. Net leases vary as to exactly what expenses the tenant is responsible for. The extreme form of net lease requires tenants to cover all expenses, including major repairs and property taxes.
Net leases are common for office and industrial properties. They are sometimes also used for single family dwellings.

In practice, the terms net and gross lease can be misleading: some gross leases still require tenants to pay some expenses such as utilities and repairs. Similarly, some net leases require the landlord to pay certain expenses. Prudent tenants and landlords look at all expense obligations in relation to the level of rent to be charged.

Percentage lease. A percentage lease allows the landlord to share in the income generated from the use of the property. A tenant pays **percentage rent**, or an amount of rent equal to a percentage of the tenant's periodic gross sales. The percentage rent may be:

- a fixed percent of gross revenue without a minimum rent
- a fixed minimum rent plus an additional percent of gross sales
- a percentage rent or minimum rent, whichever is greater

Percentage leases are used only for retail properties.

Residential lease. A residential lease may be a net lease or a gross lease. Usually, it is a form of gross lease in which the landlord pays all property expenses except the tenant's utilities and water. Since residential leases tend to be short in term, tenants cannot be expected to pay for major repairs and improvements. The landlord, rather, absorbs these expenses and recoups the outlays through higher rent.

Residential leases differ from commercial and other types of lease in that:

- lease terms are shorter, typically one or two years
- lease clauses are fairly standard from one property to the next, in order to reflect compliance with local landlord-tenant relations laws
- lease clauses are generally not negotiable, particularly in larger apartment complexes where owners want uniform leases for all residents

Commercial lease. A commercial lease may be a net, gross, or percentage lease, if the tenant is a retail business. As a rule, a commercial lease is a significant and complex business proposition. It may involve hundreds of thousands of dollars for improving the property to the tenant's specifications. Since the lease terms are often long, total rent liabilities for the tenant can easily be millions of dollars.

Some important features of commercial leases are:

- long term, ranging up to 25 years

- require tenant improvements to meet particular usage needs
- virtually all lease clauses are negotiable due to the financial magnitude of the transaction
- default can have serious financial consequences; therefore, lease clauses must express all points of agreement and be very precise

Ground lease. A ground lease, or **land lease**, concerns the land portion of a real property. The owner grants the tenant a leasehold interest in the land only, in exchange for rent.

Ground leases are primarily used in three circumstances:

- an owner wishes to lease raw land to an agricultural or mining interest
- unimproved property is to be developed and either the owner wants to retain ownership of the land, or the developer or future users of the property do not want to own the land
- the owner of an improved property wishes to sell an interest in the improvements while retaining ownership of the underlying land

In the latter two instances, a ground lease offers owners, developers, and users various financing, appreciation, and tax advantages. For example, a ground lease lessor can take advantage of the increase in value of the land due to the new improvements developed on it, without incurring the risks of developing and owning the improvements. Land leases executed for the purpose of development or to segregate ownership of land from ownership of improvements are inherently long term leases, often ranging from thirty to fifty years.

Proprietary lease. A proprietary lease conveys a leasehold interest to an owner of a cooperative. The proprietary lease does not stipulate rent, as the rent is equal to the owner's share of the periodic expenses of the entire cooperative. The term of the lease is likewise unspecified, as it coincides with the ownership period of the cooperative tenant: when an interest is sold, the proprietary lease for the seller's unit is assigned to the new buyer.

Leasing of rights. The practice of leasing property rights other than the rights to exclusive occupancy and possession occurs most commonly in the leasing of water rights, air rights, and mineral rights.

For example, an owner of land that has deposits of coal might lease the mineral rights to a mining company, giving the mining company the limited right to extract the coal. The rights lease may be very specific, stating how much of a mineral or other resource may be extracted, how the rights may be exercised, for what period of time, and on what portions of the property. The lessee's rights do not include common leasehold interests such as occupancy, exclusion, quiet enjoyment, or possession of the leased premises.

Another example of a rights lease is where a railroad wants to erect a bridge over a thoroughfare owned by a municipality. The railroad must obtain an air rights agreement of some kind, whether it be an easement, a purchase, or a lease, before it can construct the bridge.

Lease clauses

The clauses of a lease define the contractual relationship between landlord and tenant. The most important and basic clauses are the following.

Rent and security deposit. A rent clause stipulates the time, place, manner and amount of rent payment. It defines any grace period that is allowed, and states the penalties for delinquency.

The lease may also call for a security deposit to protect the landlord against losses from property damage or the tenant's default. State law regulates the handling of the security deposit: where it is deposited, and whether the tenant receives interest on the deposit. A landlord may require additional financial security from a tenant of dubious creditworthiness in the form of personal guarantees, third party guarantees, or pledges of other property as collateral.

Lease term. In the absence of an explicit term with beginning and ending date, a court will generally construe the lease to be a tenancy at will, cancelable upon proper notice.

Repairs and maintenance. Repairs and maintenance provisions define the landlord's and tenant's respective responsibilities for property repairs and maintenance. Generally, the tenant is responsible for routine maintenance of the premises while the landlord is responsible for general repairs. In residential leases, the landlord is responsible for major repairs and capital improvements. Payment of repairs and maintenance costs, however, is entirely negotiable between landlord and tenant.

Subletting and assignment. Subletting (subleasing) is the transfer by a tenant, the **sublessor**, of a *portion* of the leasehold interest to another party, the **sublessee**, through the execution of a **sublease**. The sublease spells out all of the rights and obligations of the sublessor and sublessee, including the payment of rent to the sublessor. The sublessor remains *primarily liable* for the original lease with the landlord. The subtenant is *liable* only to the sublessor.

For example, a sublessor subleases a portion of the occupied premises for a portion of the remaining term. The sublessee pays sublease rent to the sublessor, who in turn pays lease rent to the landlord.

An assignment of the lease is a transfer of the *entire leasehold interest* by a tenant, the **assignor**, to a third party, the **assignee**. There is no second lease, and the assignor retains no residual rights of occupancy or other leasehold rights unless expressly stated in the assignment agreement. The assignee becomes primarily liable for the lease and rent, and the assignor, the original tenant, remains secondarily liable. The assignee pays rent directly to the landlord.

All leases clarify the rights and restrictions of the tenant regarding subleasing and assigning the leasehold interest. Generally, the landlord cannot prohibit either act, but the tenant must obtain the landlord's written approval. The reason for this requirement is that the landlord has a financial stake in the creditworthiness of any prospective tenant.

Rules and regulations. A tenant must abide by all usage restrictions imposed by the lease's rules and regulations for the property. These rules aim to protect the property's condition as well as the rights of other tenants.

Improvements and alterations. A landlord typically wants to prevent a tenant from making alterations that later tenants may not desire. By the same token, a tenant who pays for an improvement wants to know who will own it at the end of the lease term. An improvements and alterations clause therefore identifies necessary permissions and procedures, and who owns improvements. Customarily, tenant improvements become the property of the landlord in the absence of an express agreement to the contrary.

Options. An option clause offers a tenant the opportunity to choose a course of action at some time in the future under certain terms. Typical options are the right to renew the lease, buy the property, and lease additional adjacent space. A tenant does not have to exercise an option, but the landlord must comply if the tenant does exercise it.

Damage and destruction. A damage and destruction provision defines the rights and obligations of the parties in the event the leased premises are damaged or destroyed. State laws regulate such provisions.

ADVANCED CONSIDERATIONS IN SALES CONTRACTING

Multiple offers

In a seller's market, multiple offers are inevitable if a property is priced appropriately.

It is common for a listing agent to call for "highest and best" offer upon receiving multiple offers. This tells the buyer's agents that there are other offers and they need to put their best foot forward and submit their best offer. Highest and best does not necessarily just mean the highest purchase price though. There are many other terms that are equally as important in a contract. Some sellers might prefer a quicker closing and would take a lower purchase price if it meant they could move faster. Others might prefer a zero-day inspection period. All of these terms are important to present to the sellers.

The best way a listing agent can handle multiple offers on a property is by organizing a spreadsheet with the varying categories (i.e. price, due diligence period, financing terms, etc.). This organized spreadsheet will make the offers easier to understand for sellers. It is up to the listing agent to go over the pros and cons of each offer and let the sellers decide which one they want to negotiate with.

Backup offers

In a seller's market, it is common for buyer's agents to submit backup offers. Backup offers are a way to lock the property in if the original contract falls through. For example, Abigail offers on a property, but her purchase price is $5,000 lower than the winning offer. The sellers might choose to lock Abigail in as a backup so that they do not have to re-list the property if the winning offer falls through. Common reasons an original offer might fall through include inspection issues, financing complications, or a buyer changing their mind!

If Abigail gets locked in as the backup offer, she will automatically go under contract if the original contract falls through. This means that they do not have to re-negotiate any terms and they can move forward quickly.

Backup offers benefit the sellers as well because they have the safety of knowing someone else will swoop in and purchase the property if the original contract becomes shaky. It also gives them more power in negotiations since they have something to fall back onto.

Backup offers are great for buyers because it means they automatically go under contract on a home they loved if the first offer falls through.

CONTRACT WRITING LAB

VA contract completion restrictions

In terms of validity and enforceability, a court may construe the legal status of a contract in one of four ways:

- valid
- valid but unenforceable
- void
- voidable

Required language in VA sales contracts

A valid contract that is in writing is enforceable within a statutory time period.

Under the Code of Virginia (§ 54.1-2101.1), real estate licensees may prepare written contracts for the sale, purchase, option, exchange, or rental of real estate, provided that the contract preparation is incidental to or associated with a real estate transaction. The licensee preparing the contract must be involved in the transaction and may not charge a separate fee for preparing the contract.

The licensee should ensure that all fields on a contract form are completed. If one section does not apply to a particular transaction, then the field should be noted with an N/A.

Writing finance and inspection contingencies

A financing contingency clause states under what conditions the buyer can cancel the contract without default and receive a refund of the earnest money. If the buyer cannot secure the stated financing by the deadline, the parties may agree to extend the contingency by signing next to the changed dates. It is common to have the financing contingency end on the day of closing so that the buyer is protected. Although, if a buyer wants to create a stronger offer, they will opt to make a shorter financing contingency time period is. But, the buyer's earnest money would then be at risk.

The contract should contain a property inspection contingency, and the buyer should have the property inspected for its physical and structural condition, specifically inspecting for the presence of wood-destroying pests, lead-based paint, and other environmental hazards; the existence of defective drywall; the condition of major systems such as electrical and plumbing; water and mold issues in the basement; faulty roof; and so on. The discovery of any such issues can play a critical part in agreeing on the property's purchase price.

The inspection contingency protects the buyer's earnest money if there are any issues discovered during it. Again, the shorter the contingency time period is the stronger the offer is for the sellers.

Common contract addenda

The contract form is the basis for the contract, but the form alone does not constitute the entire contract. Any contingencies, addenda, and amendments to the contract must also be included with the contract. Federal and state real estate laws require certain disclosures to be provided to the buyer. Although some of the disclosures may be given to the buyer directly, including them in the contract serves as proof the disclosures were actually provided.

Required disclosures, applicable to the specific transaction and property, include:

- brokerage relationship disclosure
- dual or designated representation disclosure
- limited service representation disclosure
- residential property disclosure
- lead-based paint disclosure
- POA or condominium resale certificate request
- defective drywall disclosure
- aircraft noise/crash disclosure
- repeated claims made with the National Flood Insurance Program
- septic system disclosure
- pending building or zoning violations
- on-site methamphetamine manufacture

Common pitfalls and mistakes made

One of the most common mistakes agents make when writing contracts is forgetting the difference between real and personal property. Real property includes everything that is permanently attached to the property (i.e. a TV mount or a gazebo). Personal property is defined as items that are not permanently attached and can be removed easily. These are items like a washer and dryer, or an actual TV that has been mounted. Personal property does not automatically convey unless it was explicitly mentioned in the contract. Agents must be careful to list every personal item they want included in the contract. Washers and dryers are commonly forgotten by newer agents.

Tips for writing clear contracts

If a buyer or seller have any doubts about specific contract terms, it is always best to clarify them in the contract itself.

Case Illustration

Polly's client is reviewing the MLS listing of the home her client is offering on and she notices the washer and dryer are not currently listed. Polly knows her client is adamant about purchasing a home with an included washer and dryer so she is meticulous and adds it into the contract.

As displayed below, the "Personal Property" section of the Virginia sales contract allows for personal property to be listed. Washers and dryers are common items agents typically forget to include.

2. **PERSONAL PROPERTY**: The following items of personal property are included in this sale:
washer and dryer to convey

_____

_____

_____

_____

_____

SNAPSHOT REVIEW: UNIT EIGHT

CONTRACT WRITING

ESSENTIALS OF CONTRACT LAW

Validity criteria: contracts in general
- Competent parties- legal age, mental competency, legitimate authority
- Mutual consent
- Valuable consideration
- Legal purpose
- Voluntary, good faith

Validity of a conveyance contract
- Written
- Legal description of property
- Signed by one+ of the parties

Electronic contracting (UETA)
- Electronic records and signatures are legal and must be accepted

Enforceability criteria
- Statute of limitations- restricts time period for which injured party in contract has right to rescind contract
- Statute of frauds- contracts in writing to be enforceable

Contract creation
- Offer; acceptance/counteroffer/revocation/termination

Contract contingencies
- Must be met before contract enforceable
- Financing
- Explicit; expiration date; require diligence to fulfill requirement

Default
- Buyer default- buyer fails to perform under terms of sale contract; breach entitles seller to legal recourse for damages. Forfeiture of buyer's deposit as liquidated damages
- Seller default- buyer sue for specific performance, damages, cancellation

PRIMARY, SECONDARY SALES CONTRACT PROVISIONS
Primary provisions
- Parties, consideration, property
- Legal description
- Price and terms
- Loan approval
- Earnest money deposit
- Escrow
- Closing and possession dates
- Conveyed interest; type of deed
- Title evidence
- Closing costs
- Damage and destruction

- Default
- Broker's representation and negotiated commissions
- Seller's representation

Secondary provisions
- Inspections
- Owner's association disclosure
- Survey
- Environmental hazards
- Compliance with laws
- Due-on-sale clause
- Seller financing disclosure
- Rental property; tenants rights
- FHA/VA financing condition
- Flood plain; flood insurance
- Condominium assessments
- Foreign seller withholding
- Tax deferred exchange
- Merger of agreements
- Notices
- Time is of the essence
- Fax transmission
- Survival
- Dispute resolution
- C.L.U.E Report
- Addenda

OPTION-T0-BUY CONTRACT

Overview
- Enforceable contract in which potential seller (optionor) grants potential buyer (optionee), right to purchase property before stated time for stated price and terms

Contract requirements
- Actual, non-refundable consideration
- Include price and terms of the sale
- Have an expiration date
- Be in writing
- Legal description
- General contract validity requirements

Common provisions
- How to deliver notice of election
- Forfeiture terms
- Property and title condition warranties
- How option consideration will be credited

CONTRACTS FOR DEED
- *Land contract, installment sale, conditional sales contract, agreement for deed.*
- Bilateral agreement between seller, vendor, buyer, vendee, in which vendor defers receipt of purchase price over specified period of time

VIRGINIA SALES CONTRACTS
Statute of Frauds
- Requires contracts for sale/lease of real estate be in writing to be enforceable
Preparation of contracts
- Licensees may prepare written contracts for sale, purchase, option, exchange, rental
Residential purchase contract
- Potential buyers submit an offer to purchase specific property
Attachments and addenda
- Contingencies, addenda, amendments be included with contract
Contracting procedure
- Offer and acceptance
- Document distribution
- Earnest money deposits
- Trust funds
- Contingencies
- Default
Buyer protections
- Attorney review
- Property inspection
- Statutory warranty
- Builder warranties
- Home warranties
Required disclosures
- Brokerage relationship disclosure; dual/designated representation disclosure; lead-based paint disclosure; defective drywall disclosure; septic system disclosure; etc.
- Property disclosure
- HOAs
- Selling with an interest
- Stigmatized properties
KEY CONTRACT PROVISIONS OF THE VA SALES CONTRACT
- Parties
- Consideration
- Property
- Loan approval
- Escrow
- Closing and possession dates
- Conveyed interest and type of deed
- Title evidence
- Closing costs
- Damage and destruction
- Seller's representation
LEASING CONTRACTS
Requirements
- State contract laws determine requirements for valid lease
- Parties
- Property description

- Exclusive possession
- Legal and permitted use
- Consideration
- Offer and acceptance
- Signatures
- Oral versus written form

Lease types
- Gross/full service lease- requires landlord to pay property's operating expenses (utilities, repairs, maintenance); office and industrial properties; residential leases are similar but tenants pay utilities
- Net lease- tenant pay for utilities, internal repairs, proportionate share of taxes, insurance, operating expenses; office and industrial properties
- Percentage lease- landlord shares income generated from use of property; retail properties
- Residential lease- net, gross lease; usually gross lease but tenant pays utilities and water
- Commercial lease- net, gross, or percentage lease
- Ground/land lease- owner grants tenant leasehold interest in land only
- Proprietary lease- conveys leasehold interest to owner of cooperative; rent equal to owner's share of periodic expenses of cooperative
- Leasing of rights- common in water, air, mineral rights

Lease clauses
- Rent and security deposit
- Lease term
- Repairs and maintenance
- Subletting and assignment
- Rules and regulations
- Improvements and alterations
- Options
- Damage and destruction

ADVANCED CONSIDERATIONS IN SALES CONTRACT

Multiple offers
- Common in seller's market

Backup offers
- Way to lock in property if original contract falls through

CONTRACT WRITING LAB

Virginia contract completion restrictions
- Contract either valid, valid but enforceable, void, voidable

Writing finance and inspection contingencies
- Financing contingency states under what conditions buyer can cancel contract without default and receive refund earnest money
- If buyer cannot secure financing by deadline, parties may agree to extend contingency by signing next to changed dates
- Inspection contingency protects buyer's earnest money if there are any issues discovered during inspections

Common contract addenda
- POAA/HOA or Condominium Resale Certificate; residential property disclosure; pending zoning violations, etc.

Common pitfalls and mistakes made
- Real versus personal property

Tips for writing clear contracts
- Clarify all terms

Check Your Understanding Quiz:

Unit Eight: Contract Writing

Carefully read each question then provide your best answer based on what you learned in this unit. Then check your answers against the Answer Key which immediately follows the quiz questions.

1. Which statute allows for electronic contracting?

    a. DocuSign Law
    b. Digital Signature Act
    c. Uniform Electronic Transactions Act (UETA)
    d. Online Contract Law

2. Which of the following is a common <u>secondary</u> provision to a contract?

    a. Inspection
    b. Price
    c. Loan approval
    d. Escrow

3. What is another name for a land contract?

    a. Contract for deed
    b. Option-to-buy
    c. Contingency contract
    d. Offer-to-purchase

4. Which statute requires that certain contracts must be in writing to be enforceable?

    a. Statute of limitations
    b. Statute of Frauds
    c. Enforceability Act
    d. Written deed law

5. What is another name for the claims history database insurance companies use when underwriting insurance policies?

    a. Insurance History Report
    b. Claims Report
    c. C.L.U.E. Report
    d. C.H.D.I. Report

6. The parties to a contract must have the capacity to contract -- which is determined by legal age, mental competency and _____.

    a. legitimate authority.
    b. valuable consideration.
    c. occupation.
    d. mutual consent.

7. By changing any of the terms of an offer, the offeree creates a _____.

    a. valid offer.
    b. counteroffer.
    c. terminated offer.
    d. revocation.

8. A Veteran's Administration sales contract financing contingency clause allows the buyer to cancel the contract if the price exceeds the _____ estimate of the property's value.

    a. conventional appraiser's
    b. USDA's
    c. BPO's
    d. VA's

9. A contract for the sale of a new home contains a one year warranty called a _____.

    a. builder warranty.
    b. home warranty.
    c. statutory warranty.
    d. systems warranty.

10. Which lease allows the landlord to share in the income generated from the use of the property?

    a. Percentage lease
    b. Residential lease
    c. Proprietary lease
    d. Ground lease

11. A(n) _____ clause offers a tenant the opportunity to choose a course of action at some time in the future.

    a. damage
    b. option
    c. delayed
    d. backup

12. If a section in the contract does not apply, what should the licensee do?

   a. Strike through it
   b. Leave it blank
   c. Cross it out and write "VOID"
   d. Write "N/A" in the section

13. Which lease type conveys a leasehold interest to an owner of a cooperative?

   a. Land lease
   b. Commercial lease
   c. Proprietary lease
   d. Net lease

14. Which type of properties are percentage leases used for?

   a. Retail properties
   b. Offices
   c. Residential properties
   d. Warehouses

15. A legal description sufficient for a competent _____ to identify the property must be included in the contract.

   a. appraiser
   b. licensee
   c. broker
   d. surveyor

==

UNIT 9:

CURRENT INDUSTRY ISSUES AND TRENDS

Unit Nine Learning Objectives: When the student has completed this unit, he or she will be able to:

- Identify the best ways to price a property in a seller's market.
- Define short sale transactions.
- Discuss licensee safety measures.

PRICING PROPERTIES IN A SELLER'S MARKET

It is almost always necessary for an agent seeking a listing to suggest a listing price or price range for the property. It is important to make a careful estimate, because underpricing a property is not in the best interests of the seller, and overpricing it often prevents a transaction altogether.

An agent usually relies on an analysis of comparable properties which have recently sold in the same neighborhood. By making adjustments for the differences between the subject property and the comparables, the agent arrives at a general price range.

In a seller's market, when the inventory is low, sellers are prone to push the price above the estimated market value. While that might still garner them multiple offers, it could lead to appraisal issues. If a buyer has an appraisal contingency, their earnest money is protected in case of a low appraisal. Listing agents must make the sellers aware that even though a buyer might be willing to offer a higher price, a lender will fall back on the appraised value before granting a loan.

Agents must be careful to caution sellers that they are not appraisers, and that the suggested price range is not an expert opinion of market value. If a more precise estimate of market value is desired, the seller should hire a licensed appraiser.

REAL ESTATE TEAMS AND REGULATORY COMPLIANCE

A real estate team is when there are multiple entities working together to represent clients under one name. All real estate teams must have a business entity salesperson license in order to be compliant. They can apply for one through the DPOR.

Real estate teams have to be careful when advertising to not mislead consumers into thinking they are a brokerage firm. Virginia does not currently prohibit any specific words regarding team advertising as long as it is not misleading.

FAIR HOUSING COMPLIANCE

The Fair Housing Board currently consists of twelve members and they investigate any fair housing violations and attempts to prevent them through education programs. The issues that they focus on include discrimination based on race, color, sources of funds, sexual orientation, national origin, disability, sex, familial status, elderliness, gender identity, and military status.

These classes are protected against discrimination from property managers, mortgage lenders, appraisers, real estate agents, landlords, and insurance companies.

Some instances this discrimination could occur would be a landlord falsely claiming that there are no apartments available to steer them away from applying; a mortgage lender denying a loan without properly reviewing their file, or an appraiser devaluing a property based on their biases.

LICENSEE SAFETY MEASURES

Unfortunately, real estate agents can be easy targets for criminals. It is important for licensees to be cautious when showing homes and attending listing appointments. Real estate agents have to be on especially high alert when meeting new clients. It is encouraged to meet in a public place first before moving on to showings. Other safety measures include parking on the street so no one can block the car in, letting someone know where you are at all times (keep your phone location turned on), bringing a fellow agent or lender to sit in open houses.

Vacant listings present another danger as well, licensees should be aware of their surroundings at all times when showing vacant properties.

SHORT SALES

A **short sale** is what must transpire whenever a property owner attempting to convey his or her property owes more than resale value and loan pay-off amount. In the short sale transaction, the seller agrees to let the lender dictate or approve the terms of the transaction in exchange for the lender's promise to release the owner from the mortgage lien and to convey marketable title to the buyer.

The lender, however, may or may not agree to accept the deficient price as a satisfactory loan payoff and may require the seller to make up deficient amounts by way of a deficiency judgment. In other instances, there may be tax consequences for the seller if the lender agrees to grant an increment of loan forgiveness – which can amount to taxable income for the seller. To avoid the deficiency charge in the short sale, the seller must make sure that the agreements include a full release of the underlying debt and a statement that it was fully satisfied.

The parties to a short sale are the buyer, the seller, their agents and the lender. The lender is a third-party contingency who must approve the sale. The process of a short sale generally unfolds as follows.

Short sale transaction benchmarks

1. The borrower-sellers or their agents contact the lender to discuss the short sale option.
2. If willing, the lender sets the required terms of the short sale.
3. For an updated valuation estimate, the real estate agent provides the lender with a Broker's Price Opinion (BPO).
4. Subsequently, the agent lists the property for sale at the highest possible price that the market will bear.
5. The agent places the listing into the MLS with a special note to the brokerage community stating that the lender will consider a short sale.
6. At some point, a buyer submits takes an interest in the property and submits an offer.
7. After negotiating price and terms, the owner and buyer agree to the terms of a contract
8. The lender is then brought into the proceedings to evaluate and (hopefully) approve the final terms of the short sale.
9. The closing date is established, the pre-closing period is completed, and ideally, the transaction closes.
10. The final terms may or may not include a deficiency proceeding to recover unacceptable shortfalls in the sales proceeds.

The success of a short sale transaction depends on the collaboration of the seller, buyer, agents, and all lenders involved (1st, 2nd, 3rd position lienholders). Each party has a specific role to ensure the transaction can go smoothly.

To get the transaction off to a good start, the seller must accurately identify exactly how much is owed on the property. The lenders can certainly provide this information.   It is vital that the seller be upfront with all parties about every property-secured loan they have, as well as any equipment they are leasing (water softeners, solar panels, adjunct power systems, etc., all of which will have to be paid off with the sale of the home).

The seller should request payoff amounts from all lenders and provide this information to the listing agent so they can together create a net sheet. The net sheet will help the seller determine what they can afford to pay back to the various lenders once the closing costs are built in.

One common characteristic of a short sale is that the homeowner is experiencing some form of hardship that is putting pressure on the owners to sell in the short term as opposed to waiting until financial conditions improve. These circumstances should not be concealed. In order to get the short sale approved by the lender, the seller will need to provide documentation supporting the fact that they are experiencing financial hardship. Subsequently, to have a successful transaction under these adverse conditions, the seller's role will need to involve open and honest collaboration with the lender's representatives. In addition, the seller will need to understand that the short sale will require more time to complete than conventional conveyances.

Buyer's role in a short sale

Once the buyers decide to submit an offer for a short sale property, they can choose whether they would like to hire a short sale negotiator. Since short sales have become more commonplace in recent years, title companies and law firms have augmented their staffs with short sale specialists. These negotiators can be very beneficial to both principal parties – for the seller they can secure a top-dollar price, and for the buyer they can negotiate difficult agreements that might otherwise fail. The job of the short sale negotiator is to argue with the lenders and persuade them to approve the buyer's offer price.

Once a short sale is approved by all lenders, the buyer will go under contract. Since it is a short sale, the buyer should be prepared for a longer transaction and for additional paperwork. The buyer should also be aware that it is rare for any repairs or price accommodations for repairs to be accepted.

Above all, the buyer should be prepared for a very common outcome – that the short sale negotiations fail and the transaction falls apart. A consummated short sale is never a guaranteed proposition since the lenders can change their requirements at any point. Buyers (and sellers) must understand that the lender does not have to agree to lose money. While the risk of a defaulted loan is higher, lenders are under stockholder pressure to generate earnings, like everyone else. The lender can just wait it out until conditions improve. Such changes can result in lost time and not insignificant losses of money for the buyer.

Listing agent's role

One of the most important roles of a listing agent is to provide a net sheet for the sellers. They can either create their own net sheet or request one from a title company. When creating this net sheet, the listing agent should ask the seller to disclose all current mortgages. This net sheet will help the seller to better understand what position they are in.

The listing agent is responsible for generating a Broker's Price Opinion on the property. They do this by selecting the best comparable properties and adjusting them accordingly to determine an appropriate price. Once the agent completes the BPO, they will submit it, along with the seller's documentation of hardship, to the seller's lender. The lender will then review the information and either counter or accept the BPO. The review process could take weeks or months depending on the situation, the backlog in the market, and the number of lenders involved. Each lender will have to agree to collaborate with the short sale terms and parties. The more mortgagees involved, the longer it could take to approve the short sale.

Within the short sale transaction scenario, the seller can either wait for the official approval from the lender, or opt to list the property immediately. Here, the listing agent is responsible for submitting the listing into the MLS and marking it as a short sale. The listing agent should be upfront with all buyers whether the short sale is lender-approved or still under review. They must also be ready to explain the short sale process to all potential buyers as well as notify them that repair and price negotiations are unlikely.

It is also important to note that, as yet another negative characteristic of the short sale transaction, the real estate agent's commission might be lower than what practitioners typically charge for residential conveyances. Indeed, all parties must give and take in order to make short sales happen.

Buyer agent's role

The buyer's agent role in the short sale transaction – in addition to all the duties inherent in a conventional transaction -- is to inform the buyer of how the short sale process works and what they should expect. In particular, short sale properties are not always in the best condition, and most sellers cannot afford to make whatever repairs that might be identified as necessary by the inspection. Thus, the short sale is, in effect, an "as-is" conveyance, and buyers should be aware of the fact that the price may not be their last expense in completing their move.

The buyer's agent should also disclose to the buyer whether or not the listing already has an approved short sale price. If the price is not yet approved by the lender, then the process can take months of negotiating with the lender. The buyer should understand that this circumstance is much like a financing contingency that must be removed for the closing to take place.

Again, it is also important to note that a real estate agent's commission might be lower with the short sale compared to conventional transactions.

Lender's role

Each lender will have to collaborate with the sellers to agree on a short sale price.

They will also typically discuss the listing agent's BPO. If necessary, the lender will generate its own BPO to validate the listing agent's value estimate.

As an interesting possibility in the short sale transaction, one should realize that the final price going onto the market may not be less than market value. If the lender does not agree to a certain price, the seller might have to list it at market value – then see what happens. But from the buyer's perspective, the short sale is not necessarily a below-market bargain or fire sale.

If there are multiple lenders who are owed money in the transaction, it can become difficult to have them all agree on their smaller payoff amounts. This negotiation process can significantly expand the time required to consummate the short sale transaction.

Another important consideration from the lender's perspective is that, in fact, the common alternative to a short sale is a default and foreclosure, both of which can cost more than loan forgiveness amounts lost in the short sale. Thus, the lender has no real win-win outcomes, and the ultimate decision to approve the upside-down short sale price must be measured against indeterminable losses incurred by a default.

VA LOANS AND BUYER-BROKER FEES

The U.S. Department of Veteran's Affairs announced that those seeking to buy homes with VA loans may now pay buyer-broker fees. The fees are negotiable, must be paid in cash at closing. They are also subject to certain safeguards.

This change is in response to the NAR class-action settlement, which likely affects the way buyers' agents are compensated. The settlement put VA borrowers at a disadvantage. The new rule allowing VA borrowers to pay brokers' fees is "valid until rescinded." It aims to keep veteran buyers competitive in the housing market. For more info, visit:

https://www.benefits.va.gov/HOMELOANS/documents/circulars/26-24-15.pdf

SOCIAL MEDIA POSTS

Many real estate salespersons and brokers create online content to engage with future clients as well as generate awareness about properties for sale. Social media posting allows salespersons and brokers to quickly engage with buyers and sellers in an informal setting. In this context, agents are able to raise awareness for their firms and build a personal brand. Potential clients can get a sense of a licensee's personality and reputation from their social media presence.

On these platforms, it is crucial to uphold all Virginia laws and keep in accordance with ethical standards of the profession. With these ideas in mind, social media is a powerful tool that can be used to showcase agents' strengths and connect with individuals.

A guide can be accessed at:

https://virginiarealtors.org/wp-content/uploads/dlm_uploads/2020/12/Social-Media-Advertising-Instructor-Guide.pdf

NAR CLASS ACTION SETTLEMENT

The National Association of REALTORS® has reached a $418 million settlement in response to an antitrust lawsuit. The lawsuit claims the NAR promulgated rules and practices that are anticompetitive. The NAR's website assures readers that the settlement is the best path forward to protect its membership, which is over 1 million strong.

The settlement releases the vast majority of members from future liability for these alleged violations. The effects of this change are fast-evolving and may decrease the likelihood that buyers' representatives will be compensated in real estate transactions. It emphasizes buyers' and sellers' ability to negotiate commissions. The situation is dynamic, and some of the outcomes are yet to be seen.

Interactive Exercise

Unit 9: Current Industry Issues and Trends

9.1) SITUATION EXAMPLE: Pricing properties in a seller's market.

Michael is preparing for a listing appointment and during his comparative market analysis, he realizes the property is worth $50,000 less than what the sellers had originally mentioned they wanted to sell for. Since it is a seller's market and the inventory is low, Michael believes he can find a buyer for that price. He needs to decide whether he aggressively supports the seller's opinion of the price or if he should explain to them the effects of pricing too high.

What would you tell the sellers if you were Michael?

_____

_____

_____

_____

_____

_____

_____

_____

_____

SNAPSHOT REVIEW: UNIT NINE

Current Industry Issues and Trends

PRICING PROPERTIES IN A SELLER'S MARKET
- Underpricing not in best interests of seller, overpricing prevents transaction
- Sellers prone to overprice home in seller's market
- Overpriced homes lead to appraisal issues

REAL ESTATE TEAMS AND REGULATORY COMPLIANCE
- Teams must have business entity salesperson license
- Advertising must not mislead consumers into thinking teams are brokerage firms

FAIR HOUSING COMPLIANCE
- Fair Housing Board is 12 members
- Investigate and prevent fair housing issues through education programs
- Focus on discrimination based on race, color, sources of funds, sexual orientation, national origin, disability, sex, familial status, elderliness, gender identity, military status

LICENSEE SAFETY MEASURES
- Licensees to be cautious when showing homes, attending listing appointments, meeting new clients

SHORT SALES
- When owner attempting to convey property owes more than resale value and loan pay-off amount
- Homeowner experiencing hardship putting pressure on owners to sell in short term as opposed to waiting until financial conditions improve
- Seller to provide documentation supporting financial hardship

VA LOANS AND BUYER BROKER FEES
- VA borrowers may temporarily pay broker fees if the seller will not
- Amount must be customary and paid in cash at closing
- Intended to keep veterans competitive in housing market after NAR settlement

EFFECTIVE SOCIAL MEDIA POSTING
- Licensees to comply with laws and Code of Ethics
- Can help connect with clients

NAR SETTLEMENT
- Agreed upon to protect NAR members from future litigation
- Expected to increase competition for commissions

Check Your Understanding Quiz:

Unit Nine: Current Industry Issues and Trends

Carefully read each question then provide your best answer based on what you learned in this unit. Then check your answers against the Answer Key which immediately follows the quiz questions.

1. If a property owner owes more on his or her home than the current resale and loan pay-off amount, then what type of conveyance transaction would be necessitated to successfully sell the property?

   a. Foreclosure
   b. Contract for deed
   c. Tax sale
   d. Short-sale

2. In a seller's market, home inventory is _____ compared to inventory in a buyer's market.

   a. low
   b. high
   c. the same
   d. Inventory does not determine the type of market.

3. Which type of license must all real estate teams have in order to be compliant?

   a. NAR team license
   b. Business entity salesperson license
   c. Team license
   d. Brokerage salesperson license

4. In a short-sale transaction, what must the real estate agent provide the lender with?

   a. A CMA
   b. An appraisal
   c. A BPO
   d. A market analysis

5. In order to get the short sale approved by the lender, the sellers will need to _____.

   a. declare bankruptcy.
   b. start the foreclosure process.
   c. sell all of their items of value.
   d. provide documentation of financial hardship.

6. What is the risk of pricing a home above market value?

   a. Appraisal issues
   b. Too many offers
   c. Inspection contingency issues
   d. Short time on the market

7. Fiona just finished text messaging a new client who wants to see a house that afternoon. What should she do to ensure her safety?

   a. Fiona should talk to him on the phone first.
   b. She should meet the client in a public place first before showing any homes.
   c. Fiona should video chat with him to ensure he does not look dangerous.
   d. She should show him the home immediately before it sells.

8. What is one of the most important things buyer's agents should share with their clients about short sales?

   a. The buyer's agent should tell their client to stay away from short sales.
   b. The buyer's agent needs to share all of the documents proving the seller's financial hardship with the buyer.
   c. The buyer's agent needs to create a BPO and share it with the buyer.
   d. The short sale price listed might not be approved by all of the lienholders.

9. Carla wants to create social media content for her real estate business. What must she first research?

   a. How to increase engagement with her account
   b. How to share market statistics
   c. The compliance requirements according to Virginia Law and the Code of Ethics
   d. The most viral social media posts concerning real estate

10. Who is responsible for creating the BPO in a short sale transaction?

    a. Listing agent
    b. Title agent
    c. Buyer's agent
    d. Seller

11. What temporary change helps VA borrowers stay competitive after the NAR class-action settlement?

    a. They may pay broker fees if certain requirements are met
    b. They may pay broker fees that are higher than is customary for the area
    c. They may become licensed brokers with all requirements waived
    d. They may apply to gain access to exclusive VA listing service

Interactive Exercises – Case Debriefs

Case Debrief 3.1:

If Alex's buyer has an inspection contingency in place, then he is able to receive a full refund. Alex will need to type up a contract cancellation with instructions on the disbursement of funds. Since the transaction did not close, the escrow funds stay in the account until all principals to the transaction agree in writing how the funds are to be disbursed. If Alex does not have an inspection contingency, then the escrow will be deemed non-refundable and will be disbursed to the sellers. Sometimes the escrow deposit is split between the sellers and the listing agent. Inspection contingencies are a valuable way to protect the buyer's escrow money. They are especially important in older homes where issues are more likely to arise.

Case Debrief 5.1:

Jamie should conduct some research and find out whether Olivia violated any laws. After completing the due diligence, he would discover that Olivia violated the Fair Housing Act by deliberately failing to bring a listing to his attention. He can now file a complaint with the Real Estate Board within the next year, so she receives the appropriate disciplinary actions.

Case Debrief 5.2:

Federal and state governments have enacted laws prohibiting discrimination in the national housing market. The aim of these fair housing laws, or equal opportunity housing laws, is to give all people in the country an equal opportunity to live wherever they wish, provided they can afford to do so, without impediments of discrimination in the purchase, sale, rental, or financing of the property. One of the protected classes under the Fair Housing Act is race. Since it is a protected class, Mallory cannot risk answering Chase's questions.

So, what should she do? One way to tackle this situation is to urge Chase to complete his due diligence by running online searches on the local neighborhood's demographics. There is a lot of market data available online, and Chase can discover the answers for himself without putting Mallory's license at risk.

Case Debrief 6.1
1. Eric should have presented both offers. He then should have explained the pros and cons of each offer. The final decision is up to the sellers on whom they want to buy their house.

2. In this situation, the Professional Standards board determined that Eric violated Articles 1 and 3 of the NAR Code of Ethics.

3. The Standards of Practice violated are:
   SP 1.6 – Submit all offers and counteroffers objectively and as quickly as possible.
   SP 1.7 – The listing brokers must continue to submit offers they receive up to closing.
   SP 1.15 – When asked by the cooperating broker, the listing broker should disclose that he has other offers.
   SP 3.6 – The REALTOR® should reveal the existence of accepted offers.

Case Debrief 6.2:

1.   Article 10 of the Code of Ethics was violated.

2.   The agent violated Standard of Practice 10.5.

3.   The agent may state their mind in the public forum; however, she may not use slurs or hate speech. She should have remained civil and not use derogatory comments against the County Commissioner. She would be guilty because she advocated violence against the Commissioner.

Case Debrief 6.3:

1.   Article 16 of the Code of Ethics was violated.

2.   The agent violated Standard of Practice 16.13.

3.   At the hearing, Janet defended her actions because she had been invited to present the offer to the seller and begin the negotiations to sell the property. Janet had assumed that she had Dan's permission to talk with Joey about the property's sale. The ability of a REALTOR® to speak with another agent's customer must be expressed and not implied.

Note: Each student's opinion on how to handle this case will vary; however, each student should support their stand.

Case Debrief 7.1:

Since Abigail is not a contractor she should not speak on the repair estimates for the home. Unintentional misrepresentation occurs when a licensee unknowingly conveys inaccurate information to a consumer concerning a property, financing or agency service. False or inaccurate information that the licensee, as a professional, should have known to be false or inaccurate may be included in the definition. Those found guilty generally have to pay fines and may be disciplined by state real estate regulators and professional organizations.

Instead of trying to win the client over with inaccurate estimates, Abigail should state that she is not a contractor but knows a few trusted contractors she could schedule to come out there for accurate estimates. This will show the potential client that she is resourceful and has his best interest at heart. It will also help protect her from any liability or misrepresentation issues.

Case Debrief 9.1:

Pricing property in a seller's market can be difficult since every seller wants to maximize their profits. Agents should always present all comparable properties to the sellers and explain to them the dangers of overpricing a property. If there are any appraisal issues, then the deal could potentially fall through and the property will then be stigmatized when it is re-listed on the MLS. It is important to be upfront about the current market pricing trends with sellers.

At the end of the day, the listing price is determined by the sellers, but the licensee's job is to help them make the most informed decision possible. The licensee should remain neutral and focus on educating the clients rather than steering them one way or another.

Quiz Answer Key

Unit One: Real Estate Law and Regulations

1. b. Submitting listings to MLS
2. a. Megan's Law
3. d. Common Interest Communities
4. b. The Virginia Time-Share Act
5. d. 15 years.
6. a. possession
7. a. DPOR
8. b. 3 years
9. c. Seller
10. b. Tax liens
11. a. 65
12. d. A public offering statement
13. c. Chesapeake Bay Preservation Act
14. b. Determining license fees
15. a. historic district ordinances.
16. d. CIC Ombudsman
17. c. The Virginia Underground Utility Damage Prevention Act
18. b. Virginia homestead laws
19. a. $100,000
20. d. Only the homeowners in that neighborhood
21. a. Computing commission checks
22. b. Arbitrate disputes between salespersons and brokers
23. b. 4 years
24. c. Two
25. a. SCRA
26. d. Removing all waste from the dwelling in appropriate receptacles
27. b. Providing certification that all smoke alarms are in working order
28. c. Within any agreed upon number of days
29. a. Virginia Time-Share Act
30. d. joint tenancy with survivorship
31. a. Virginia Resale Disclosure Act

Unit Two: Agency Law

1. c. independent contractor.
2. a. CSIC.
3. c. Dual standard agency
4. d. A customer asking licensee to show her homes that meet her criteria so she can submit an offer.
5. b. Open listing
6. a. Designated standard agency
7. a. Net listing
8. c. Disclosing whether or not the buyer intends to occupy the property as a principal residence
9. b. Net listing

10. c. Being available for property showings
11. a. A buyer agency agreement
12. b. Emily can sign a referral agreement with the other agent to ensure she gets paid a fee at closing.
13. c. Bait and switch
14. d. limited to the duties agreed upon at the time the written brokerage agreement is created.
15. b. Kaitlin cannot advise what terms to offer.

Unit Three: Escrow Requirements

1. c. commingling.
2. b. Recording the transaction
3. a. RESPA
4. a. fifth business banking day.
5. d. For 3 years from the date of execution
6. b. REB
7. b. conversion.
8. c. Paying the principal
9. a. Payoff statement
10. d. Confirming performance
11. b. As close to the closing date as possible
12. c. When a foreclosure terminates a contract
13. a. title commitment
14. b. beneficiary statement
15. d. An unpaid lien

Unit Four: Real Estate Finance

1. d. hypothecation.
2. b. interest rate.
3. a. Income ratio
4. c. LTV
5. d. Conditional commitment
6. a. RESPA
7. b. lien-theory
8. d. Adjustable rate loan
9. a. A "lock-in" commitment
10. c. ECOA

Unit Five: Fair Housing, ADA and Civil Rights

1. d. Sexual identity
2. b. Steering
3. a. The Fairhaven Program
4. d. race
5. c. The Americans with Disabilities Act
6. b. Redlining

7. a. Executive Order 11063
8. b. Jones v. Mayer
9. c. compulsive hoarding
10. a. commercial facilities

Unit Six: Ethics and Standards of Conduct

1. a. duties to REALTORS®.
2. b. REALTORS® are not obligated to discover latent defects.
3. c. Property.
4. b. Commitment to Excellence
5. d. REALTORS® must not disclose information ascertained from a hearing.
6. a. To protect the public and promote homeownership
7. b. procuring cause.
8. c. mediation
9. b. Article 15 of the Code of Ethics
10. d. The Preamble
11. c. The prohibition against undisclosed compensation
12. a. Anyone
13. b. $15,000
14. d. Expulsion from membership for one to three years
15. c. Ombudsman

Unit Seven: Risk Management

1. c. retention.
2. a. Errors & Omissions insurance
3. c. Obedience
4. b. Transference
5. a. Antitrust law
6. c. 1978
7. a. Education
8. b. Consequential loss, use, and occupancy insurance
9. d. Appraisal
10. c. Unauthorized practice of law
11. a. The FTC brings civil enforcement actions
12. b. Handling earnest money improperly
13. c. Accounting
14. a. Claims that the licensee failed to carry out fiduciary duties
15. b. RESPA

Unit Eight: Contract Writing

1. c. Uniform Electronic Transactions Act (UETA)
2. a. Inspection
3. a. Contract for deed
4. b. Statute of Frauds
5. c. C.L.U.E. Report

6. a. legitimate authority.
7. b. counteroffer.
8. d. VA's
9. c. statutory warranty.
10. a. Percentage lease
11. b. option
12. d. Write "N/A" in the section
13. c. Proprietary lease
14. a. Retail properties
15. d. surveyor

Unit Nine: Current Industry Issues and Trends

1. d. Short-sale
2. a. low
3. b. Business entity salesperson license
4. c. A BPO
5. d. provide documentation of financial hardship.
6. a. Appraisal issues
7. b. She should meet the client in a public place first before showing any homes.
8. d. The short sale price listed might not be approved by all of the lienholders yet.
9. c. The compliance requirements according to Virginia Law and the Code of Ethics
10. a. Listing agent
11. a. They may pay broker fees if certain requirements are met